D0518333

VOLUME 4

THE AGE OF
DIVERGING TRADITIONS

THE ILLUSTRATED
HISTORY OF THE WORLD

VOLUME 4

THE AGE OF
DIVERGING TRADITIONS

J. M. ROBERTS

3 1336 05118 3888

New York
Oxford University Press

The Illustrated History of the World

This edition first published in 1999 in the United States of America by
Oxford University Press, Inc.,
198 Madison Avenue, New York, N.Y. 10016
Oxford is a registered trademark of Oxford University Press

All rights reserved. No part of this book may be reproduced or utilized in any form or
by any means electronic or mechanical, including photocopying, recording, or by any
information storage and retrieval system now known or hereafter invented, without the
prior permission of the publishers.

THE AGE OF DIVERGING TRADITIONS
Copyright © Editorial Debate SA 1998
Text Copyright © J. M. Roberts 1976, 1980, 1983, 1987, 1988, 1992, 1998
Artwork and Diagram Copyright © Editorial Debate SA 1998
(for copyright of photographs and maps, see acknowledgments on page 192, which are
to be regarded as an extension of this copyright)

Art Direction by Duncan Baird Publishers
Produced by Duncan Baird Publishers, London, England,
and Editorial Debate, Madrid, Spain

Series ISBN 0-19-521529-X
Volume ISBN 0-19-521522-2

DBP staff:
Senior editor: Joanne Levêque
Assistant editor: Georgina Harris
Senior designer: Steven Painter
Assistant designer: Anita Schnable
Picture research: Julia Ruxton
Sales fulfilment: Ian Smalley
Map artwork: Russell Bell
Decorative borders: Lorraine Harrison

Editorial Debate staff:
Editors and picture researchers:
Isabel Belmonte Martínez, Feliciano Novoa Portela,
Ruth Betegón Díez, Dolores Redondo
Editorial coordination: Ana Lucía Vila

Typeset in Sabon 11/15 pt
Color reproduction by Trescan, Madrid, Spain
Printed in Singapore by Imago Limited

NOTE
The abbreviations CE and BCE are used throughout this book:
CE Common Era (the equivalent of AD)
BCE Before Common Era (the equivalent of BC)

10 9 8 7 6 5 4 3 2 1

CONTENTS

Introduction 6

Chapter 1
Islam and the Re-making of the Near East 8

Chapter 2
The Arab Empires 28

Chapter 3
Byzantium and its Sphere 48

Chapter 4
The Disputed Legacies of the Near East 96

Chapter 5
The Making of Europe 130

Time chart 180

Chapters and contents 182

Series contents 184

Index 186

Acknowledgments 192

THE AGE OF DIVERGING TRADITIONS

T HE "ROMANS" OF JUSTINIAN'S DAY knew they were very different from other people and were proud of it. They belonged to a particular civilization; some of them, at least, thought it was the best conceivable. They were not unique in this. Undoubtedly there would have been people belonging to other civilizations who felt much the same, and there were, long before the birth of Christ, well-developed civilizations everywhere except in the Americas and Australasia. Because of this, the differences which had already appeared between patterns of life in different parts of the world in prehistoric times were to deepen and become richer and more complex.

Yet though civilizations were at work and dominant for long periods of time in certain parts of the globe, they tended before the age of modern history to be confined to them. From two or three centuries before the birth of Christ, the civilizations of different parts of the Eurasian landmass survived largely independently of one another. Though there were occasional and restricted contacts between them, they tended to occur because of the travels of enterprising merchants, wandering scholars, ambitious diplomats or enthusiastic missionaries, and such dependence on individuals meant that intercommunication between cultures was slight. Such sporadic contact could hardly be expected to overcome the great distances which separated some of them. Only when civilizations were actually contiguous – as were the Christian cultures of the Latin and Catholic West and the Greek and Orthodox East, for example – were there really possibilities of influencing one another profoundly.

Yet for all the differences of style and detail between them, in certain fundamental and shaping ways all civilizations were for a long time much alike. All civilizations until very recent times relied on subsistence agriculture for the most part; similarly, all of them had to find their energy supplies in wind, running water and human and animal muscle-power. None of them had for a long time any outstanding advantage over the others. As a result, technological sophistication or lack of it mattered less than in later times, when advantages would be deployed across huge distances to impose the ways of one civilization on another. Yet the insulation of one civilization from another was never absolute; there was always just a little interaction going on, some sharing of knowledge or techniques, even if merely those of war-making.

The major impact of civilizations on one another came about when migration actually changed the location of peoples and gave them new neighbours, or when nomadic peoples broke into settled societies. Then, sometimes, first a clash and then a symbiosis of civilizations might take place. These could be stimulating. Often, though, the effects of incursions by alien and barbarian peoples were destructive and negative. Such, for the most part, was the impact on the Middle East and eastern Europe of the Mongol peoples who poured out more than once from their Central Asian fastnesses to harry both Asia and Europe. Sometimes, though, the effects were more positive and enduring, as was the case when one of the Turkish peoples from the heart of Asia established itself in Anatolia and built on it a new empire which was to replace that of Byzantium. But the most important of all these world-historical clashes was one with which the story contained in this volume has to begin. It was to disturb peoples from Spain to Indonesia, and from the Niger basin to China, but it was also to be one of the first great carriers of cultural fertilization between civilizations.

During the Middle Ages, civilized society consisted of and was determined by three cultures: Christianity, Islam and Judaism. This Christian manuscript illustration is from 9th-century Spain. It is taken from the "Codex of the Council of Abelda", which forms part of a collection of manuscripts held at the El Escorial Monastery related to the Roman Catholic Councils of Toledo.

1 ISLAM AND THE RE-MAKING OF THE NEAR EAST

WITH RELATIVELY BRIEF interruptions, the great empires based in Iran hammered away at the West for a thousand years before 500. Wars can sometimes bring civilizations closer, and in the Near East two cultural traditions had so influenced one another that their histories, though distinct, are inseparable. Through Alexander and his successors, the Achaemenids had passed to Rome the ideas and style of a divine kingship whose roots lay in ancient Mesopotamia; from Rome they went on to flower in the Byzantine Christian empire which fought the Sassanids. Persia and Rome fascinated and, in the end, helped to destroy one another; their antagonism was a fatal commitment to both of them when their attention and resources were urgently needed elsewhere. In the end both succumbed.

THE SASSANIDS

THE FIRST SASSANID, Ardashir, or Artaxerxes, had a strong sense of continuing Persian tradition. He deliberately evoked memories of the Parthians and the Great King, and his successors followed him in cultivating them by sculpture and inscription. Ardashir claimed all the lands once ruled by Darius and went on himself to conquer the oases of Merv and Khiva, and invade

The survival of the Sassanid monarchy depended on its control of the army and of religion. The latter was used to sanction the divine status of royal authority. In this Persian bas-relief from Naqsh-i-Rustam, the gods Mithras and Ahura Mazda are depicted offering a crown to King Ardashir II (379–383).

The Sassanid Empire at the time of Khusrau I

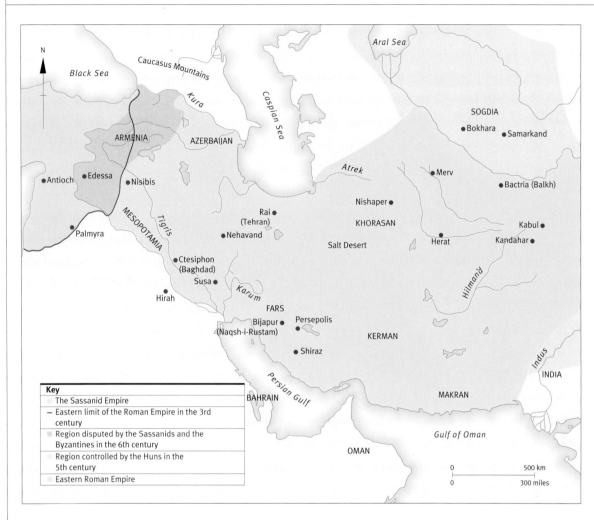

The Sassanid Empire reached the height of its expansion in the 6th century, during the reign of Khusrau I (531–579). In the 3rd century, the Sassanids had expanded their territories into Syria and Armenia. This brought them into conflict with the Roman Empire and other powers anxious to retain access to the commercial silk route. In the 4th century, the Sassanids fought the Byzantines in the west. During the same period, the northeastern Sassanid border was threatened by the Huns. The Sassanid Empire finally succumbed to Arab conquerors in 642, following the battle of Nehavand.

the Punjab; the conquest of Armenia took another hundred and fifty years to confirm but most of it was in the end brought under Persian hegemony. This was the last reconstitution of the ancient Iranian Empire which in the sixth century even dominated the Yemen.

SASSANID GOVERNMENT

Geographical and climatic variety always threatened this huge sprawl of territory with disintegration, but for a long time the Sassanids solved the problems of governing it. There was a bureaucratic tradition running

Time chart (224–651)

200	300	400	500	600	700
	260 Shapur I defeats the Roman emperor Valerian			**578** Sassanid expedition against Ceylon	**651** Yazdigird III, the last Sassanid emperor, is murdered and the Arabs conquer Persia
	224 Ardashir I defeats Artabanus V, the last Parthian emperor, marking the birth of the Sassanid Empire	**363** Shapur II defeats the Roman emperor Julian		**591** Khusrau II wins back the throne, with the help of Roman emperor Maurice	

back to Assyria to build on and a royal claim to divine authority. The tension between these centralizing forces and the interests of great families was what the political history of the Sassanid state was about. The resultant pattern was of alternating periods of kings encumbered or unsuccessful in upholding their claims. There were two good tests of this. One was their ability to appoint their own men to the major offices of state and resist the claims on them of the nobility. The other was their retention of control over the succession. Some kings were deposed and though the kingship itself formally passed by nomination by the ruler, this gave way at times to a semi-electoral system in which the leading officers of state, soldiers and priests made a choice from the royal family.

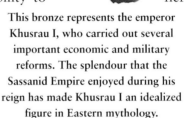

This bronze represents the emperor Khusrau I, who carried out several important economic and military reforms. The splendour that the Sassanid Empire enjoyed during his reign has made Khusrau I an idealized figure in Eastern mythology.

The dignitaries who contested the royal power and often ruled in the satrapies came from a small number of great families which claimed descent from the Parthian Arsacids, the paramount chiefs of that people. They enjoyed large fiefs for their maintenance but their dangerous weight was balanced by two other forces. One was the mercenary army, which was largely officered by members of the lesser nobility, who were thus given some foothold against the greater. Its corps d'élite, the heavy-armed household cavalry, was directly dependent on the king. The other force at work to counteract the dignitaries' power was that of the priesthood.

As well as providing fresh meat, a hunt was a means of demonstrating the king's strength and skill to the court. The decoration on this Sassanid plate portrays Khusrau II taking part in a hunt.

ZOROASTRIANISM

Sassanid Persia was a religious as well as a political unity. Zoroastrianism had been formally restored by Ardashir, who gave important privileges to its priests, the *magi*. They led in due course to political power as well. Priests confirmed the divine nature of the kingship, had important judicial duties, and came, too, to supervise the collection of the land-tax which was the basis of Persian finance. The doctrines they taught seem to have varied considerably from the strict monotheism attributed to Zoroaster but focused on a creator, Ahura Mazda, whose viceroy on earth was the king. The Sassanids' promotion of the state religion was closely connected with the assertion of their own authority.

THE EMERGENCE OF MANICHAEISM

The ideological basis of the Persian state became even more important when the Roman Empire became Christian. Religious differences began to matter much more; religious disaffection came to be seen as political. The wars with Rome made Christianity treasonable. Though Christians in Persia had at first been tolerated, their persecution became logical and continued well into the fifth century. Nor was it only Christians who were tormented. In 276 a Persian religious teacher called Mani was executed – by the particularly agonizing method of being flayed alive. He was to become known in the West under the Latin form of his name, Manichaeus, and the teaching attributed to him had a great future as a Christian heresy. Manichaeism brought together Judaeo-Christian beliefs and Persian mysticism and saw the whole cosmos as a great drama in which the forces of Light and Darkness struggled for domination. Those who apprehended this truth sought to participate in the struggle by practising austerities which would open to them the way to perfection and to harmony with the cosmic

Ahura Mazda was the ancient Persians' principal deity. He later became known as Ormazd, sole creator and god of good. In this stone bas-relief Ahura Mazda is represented by a symbol depicting the winged spirit of light.

drama of salvation. Manichaeism sharply differentiated good and evil, nature and God; its fierce dualism appealed to some Christians who saw in it a doctrine coherent with what Paul had taught. St Augustine was a Manichee in his youth and Manichaean traces have been detected much later in the heresies of medieval Europe. Perhaps an uncompromising dualism has always a strong appeal to a certain cast of mind. However that may be, the distinction of being persecuted both by a Zoroastrian and a Christian monarchy preceded the spread of Manichaean ideas far and wide. Their adherents found refuge in Central Asia and China, where Manichaeism appears to have flourished as late as the thirteenth century.

ORTHODOX CHRISTIANS IN PERSIA

As for orthodox Christians in Persia, although a fifth-century peace stipulated that they should enjoy toleration, the danger that they might turn disloyal in the continual wars

St Augustine, who is depicted in this miniature, was one of a number of distinguished Christians to be influenced by Mani, the son of an important Sassanid family. Before Mani was executed for his beliefs, he had spread his teachings in the East (where he visited China, India and Tibet) as well as in the West (he went to Spain and southern Italy).

This cameo represents the defeat at Edessa in 260 of the Roman emperor Valerian (seen here on the left) at the hands of Shapur I. The victorious Sassanids took Valerian prisoner and went on to plunder 36 cities in the territory abandoned by the Romans.

with Rome made this a dead letter. Only at the end of the century did a Persian king issue an edict of toleration and this was merely to conciliate the Armenians. It did not end the problem; Christians were soon irritated by the vigorous proselytizing of Zoroastrian enthusiasts. Further assurances by Persian kings that Christianity was to be tolerated do not suggest that they were very successful or vigorous in seeing that it was. Perhaps it was impossible against the political background: the exception which proves the rule is provided by the Nestorians, who *were* tolerated by the Sassanids, but this was just because they were persecuted by the Romans. They were, therefore, thought likely to be politically reliable.

THE PERSIAN-ROMAN WARS

Though religion and the fact that Sassanid power and civilization reached their peak under Khusrau I in the sixth century both help to give the rivalry of the empires something of the dimensions of a contest between civilizations, the renewed wars of that century are not very interesting. They offer for the most part a dull, ding-dong story, though they

were the last round but one of the struggle of East and West begun by the Greeks and Persians a thousand years earlier. The climax to this struggle came at the beginning of the seventh century in the last world war of antiquity. Its devastations may well have been the fatal blow to the Hellenistic urban civilization of the Near East.

Khusrau II, the last great Sassanid, then ruled Persia. His opportunity seemed to have come when a weakened Byzantium – Italy was already gone and the Slavs and Avars were pouring into the Balkans – lost a good emperor, murdered by mutineers. Khusrau owed a debt of gratitude to the dead Maurice, for he had been restored to the Persian throne with his aid. He seized on the crime as an excuse and said he would avenge it. His armies poured into the Levant, ravaging the cities of Syria. In 615 they sacked Jerusalem, bearing away the relic of the True Cross which was its most famous treasure. The Jews, it may be remarked, often welcomed the Persians and seized the chance to carry out pogroms of Christians no doubt all the more delectable because the boot had for so long been on the other foot. The next year Persian armies went on to invade Egypt; a year later still, their advance-guards paused only a mile from Constantinople. They even put to sea, raided Cyprus and seized Rhodes from the empire. The empire of Darius seemed to be restored almost at the moment when, at the other end of the Mediterranean, the Roman Empire was losing its last possessions in Spain.

HERACLIUS

This was the blackest moment for Rome in her long struggle with Persia, but a saviour was at hand. In 610 the imperial viceroy of Carthage, Heraclius, had revolted against

Maurice's successor and ended that tyrant's bloody reign by killing him. In his turn he received the imperial crown from the Patriarch. The disasters in Asia could not at once be stemmed but Heraclius was to prove one of the greatest of the soldier emperors. Only sea-power saved Constantinople in 626, when the Persian army could not be transported to support an attack on the city by their Avar allies. Next year Heraclius broke into Assyria and Mesopotamia, the old disputed heartland of Near Eastern strategy. The Persian army mutinied, Khusrau was murdered and his successor made peace. The great days of Sassanid power were over. The relic of the True Cross – or what was said to be such – was restored to Jerusalem. The long duel of Persia and Rome was at an end and the focus of world history was to shift at last to another conflict.

Following Khusrau II's defeat by the emperor Heraclius, who is represented on this coin, the descendants of the Sassanid Empire's last king fled to China.

THE ASIAN NOMADS

The Sassanids went under in the end because they had too many enemies. The year 610 had brought a bad omen: for the first time an Arab force defeated a Persian army. But for centuries Persian kings had been much more preoccupied with enemies on their northern frontiers than with those of the south. They had to contend with the nomads of Central Asia who have already made their mark on this narrative, but whose history it is hard to see either as a whole or in detail. None the less, one salient fact is clear – for nearly fifteen centuries these peoples provided an impetus in world history which was felt spasmodically and confusedly and had results ranging from the Germanic invasions of the West to the revitalizing of Chinese government in East Asia.

The best starting-point is geography. The place from which they came, "Central Asia", is not very well named. The term is imprecise. "Land-locked Asia" might be better, for it is its remoteness from oceanic contact which distinguishes the crucial area. In the first place, this remoteness produced a distinctive and arid climate; secondly, it ensured until modern times an almost complete seclusion from external political pressure, though Buddhism, Christianity and Islam all showed that it was open to cultural influence from the outside.

One way to envisage the area is in a combination of human and topographic terms. It is that part of Asia which is suitable for nomads and it runs like a huge corridor from east to west for four thousand miles or so. Its

Caravanserais, which were large inns built around internal courtyards, provided accommodation for the many caravans that passed through the trade cities in Asia's oases. This elaborately decorated portal formed the entrance to the Rabati-Malik caravanserai near Bokhara in Uzbekistan.

northern wall is the Siberian forest mass; the southern is provided by deserts, great mountain ranges, and the plateaux of Tibet and Iran. For the most part it is grassy steppe, though the boundary with the desert fluctuates and it extends into it to important oases which have always been a distinctive part of its economy. They sheltered settled populations whose way of life both aroused the antagonism and envy of the nomads and also complemented it. The oases were most frequent and richest in the region of the two great rivers known to the Greeks as the Oxus and the Jaxartes. Cities rose there which were famous for their wealth and skills – Bokhara, Samarkand, Merv – and the trade-routes which bound distant China to the West passed through them.

for their culture than for their genetic stock. By the first millennium BCE they were specialists in the difficult art of living on the move, following pasture with their flocks and herds and mastering the special skills this demanded. It is almost completely true that until modern times they remained illiterate and they lived in a mental world of demons and magic except when converted to the higher religions. They were skilled horsemen and especially adept in the use of the composite bow, the weapon of the mounted archer, which took extra power from its construction not from a single piece of wood but from strips of wood and horn. They could carry out elaborate weaving, carving and decoration, but, of course, did not build, for they lived in their tents.

NOMADIC CULTURE

No one knows the ultimate origins of the peoples of Central Asia. They seem distinctive at the moment they enter history, but more

When a Scythian leader died, a funeral ceremony was held beside his tomb. The rituals performed included the sacrifice of his wives, servants and horses, as depicted in the decoration of this 5th- or 4th-century BCE gold comb, found in a royal tomb.

THE SCYTHIANS

The first to be named among these peoples were the Scythians, though it is not easy to say very precisely who they were. Scythians have been identified by archaeologists in many parts of Asia and Russia, and as far into Europe as Hungary. They seem to have had a long history of involvement in the affairs of the Near East. Some of them are reported harrying the Assyrian borders in the eighth century BCE. Later they attracted the attention of Herodotus, who had much to say about a people who fascinated the Greeks. Possibly they were never really one people, but a group of related tribes. Some of them seem to have settled in south Russia long enough to build up regular relations with the Greeks as farmers, exchanging grain for the beautiful gold objects made by the Greeks of the Black Sea coasts which have been found in Scythian graves. But they also most impressed the Greeks as warriors, fighting in the way which was to be characteristic of the Asian nomads,

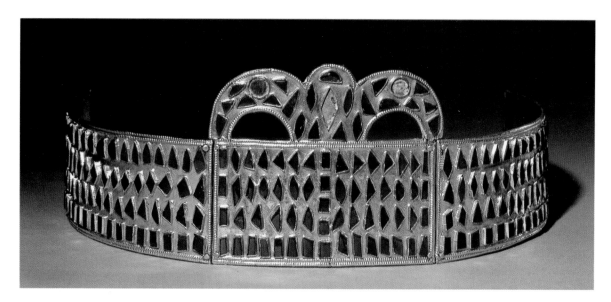

This stunning gold crown, decorated with precious stones, is thought to have belonged to the Hun people. It was found in Hungary.

using bow and arrow from horseback, falling back when faced with a superior force. They harassed the Achaemenids and their successors for centuries and shortly before 100 BCE overran Parthia.

The Scythians can serve as an example of the way in which such peoples are set in motion, for they were responding to very distant impulses. They moved because other peoples were moving them. The balance of life in Central Asia was always a nice one; even a small displacement of power or resources could deprive a people of its living-space and force it to long treks in search of a new livelihood. Nomads could not travel fast with flocks and herds, but seen from a background of long immunity their irruptions into settled land could seem dramatically sudden. It is through its large-scale periodic upheavals rather than the more or less continuous frontier raiding and pillaging that Central Asia has made its impact on world history.

THE HSIUNG-NU

In the third century BCE another nomadic people was at the height of its power in Mongolia, the Hsiung-Nu, in whom some recognize the first appearance on the historical stage of those more familiar as Huns. For centuries they were a byword; all sources agree at least that they were most unpleasant opponents, ferocious, cruel and, unfortunately, skilled warriors. It was against them that the Chinese emperors built the Great Wall, a fourteen-hundred-mile-long insurance policy. Later Chinese governments none the less found it inadequate protection and suffered at the Huns' hands until they embarked on a forward policy, penetrating Asia so as to outflank the Hsiung-Nu. This led to a Chinese occupation of the Tarim basin up to the foothills of the Pamirs and the building on its north side of a remarkable series of frontier works. It was an early example of the generation of imperialism by suction; great powers can be drawn into areas of no concern to them except as sources of trouble. Whether or not this Chinese advance was the primary cause, the Hsiung-Nu now turned on their fellow nomads and began to push west. This drove before them another people, the Yueh-chih, who in turn pushed out of their way more Scyths. At the end of the line stood the post-Seleucid Greek state of Bactria; it disappeared towards 140 BCE and the Scythians then went on to invade Parthia.

The Huns advanced determinedly towards western Europe from the 4th century. In the year 451, led by Attila, they reached Gaul, where they were detained by an alliance of Franks and Romans. The following year, Attila attempted to invade Italy – Pope Leo I is widely believed to have begged him not to do so. The scene is depicted in this 16th-century fresco by Raphael.

They also pushed into south Russia, and into India, but that part of the story may be set aside for a moment. The history of the Central Asian peoples quickly takes non-specialists out of their depth; experts are in much disagreement, but it is clear that there was no comparable major upheaval such as that of the third century BCE for another four hundred years or so. Then about 350 CE came the re-emergence of the Hsiung-Nu in history, when Huns began to invade the Sassanid Empire (where they were known as Chionites). In the north, Huns had been moving west-wards from Lake Baikal for centuries, driven before more successful rivals as others had been driven before them. Some were to appear west of the Volga in the next century; we have already met them near Troyes in 451. Those who turned south were a new handicap to Persia in its struggle with Rome.

THE TURKS

Only one more major people from Asia remains to be introduced, the Turks. Again, the first impact on the outside world was indirect. The eventual successors of the Hsiung-Nu in Mongolia had been a tribe called the Juan-Juan. In the sixth century its survivors were as far west as Hungary, where they were known as Avars; they are noteworthy for introducing a revolution in cavalry warfare to Europe by introducing there the stirrup, which had given them an impor-tant advantage. But they were only in Europe because in about 550 they had been displaced in Mongolia by the Turks, a clan of iron-workers who had been their slaves. Among them were tribes – Khazars, Pechenegs, Cumans – which played important parts in the later history of the Near East and Russia.

The Khazars were Byzantium's allies against Persia, when the Avars were allies of the Sassanids. What is called the first Turkish Empire seems to have been a loose dynastic connexion of such tribes running from the Tamir river to the Oxus. A Turkish khan sent emissaries to Byzantium in 568, roughly nine centuries before other Turks were to enter Constantinople in triumph. In the seventh century the Turks accepted the nominal suzerainty of the Chinese emperors, but by then a new element had entered Near Eastern history, for in 637 Arab armies overran Mesopotamia.

This follow-up to the blows of Heraclius announced the end of an era in Persian

The Euro-Asiatic nomadic peoples

In the 4th century there was already a number of various "barbarian" peoples living in the Euro-Asiatic region who were to play an important role in its future political and economic structure. These peoples all shared a nomadic way of life and an economy based on animal husbandry or rudimentary trade.

At the end of the 4th century there was a huge population explosion among the region's nomadic peoples. This encouraged many of them, including the notorious Huns, to break through the frontiers of the great empires of the time – Chinese, Indian (Gupta),

This detail from a fresco at the Moldovita Monastery in Romania shows Turkish warriors slaughtering Christians during a siege of the Byzantine capital, Constantinople.

Persian (Sassanid) and Roman – all of which offered cities to sack and peoples to enslave. When, in around 550, the Turks from Alta (near present-day Mongolia) started to move westwards, it was the culmination of centuries of often aggressive migration by the Euro-Asiatic nomads. By the 10th century, the Turks had arrived at the frontiers of Byzantium.

Numerous legends surround the birth of the prophet Muhammad, depicted in this manuscript – it is even said that the baby was washed by the angels themselves. Tradition also tells how Muhammad's grandfather, al-Muttalib, noticed that his grandson's footprint was identical to that of the patriarch Abraham, supposedly preserved in the shrine of the Kaaba at Mecca.

history. In 620 Sassanid rule stretched from Cyrenaica to Afghanistan and beyond; just thirty years later it no longer existed. The Sassanid Empire was gone, its last king murdered by his subjects in 651. More than a dynasty passed away, for the Zoroastrian state went down before a new religion as well as before the Arab armies and it was one in whose name the Arabs would go on to yet greater triumphs.

ISLAM

ISLAM HAS SHOWN greater expansive and adaptive power than any other religion except Christianity. It has appealed to peoples as different and as distant from one another as Nigerians and Indonesians; even in its heartland, the lands of Arabic civilization between the Nile and the Hindu Kush, it encompasses huge differences of culture and

climate. Yet none of the other great shaping factors of world history was based on fewer initial resources, except perhaps the Jewish religion. Perhaps significantly, the Jews' own nomadic origins lay in the same sort of tribal society, barbaric, raw and backward, which supplied the first armies of Islam. The comparison inevitably suggests itself for another reason, for Judaism, Christianity and Islam are the great monotheistic religions. None of them, in their earliest stages, could have been predicted to be world-historical forces, except perhaps by their most obsessed and fanatical adherents.

THE PROPHET MUHAMMAD

The history of Islam begins with Muhammad, but not with his birth, for its date is one of many things which are not known about him. His earliest Arabic biographer did not write until a century or so after he died and even his account survives only indirectly. What is known is that round about 570 Muhammad was born in the Hejaz of poor parents, and was soon an orphan. He emerges as an individual in young manhood preaching the message that there is one God, that He is just and will judge all men, who may assure their salvation by following His will in their religious observance and their personal and social behaviour. This God had been preached before, for he was the God of Abraham and the Jewish prophets, of whom the last had been Jesus of Nazareth.

Muhammad belonged to a minor clan of an important Bedouin tribe, the Quraysh. It was one of many in the huge Arabian peninsula, an area six hundred miles wide and over a thousand long. Those who lived there were subjected to very testing physical conditions; scorched in its hot season, most of Arabia was desert or rocky mountain. In much of it even survival was an achievement. But round its fringes there were little ports, the homes of Arabs who had been seafarers even in the second millennium BCE. Their enterprise linked the Indus valley to Mesopotamia and brought the spices and gums of East Africa up the Red Sea to Egypt. The origins of these peoples and those who lived inland is disputed, but both language and the traditional genealogies which go back to Old Testament patriarchs suggest ties with other early Semitic pastoralists who were also ancestors of the Jews, however disagreeable such a conclusion may be to some Arabs today.

Arabia had not always been so uninviting. Just before and during the first centuries of the Common Era it contained a group of prosperous kingdoms. They survived until, possibly, the fifth century CE; both Islamic tradition and modern scholarship link their disappearance with the collapse of the irrigation arrangements of southern Arabia. This produced migration from south to north, which created the Arabia of Muhammad's day. None of the great empires had penetrated more than briefly into the peninsula, and Arabia had undergone little sophisticating fertilization from higher civilizations. It declined swiftly into a tribal society based on nomadic pastoralism. To regulate its affairs, patriarchal and kinship arrangements were enough so long as the Bedouin remained in the desert.

MECCA

At the end of the sixth century new changes can be detected. At some oases, population was growing. There was no outlet for it and this was straining traditional social practice. Mecca, where the young Muhammad lived, was such a place. It was important both as an oasis and as a pilgrim centre, for people came

to it from all over Arabia to venerate a black meteoric stone, the Kaaba, which had for centuries been important in Arab religion. But Mecca was also an important junction of caravan routes between the Yemen and Mediterranean ports. Along them came foreigners and strangers. The Arabs were polytheists, believing in nature gods, demons and spirits, but as intercourse with the outside world increased, Jewish and Christian

The Great Mosque at Mecca is shown in this Persian gouache by Mustafa-al-Shukri. Pilgrims still flock to Mecca to worship at the Kaaba shrine – seen here in the centre of the image.

Arabia in the 7th century

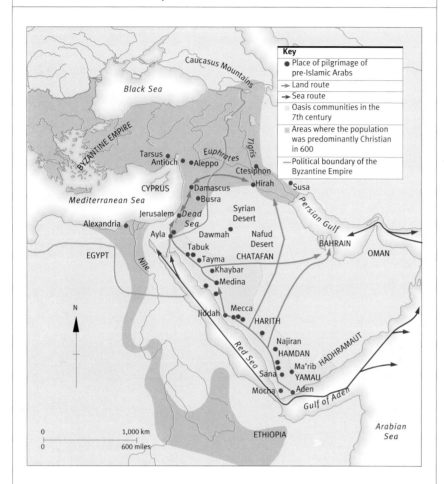

Key
- Place of pilgrimage of pre-Islamic Arabs
- Land route
- Sea route
- Oasis communities in the 7th century
- Areas where the population was predominantly Christian in 600
- Political boundary of the Byzantine Empire

For hundreds of years, the two main commercial routes through Arabia were the Nile passage and the Tigris-Euphrates route to the Persian Gulf. At the end of the 6th century, as a result of the conflicts threatening to engulf the Persian and Byzantine empires, these routes fell into disuse. The route through the oasis city of Mecca soon replaced them. Mecca itself became one of the greatest trade centres of its time and a powerful economic oligarchy emerged there. Several smaller but prosperous commercial towns also lined the route between the Yemen and the Mediterranean ports.

were compromised by commercial values. The social relationships of a pastoral society assumed noble blood and age to be the accepted concomitants of wealth and this was no longer always the case. Here were some of the formative psychological pressures working on the tormented young Muhammad. He began to ponder the ways of God to man. In the end he articulated a system which helpfully resolved many of the conflicts arising in his disturbed society and gave it a set of beliefs still alive today.

THE KORAN AND MUHAMMAD'S TEACHING

The roots of Muhammad's achievement lay in the observation of the contrast between the Jews and Christians who worshipped the God familiar also to his own people as Allah, and the Arabs; Christians and Jews had a scripture for reassurance and guidance, and Muhammad's people had none. One day while he contemplated in a cave outside Mecca a voice came to him revealing his task:

"Recite, in the name of the Lord, who created, Created man from a clot of blood."

For twenty-two years Muhammad was to recite and the result is one of the great formative books of humankind, the Koran. Its narrowest significance is still enormous and, like that of Luther's Bible or the Authorized Version, it is linguistic; the Koran crystallized a language. It was the crucial document of Arabic culture not only because of its content but because it was to propagate the Arabic tongue in a written form. But it is much more; it is a visionary's book, passionate in its conviction of divine inspiration; vividly conveying Muhammad's spiritual genius and vigour. Though not collected in his lifetime,

communities appeared in the area; there were Christian Arabs before there were Muslims.

At Mecca some of the Quraysh began to go in for commerce (another of the few early biographical facts we know about Muhammad is that in his twenties he was married to a wealthy Qurayshi widow who had money in the caravan business). But such developments brought further social strains as the unquestioned loyalties of tribal structure it was taken down by his entourage as delivered by him in a series of revelations; Muhammad saw himself as a passive instrument, a mouthpiece of God. The word *Islam* means submission or surrender. Muhammad believed he was to convey God's message to the Arabs as other messengers had earlier brought His word to other peoples. But Muhammad was sure that his position was special; though there had been prophets before him, their revelations heard (but falsified) by Jew and Christian, he was the final Prophet. Through him, Muslims were to believe, God spoke his last message to his creation.

The message demanded exclusive service for Allah. Tradition says that Muhammad on one occasion entered the Kaaba's shrine and struck with his staff all the images of the other deities which his followers were to wash out, sparing only that of the Virgin and Child (he retained the stone itself). His teaching began with the uncompromising preaching of monotheism in a polytheistic religious centre. He went on to define a series of observances necessary to salvation and a social and personal code which often conflicted with current ideas, for example in its attention to the status of the individual believer, whether man, woman or child. It can readily be understood that such teaching was not always welcome. It seemed yet another disruptive and revolutionary influence – as it was – setting its converts against those of their tribe who worshipped the old gods and would certainly go to hell for it. It might damage the pilgrim business, too (though in the upshot it improved it, for Muhammad insisted strictly on the value of pilgrimage to so holy a place). Finally, as a social tie Muhammad's teaching placed blood second to belief; it was the brotherhood of believers which was the source of community, not the kinship group.

The Koran

"Give thou good tidings to those who believe
and do deeds of righteousness, that for them
await gardens underneath which rivers flow;
whensoever they are provided with fruits therefrom
they shall say, 'This is that wherewithal
we were provided before'; that they shall be
given in perfect semblance; and there
for them shall be spouses purified; therein
they shall dwell forever.

"God is not ashamed to strike a similitude
even of a gnat, or aught above it.
As for the believers, they know it is the truth
from their Lord; but as for unbelievers,
they say, 'What did God desire by this
for a similitude?' Thereby He leads
many astray, and thereby He guides
many; and thereby He leads none astray
save the ungodly such as break the covenant of
God after its solemn binding, and such as cut
what God has commanded should be joined,
and such as do corruption in the land –
they shall be the losers."

An extract from v. 23/25, Book II ("The Cow") of the Koran, translated by Arthur J. Arberry.

Muhammad's marriage to Khadijah, which is represented in this manuscript illustration, took place in the year 595. Khadijah was a wealthy widow who had been married twice previously. She bore Muhammad four daughters and two sons, although both the boys died in infancy.

The five pillars of the Islamic faith

The Islamic religion has five precepts, known as the pillars of the faith. The first, the *shahada*, is summarized in the phrase "there is no god but God and Muhammad is His messenger". The recitation of this phrase in the presence of another Muslim, preceded by the words "I testify", is sufficient to join the faith.

The second pillar of Islam involves compulsory formal prayers (*salat*), which must be said at least five times a day – at dawn, noon, mid-afternoon, evening and night. The faithful pray facing in the direction of their most holy city, Mecca. This is considered to be Muslims' most important duty and is their way of paying homage to God.

The third pillar of the Muslim religion is the giving of alms. There are two types of alms: the *sadaqa*, which is given voluntarily, and the *zakat*, which is obligatory and is collected by the state in Islamic countries as a portion of each person's income.

Fasting (*sawm*) constitutes the fourth precept. The fasting takes place during Ramadan, the ninth month in the Muslim calendar, during which it is believed the Koran was first revealed to Muhammad. All Muslims, with the exception of children, pregnant women and the sick, must fast from dawn until sunset.

The last precept is the pilgrimage to Mecca (*hajj*), which every Muslim who is able to has to undertake at least once during his or her lifetime.

The *jihad*, although not one of the five pillars, is considered equally important by many Muslims. Often translated as "holy war", *jihad* signifies the individual's duty to defend the faith – for example, by protecting fellow Muslims who are persecuted for their beliefs.

The sacred book of the Islamic religion is the Koran, the text of which is believed to have been revealed to Muhammad by God. Throughout its 114 chapters, or suras, the beliefs and duties to which all good Muslims must adhere are detailed. The above pages are taken from a copy of the Koran that was produced in Damascus in the 18th century.

THE *HEGIRA*

It is not surprising that the leaders of his tribe turned on Muhammad. Some of his followers emigrated to Ethiopia, a monotheistic country already penetrated by Christianity. Economic boycott was employed against the recalcitrant who stayed. Muhammad heard that the atmosphere might be more receptive at another oasis about two hundred and fifty miles further north, Yathrib. Preceded by some two hundred followers, he left Mecca and went there in 622. This *Hegira*, or emigration, was to be the beginning of the Muslim calendar and Yathrib was to change its name, becoming the "city of the prophet", Medina.

It, too, was an area unsettled by economic and social change. Unlike Mecca, though, Medina was not dominated by one powerful tribe, but was a focus of competition for two; moreover, there were other Arabs there who adhered to Judaism. Such divisions favoured Muhammad's leadership. Converted families gave hospitality to the immigrants. The two groups were to form the future élite of Islam, the "Companions of the Prophet". Muhammad's writings for them show a new direction in his concerns, that of organizing a community. From the spiritual emphasis of his Mecca revelations he turned to practical, detailed statements about food, drink, marriage, war. The characteristic flavour of Islam, a religion which was also a civilization and a community, was now being formed.

THE ISLAMIC BROTHERHOOD

Medina was the base for subduing first Mecca and then the remaining tribes of Arabia. A unifying principle was available in Muhammad's idea of the *umma*, the brotherhood of believers. It integrated Arabs (and, at

first, Jews) in a society which maintained much of the traditional tribal framework, stressing the patriarchal structure in so far as it did not conflict with the new brotherhood of Islam, even retaining the traditional primacy of Mecca as a place of pilgrimage. Beyond this it is not clear how far Muhammad wished to go. He had made approaches to Jewish tribesmen at Medina, but they had refused to accept his claims; they were therefore driven out, and a Muslim community alone remained, but this need not have implied any enduring conflict with either Judaism or its continuator, Christianity. Doctrinal ties existed in their monotheism and their scriptures even if Christians were believed to fall into polytheism with the idea of the Trinity. Nevertheless, Muhammad enjoined the conversion of the infidel and for those who wished there was a justification here for proselytizing.

Muhammad's flight to Yathrib, depicted on this 16th-century Turkish manuscript, marks the start of the Muslim calendar. Although the representation of human figures is forbidden in Islamic religious art, the work from which this image is taken (*The Life of the Prophet* from the Topkapi Palace in Istanbul) is one of three manuscripts that are an exception to this rule. The face of Muhammad, however, can never be shown and in this illustration, as in others from the same source, the Prophet's head is covered.

MUHAMMAD'S LEGACY

Muhammad died in 632. At that moment the community he had created was in grave danger of division and disintegration. Yet on it two Arab empires were to be built, dominating successive historical periods from two different centres of gravity. In each the key institution was the caliphate, the inheritance of Muhammad's authority as the head of a community, both its teacher and its ruler. From the start, there was no tension of religious and secular authority in Islam, no "Church and State" dualism such as was to shape Christian policies for a thousand years and more. Muhammad, it has been well said, was his own Constantine, prophet and sovereign in one. His successors would not prophesy as he had done, but they were long to enjoy his legacy of unity in government and religion.

Following the death of Muhammad, Abu-Bakr, the father of one of the Prophet's nine wives, became the first caliph and initiated the expansion of Islam to Chaldea, Palestine and Trans-Jordan. His successor, Umar, continued the territorial conquests through Syria, Iraq, Mesopotamia, Egypt and Persia. Umar was replaced by Uthman, Muhammad's son-in-law, who was assassinated and succeeded by Ali, the Prophet's cousin. These caliphs are all depicted surrounding Muhammad in this illustration.

THE CALIPHS

The first "patriarchal" caliphs were all Quraysh, most of them related to the Prophet by blood or marriage. Soon, they were criticized for their wealth and status and were alleged to act as tyrants and exploiters. The last of them was deposed and killed in 661 after a series of wars in which conservatives contested what they saw as the deterioration of the caliphate from a religious to a secular office. The year 661 saw the beginning of the Umayyad caliphate, the first of the two major chronological divisions of Arab empire, focused on Syria, with its capital as Damascus. It did not bring struggle within the Arab world to an end for in 750 the Abbasid caliphate displaced it. The new caliphate lasted longer. Soon moved to a new location, Baghdad, it would survive nearly two centuries (until 946) as a real power and even longer as a puppet régime. Between them the two dynasties gave the Arab peoples three centuries of ascendancy in the Near East.

ISLAMIC CONQUESTS

The first and most obvious expression of Arab ascendancy was a great series of conquests in the first century of Islam which remade the world map from Gibraltar to the Indus. They had in fact begun immediately after the Prophet's death with the assertion of the first caliph's authority. Abu-Bakr set about conquering the unreconciled tribes of southern and eastern Arabia for Islam. But this led to fighting which spread to Syria and Iraq. Something analogous to the processes by which barbarian disturbances in Central Asia rolled outward in their effects was at work in the overpopulated Arabian peninsula; this time there was a creed to give it direction as well as a simple love of plunder.

The spread of early Islam

When Muhammad died in 632, members of the new faith were centred around the Arabian cities of Mecca and Medina. The early Muslims quickly began the long campaign of Islamic expansion: in 655 Muslim armies arrived in Samarkand to the east and in Tripoli to the west. Although they defeated Sassanid Persia, the Muslims were prevented from expanding into eastern Europe by the Byzantine defensive. However, between 634 and 650, they did take control of Libya, Syria, Palestine, Iraq and Egypt, among others, recruiting soldiers from new converts to the faith. In 711, the caliph's armies conquered Spain at the same time as arriving in India and China. The European conquests ended in 732 when the Franks defeated the Muslims at Poitiers.

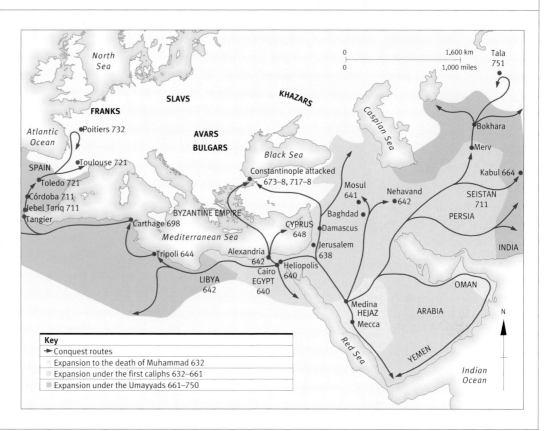

Once beyond the peninsula, the first victim of Islam was Sassanid Persia. The challenge came just as she was under strain at the hands of the Heraclian emperors who were likewise to suffer from this new scourge. In 633 Arab armies invaded Syria and Iraq. Three years later the Byzantine forces were driven from Syria and in 638 Jerusalem fell to Islam. Mesopotamia was wrested from the Sassanids in the next couple of years, and at about the same time Egypt was taken from the empire. An Arab fleet was now created and the absorption of North Africa began. Cyprus was raided in the 630s and 640s; later in the century it was divided between the Arabs and the empire. At the end of the century the Arabs took Carthage, too. Meanwhile, after the Sassanids' disappearance the Arabs had conquered Khurasan in 655, Kabul in 664; at the beginning of the eighth century they

crossed the Hindu Kush to invade Sind, which they occupied between 708 and 711. In the latter year an Arab army with Berber allies crossed the Straits of Gibraltar (its Berber commander, Tariq, is commemorated in that name, which means *Jebel Tariq*, or mount of Tariq) and advanced into Europe, shattering at last the Visigothic kingdom. Finally, in 732, a hundred years after the death of the Prophet, the Muslim army, deep in France, puzzled by overextended communications and the approach of winter, turned back near Poitiers. The Franks who faced them and killed their commander claimed a victory; at any rate, it was the high-water mark of Arab conquest, though in the next few years Arab expeditions raided into France as far as the upper Rhône. Whatever brought it to an end (and possibly it was just because the Arabs were not much interested in European conquest, once away from the warm lands of the Mediterranean littoral), the Islamic onslaught in the West remains an astonishing achievement, even if Gibbon's vision of an Oxford teaching the Koran was never remotely close to realization.

The Arab armies were at last stopped in the East, too, although at a cost of two sieges of Constantinople and the confining of the empire to the Balkans and Anatolia. From eastern Asia there is a report that an Arab force reached China in the early years of the eighth century; even if questionable, such a story is evidence of the conquerors' prestige. What is certain is that the frontier of Islam settled down along the Caucasus mountains and the Oxus after a great Arab defeat at the hands of the Khazars in Azerbaijan, and a victory in 751 over a Chinese army commanded by a Korean general on the river Talas, in the high Pamirs. On all fronts, in western Europe, Central Asia, Anatolia and in the Caucasus, the tide of Arab conquest at last came to an end in the middle of the eighth century.

FAVOURABLE CONDITIONS FOR ISLAM

The Arab drive to conquer had not been uninterrupted. There had been something of a lull in Arab aggressiveness during the internecine quarrelling just before the establishment of the Umayyad caliphate and there had been bitter fighting of Muslim against Muslim in the last two decades of the seventh century. But for a long time circumstances favoured the Arabs. Their first great enemies, Byzantium and Persia, had both had heavy commitments on other fronts and had been for centuries one another's fiercest antagonists. After Persia went under, Byzantium still had to contend with enemies in the west and to the north, fending them off with one hand while grappling with the Arabs with the other. Nowhere did the Arabs face an opponent comparable to the Byzantine Empire nearer than China. Because of this, they pressed their conquests to the limit of geographical possibility or attractiveness, and sometimes their defeat showed they had overstretched themselves. Even when they met formidable opponents, though, the Arabs still had great military advantages. Their armies were recruited from hungry fighters to whom the Arabian desert had left small alternative; the spur of overpopulation was behind them. Their assurance in the Prophet's teaching that death on the battlefield against the infidel would be followed by certain removal to paradise was a huge moral advantage. They fought their way, too, into lands whose peoples were often already disaffected with their rulers; in Egypt, for example, Byzantine religious orthodoxy had created dissident and alienated minorities. Yet when all such influences have been totted up, the Arab success remains amazing. The fundamental explanation must lie in the movement of large numbers of individuals by a religious ideal. The Arabs thought they were doing God's will and creating a new brotherhood in the process; they generated an excitement in themselves like that of later revolutionaries. And conquest was only the beginning of the story of the impact of Islam on the world. In its range and complexity it can only be compared to that of Judaism or Christianity. At one time it looked as if Islam might be irresistible everywhere. That was not to be, but one of the great traditions of civilization was to be built on its conquests and conversions.

وَكَادَ يَزعَزِعُ الجِمَالَ الشَّمَّ وَالنُّشَّدَ
مَا الحَجُّ سَيرُكَتَا وَبَيَّاوَاذلاجَا وَلَا اعَيَاَمَّ جِمَالًا وَاحِدَأَ

الحَجُّ أَنُ نَقصِدَ البَيتَ الحَرَامَ عَلَى تَحرِيمِ الحَجِّ لَا تَبغِي بِهِ حَاجَا
وَسَعِي كَاهِلِ الإِنصَافِ مُتَّخِذًا رَدعَ الهَوَى هَادِيًا وَالحَقَّ مِنهَاجَا

This illustration, dating from the 13th century, depicts the Islamic warrior Maqamat de al-Hariri and his troops going into battle.

2 *THE ARAB EMPIRES*

This image, which dates from 1237, illustrates a poem by the 10th-century writer Al-Mutanabbi about the Muslim conquest of Spain.

IN 661 THE ARAB GOVERNOR OF SYRIA, Mu-Awiyah, set himself up as caliph after a successful rebellion and the murder (though not at his hands) of the caliph Ali, cousin and son-in-law of the Prophet. This ended a period of anarchy and division, and so, thought many Muslims, excused what he did. It was also the foundation of the Umayyad caliphate.

THE UMAYYAD CALIPHATE

THIS USURPATION gave political ascendancy among the Arab peoples to the aristocrats of the Quraysh, the very people who had opposed Muhammad at Mecca. Mu-Awiyah set up his capital at Damascus and later named his son crown prince, an innovation which introduced the dynastic principle. This was also the beginning of a schism within Islam, for a dissident group, the Shi'ites, henceforth claimed that the right of interpreting the Koran was confined to Muhammad's descendants. The murdered caliph, they said, had been divinely designated as *imam* to transmit his office to his descendants and was immune from sin and error. The Umayyad caliphs, correspondingly, had their own party of supporters, called Sunnites, who believed that doctrinal authority changed hands with the caliphate. Together with the creation of a regular army and a system of supporting it by taxation of the unbelievers, a decisive movement was thus made away from an Arab world solely of tribes. The site of the Umayyad capital, too, was important in changing the style of Islamic culture, as were the personal tastes of the first caliph. Syria was a Mediterranean state, but

Time chart (c.570–c.1300)				
	661 Founding of the Umayyad caliphate of Damascus	973 Cairo becomes the capital of the Fatimid caliphate		1250 The Mamelukes come to power in Egypt
600	800	1000	1200	1400
c.570 Birth of Muhammad in Mecca	756 Founding of the Umayyad emirate of Córdoba	1010 Beginning of the era of the *taifa* kings in Spain		c.1300–1918 The Ottoman Empire

Mu-Awiyah seized power in 661. He established the capital of Islam in Damascus, the seat of his political and military power, where buildings such as the Great Mosque still serve as reminders of the city's Umayyad past. The last caliph of the Umayyad Dynasty was overthrown in 750.

Damascus was roughly on the border between the cultivated land of the Fertile Crescent and the barren expanses of the desert; its life was fed by two worlds. To the desert-dwelling Arabs, the former must have been the more striking. Syria had a long Hellenistic past and both the caliph's wife and his doctor were Christians. While the barbarians of the West looked to Rome, Arabs were to be shaped by the heritage of Greece.

UMAYYAD GOVERNMENT

The first Umayyad speedily reconquered the East from dissidents who resisted the new régime and the Shi'ite movement was driven underground. There followed a glorious century whose peak came under the sixth and seventh caliphs between 685 and 705.

Unfortunately we know little about the detailed and institutional history of Umayyad times. Archaeology sometimes throws light on general trends and reveals something of the Arabs' impact on their neighbours. Foreign records and Arab chroniclers log important events. Nevertheless, early Arab history produces virtually no archive material apart from an occasional document quoted by an Arab author. Nor did Islamic religion have a bureaucratic centre of ecclesiastical government. Islam had nothing remotely approaching in scope the records of the papacy, for example, though the analogy between the popes and the caliphs might reasonably arouse similar expectations. Instead of administrative records throwing light on continuities there are only occasional collections preserved almost by chance, such as a mass of papyri from Egypt, special

The internal courtyard of the Great Mosque in Damascus, Syria, is shown here with the fountain of ablutions on the left. The mosque dates from 705, the last year of the seventh caliph's reign, and bears testament to the wealth and ambition of the early Umayyad caliphate.

accumulations of documents by minority communities such as the Jews, and coins and inscriptions. The huge body of Arabic literature in print or manuscript provides further details, but it is much more difficult to make general statements about the government of the caliphates with confidence than, say, similar statements about Byzantium.

The characteristic feature of Arab coins is the absence of any figurative decoration. Only religious inscriptions, the name of the mint where the coin was produced, the date and the name of the ruler appear.

TAXATION AND COMMERCE

It seems, none the less, that the early arrangements of the caliphates, inherited from the orthodox caliphs, were loose and simple – perhaps too loose, as the Umayyad defection showed. Their basis was conquest for tribute, not for assimilation, and the result was a series of compromises with existing structures. Administratively and politically, the early caliphs took over the ways of earlier rulers. Byzantine and Sassanid arrangements continued to operate; Greek was the language of government in Damascus, Persian in Ctesiphon, the old Sassanid capital, until the early eighth century. Institutionally, the Arabs left the societies they took over by and large undisturbed except by taxation. Of course, this does not mean that they went on just as before. In northwestern Persia, for example, Arab conquest seems to have been followed by a decline in commerce and a drop in population, and it is hard not to associate this with the collapse of a complex drainage and irrigation system successfully maintained in Sassanid times. In other places, Arab conquest had less drastic effects. The conquered were not antagonized by having to accept Islam, but took their places in a hierarchy presided over by the Arab Muslims.

Below them came the converted neo-Muslims of the tributary peoples, then the *dhimmi*, or "protected persons" as the Jewish and Christian monotheists were called. Lowest down the scale came unconverted pagans or adherents of no revealed religion. In the early days the Arabs were segregated from the native population and lived as a military caste in special towns paid by the taxes raised locally, forbidden to enter commerce or own land.

ARAB INTEGRATION

Segregation could not be kept up. Like the Bedouin customs brought from the desert, it was eroded by garrison life. Gradually the Arabs became landowners and cultivators, and so their camps changed into new, cosmopolitan cities such as Kufa or Basra, the great *entrepôt* of the trade with India. More and more Arabs mixed with the local inhabitants in a two-way relationship, as the indigenous élites underwent an administrative and linguistic arabization. The caliphs appointed more and more of the officials of the provinces and by the mid-eighth century Arabic was almost everywhere the language of administration. Together with the standard coinage bearing Arabic inscriptions it is the major evidence of Umayyad success in laying the foundations of a new, eclectic civilization. Such changes went fastest in Iraq, where they were favoured by prosperity as trade revived under the Arab peace.

The assertion of their authority by the Umayyad caliphs was one source of their troubles. Local bigwigs, especially in the eastern half of the empire, resented interference with their practical independence. Whereas many of the aristocracy of the former Byzantine territories emigrated to Constantinople, the élites of Persia could not; they had nowhere to go and had to remain, irritated by their subordination to the Arabs who left them much of their local authority. Nor did it help that the later Umayyad caliphs were men of poor quality, who did not command the respect won by the great men of the dynasty. Civilization softened them. When they sought to relieve the tedium of life in the towns they governed, they moved out into the desert, not to live again the life of the Bedouin, but to enjoy their new towns and palaces, some of them remote and luxurious, equipped as they were with hot baths and great hunting enclosures and supplied from irrigated plantations and gardens.

THE SHI'A

Umayyad government created opportunities for the disaffected, among whom the Shi'a, the party of the Shi'ites, were especially notable. Besides their original political and religious appeal, they increasingly drew on social grievances among the non-Arab converts to Islam, particularly in Iraq. From the start, the Umayyad régime had distinguished sharply between those Muslims who were and those who were not by birth members of an Arab tribe. The numbers of the latter class grew rapidly; the Arabs had not sought to convert (and sometimes even tried to deter from conversion in early times) but the attractiveness of the conquering creed was powerfully reinforced by the fact that adherence to it might bring tax relief. Around the Arab garrisons, Islam had spread rapidly among the non-Arab populations which grew up to service their needs. It was also very successful among the local élites who

maintained the day-to-day administration. Many of these neo-Muslims, the *mawali*, as they were called, eventually became soldiers, too. Yet they increasingly felt alienated and excluded from the aristocratic society of the pure Arabs. The puritanism and orthodoxy of the Shi'ites, equally alienated from the same society for political and religious reasons, made a great appeal to them.

THE UMAYYAD CALIPHATE LOSES POWER

Increasing trouble in the east heralded the breakdown of Umayyad authority. In 749 a new caliph, Abu-al-Abbas, was hailed publicly in the mosque at Kufa in Iraq. This was the beginning of the end for the Umayyads. The pretender, a descendant of an uncle of the Prophet, announced his intention of restoring the caliphate to orthodox ways; he appealed to a wide spectrum of opposition including the Shi'ites. His full name was promising: it meant "Shedder of Blood". In 750 he defeated and executed the last Umayyad caliph. A dinner-party was held for the males of the defeated house; the guests were murdered before the first course, which was then served to their hosts. With this clearing of the decks began nearly two centuries during which the Abbasid caliphate ruled the Arab world, the first of them the most glorious.

THE ABBASID CALIPHATE

THE SUPPORT THE ABBASIDS ENJOYED in the eastern Arab dominions was reflected by the shift of the capital to Iraq, to Baghdad, until then a Christian village on the Tigris. The change had many implications. Hellenistic influences were weakened; Byzantium's prestige seemed less unquestionable. A new

General disorder, resulting from poor economic and social policies, eventually led to a loss of support for the Umayyad régime. Several insurrections took place, one of which was instigated by the Abbasid party and led by Abu-al-Abbas, who was appointed caliph by his followers in 749 in the mosque at Kufa (Iraq), shown here.

weight was given to Persian influence which was both politically and culturally to be very important. There was a change in the ruling caste, too, and one sufficiently important to lead some historians to call it a social revolution. They were from this time Arabs only in the sense of being Arabic-speaking; they were no longer Arabian. Within the matrix provided by a single religion and a single language the élites which governed the Abbasid Empire came from many peoples right across the Middle East. They were almost always Muslims but they were often converts or children of convert families. The cosmopolitanism of Baghdad reflected the new cultural atmosphere. A huge city, rivalling Constantinople, with perhaps a half-million inhabitants, it was a complete antithesis of the ways of life brought from the desert by the first Arab conquerors. A great empire had come again to the whole Middle East. It did not break with the past ideologically, though, for after dallying with other possibilities the Abbasid caliphs confirmed the Sunnite orthodoxy of their predecessors. This was soon reflected in the disappointment and irritation of the Shi'ites who had helped to bring them to power.

ABBASID RULE

The Abbasids were a violent lot and did not take risks with their success. They quickly and ruthlessly quenched opposition and bridled former allies who might turn sour. Loyalty to the dynasty, rather than the brotherhood of Islam, was increasingly the basis of the empire

This coin was minted during the era of the Abbasid caliphs, who claimed to be descendants of the prophet Muhammad. Their power lasted until the middle of the 11th century, when they were deposed by the Seljuk Turks.

and this reflected the old Persian tradition. Much was made of religion as a buttress to the dynasty, though, and the Abbasids persecuted nonconformists. The machinery of government became more elaborate. Here one of the major developments was that of the office of vizier (monopolized by one family until the legendary caliph Haroun-al-Raschid wiped them out). The whole structure became somewhat more bureaucratized, the land taxes raising a big revenue to maintain a magnificent monarchy. Nevertheless, provincial distinctions remained very real. Governorships tended to become hereditary, and, because of this, central authority was eventually forced on to the defensive. The governors exercised a greater and greater power in appointments and the handling of taxation. It is not easy to say what was the caliphate's real power, for it regulated a loose collection of provinces whose actual dependence was related very much to the circumstances of the moment. But of Abbasid wealth and prosperity at its height there can be no doubt. They rested not only on its great reserves of manpower and the large areas where agriculture was untroubled during the Arab peace, but also upon the favourable conditions it created for trade. A wider range of commodities circulated over a larger area then ever before. This revived commerce in the cities along the caravan routes which passed through the

Arab lands from east to west. The riches of Haroun-al-Raschid's Baghdad reflected the prosperity they brought.

ISLAMIC CIVILIZATION

ISLAMIC CIVILIZATION in the Arab lands reached its peak under the Abbasids. Paradoxically, one reason for this was the movement of its centre of gravity away from Arabia and the Levant. Islam provided a political organization which, by holding together a huge area, cradled a culture which was essentially synthetic, mingling, before it was done, Hellenistic, Christian, Jewish, Zoroastrian and Hindu ideas. Arabic culture under the Abbasids had closer access to the Persian tradition and closer contact with India which brought to it renewed vigour and new creative elements.

One aspect of Abbasid civilization was a great age of translation into Arabic, the new lingua franca of the Middle East. Christian and Jewish scholars made available to Arab readers the works of Plato and Aristotle, Euclid and Galen, thus importing the categories of Greek thought into Arab culture. The tolerance of Islam for its tributaries made this possible in principle from the moment when Syria and Egypt were conquered, but it was under the early Abbasids that the most important translations were made. So much it is possible to chart fairly confidently. To say what this meant, of course, is more difficult, for though the texts of Plato might be available, it was the Plato of late Hellenistic culture, transmitted through interpretations by Christian monks and Sassanid academics.

The astrolabe is a navigational instrument used for observing the position of the stars and for establishing their distance from the horizon. This astrolabe, made by Ibrahim ibn Said al-Sahli in Toledo, Spain, has a very important feature: it indicates the duration of the longest and shortest diurnal arcs of the year for various Eastern, North African and Spanish cities.

The Thousand Nights and One Night

"Then she fell silent, and King Shahryar cried, 'O Shahrazad, that was a noble and admirable story! O wise and subtle one, you have taught me many lessons, letting me see that every man is at the call of Fate; you have made me consider the words of kings and peoples passed away; you have told me some things which were strange, and many that were worthy of reflection. I have listened to you for a thousand nights and one night, and now my soul is changed and joyful, it beats with an appetite for life. I give thanks to Him Who has perfumed your mouth with so much eloquence and has set wisdom to be a seal upon your brow! ... O Shahrazad, I swear by the Lord of Pity that you were already in my heart before the coming of these children. He had given you gifts with which to win me; I loved you in my soul because I had found you pure, holy, chaste, tender, straight-forward, unassailable, ingenious, subtle, eloquent, discreet, smiling, and wise. May Allah bless you, my dear, your father and mother, your root and race! O Shahrazad, this thousand and first night is whiter for us than the day!'"

An extract from the epilogue of *The Book of the Thousand Nights and One Night* by Haroun-al-Raschid (766–809), translated by Powys Mathers from the French rendering by Dr J. C. Mardrus.

LITERARY CULTURE

Abbasid culture was predominantly literary; Arabic Islam produced beautiful buildings, lovely carpets, exquisite ceramics, but its great medium was the word, spoken and written. Even the great Arab scientific works are often huge prose compendia. The accumulated bulk of this literature is immense and much of it simply remains unread by western scholars. Large numbers of its manuscripts have never been examined at all. The prospect is promising; the absence of archive material for early Islam is balanced by a huge corpus of literature of all varieties and forms except the drama. How deeply it penetrated Islamic society remains obscure, though it is clear that educated people expected to be able to write verses and could enjoy critically the performances of singers and bards. Schools were widespread; the Islamic world was probably highly literate by comparison, for example, with medieval Europe. Higher learning, more closely religious in so far as it

Also known as *The Arabian Nights*, *The Book of the Thousand Nights and One Night* is probably the best-known literary work from the Arab world. This illustration from an 18th-century Persian manuscript shows a scene from one of the tales about Sinbad the Sailor.

Astronomy was a fundamental part of Islamic science. This 16th-century Ottoman illustration shows astronomers using various instruments to study the celestial bodies.

Arab science: the writing of Maimonides

"You have to know that as far as the spheres of Venus and Mercury are concerned there are differences of opinion amongst the ancient mathematicians, of whether they are found above the Sun or below, for the position of these two spheres has not been proved. These ancient people were of the opinion that the two spheres of Venus and Mercury are above the Sun. ... Then came Ptolemy, who asserted that they were underneath, alleging that it is more natural to place the Sun in the centre, with three planets above and three below. Later on, there appeared men in El-Andalus ... who proved that Venus and Mercury were found above the Sun, in accordance with the principles of Ptolemy.

"Ibn Aflah of Seville ... wrote a famous book on the subject; and later the eminent philosopher Abu Bakr ibn Al-Sa'ig ... examined the question and formulated some arguments ... by virtue of which the theory that Venus and Mercury lie above the Sun was revoked. But the argument that Abu Bakr cites suggests the improbability and not the impossiblity. So, as it turns out, all the ancient mathematicians placed Venus and Mercury above the Sun, and for this reason they counted five spheres: the Moon, which is undoubtedly near us; the Sun, which has to be above it; the other five planets; the fixed stars and the sphere which surrounds it all, in which there are no stars."

An extract from Chapter 9 of the *Guide for the Perplexed* by Maimonides (1135–1204).

This 13th-century Turkish illustration shows two astrologers in the "House of Wisdom".

was institutionalized in the mosques or special schools of religious teachers, is more difficult to assess. How much, therefore, the potentially divisive and stimulating effect of ideas drawn from other cultures was felt below the level of the leading Islamic thinkers and scientists is hard to say, but potentially many seeds of a questioning and self-critical culture were there from the eighth century onwards. They seem not to have ripened.

SCIENCE AND MATHEMATICS

Judged by its greatest men, Arabic culture was at its height in the East in the ninth and tenth centuries and in Spain in the eleventh and twelfth. Although Arab history and geography are both very impressive, its greatest triumphs were scientific and mathematical; we still employ the "arabic" numerals which made possible written calculations with far astronomical tables, none the less, were an Arabic achievement, an expression of the synthesis made possible by Arab empire.

The translation of Arabic works into Latin in the later Middle Ages, and the huge repute enjoyed by Arab thinkers in Europe, testify to the quality of this culture. Of the works of Al-Kindi, one of the greatest of Arab philosophers, more survive in Latin than in Arabic, while Dante paid Ibn-Sina (Avicenna in Europe) and Averroës the compliment of placing them in limbo (together with Saladin, the Arab hero of the crusading epoch) when he allocated great men to their fate after death in his poem, and they were the only men of the Common Era whom he treated thus. The Persian practitioners who dominated Arabic medical studies wrote works which remained for centuries the standard textbooks of western training. European languages are still marked by Arabic words which indicate the special importance of Arabic study in certain areas: "zero", "cipher", "almanac", "algebra" and "alchemy" are among them. The survival of a technical vocabulary of commerce, too – tariff, *douane*, magazine – is a reminder of the superiority of Arab commercial technique; the Arab merchants taught Christians how to keep accounts. Strikingly, this cultural traffic with Europe was almost entirely one way. Only one Latin text, it appears, was ever translated into Arabic during the Middle Ages, at a time when Arabic scholars were passionately interested in the cultural legacies of Greece, Persia and India. A single fragment of paper bearing a few German words with their Arabic equivalents is the only evidence from eight hundred years of Islamic Spain of any interest in western languages outside the peninsula. The Arabs regarded the civilization of the cold lands of the north as a meagre, unsophisticated affair, as no doubt it was. But Byzantium impressed them.

The prohibition of the use of the human form in Islamic art led to the development of a decorative style based on calligraphy and abstract or floral shapes, as shown in this detail of the mosaics in Córdoba's Great Mosque.

greater simplicity than did Roman numeration and which were set out by an Arab arithmetician (although in origin they were Indian). This transmission function of Arabic culture was always important and characteristic but must not obscure its originality. The name of the greatest of Islamic astronomers, Al-Khwarizmi, indicates Persian Zoroastrian origins; it expresses the way in which Arabic culture was a confluence of sources. His

ARCHITECTURE

An Arabic tradition in visual art founded under the Umayyads also flourished under the Abbasids, but it was narrower in its scope than Islamic science. Islam came to forbid the making of likenesses of the human form or face; this was not scrupulously enforced, but it long inhibited the appearance of naturalistic painting or sculpture. Of course, it did not restrict architects. Their art developed very far within a style whose essentials had appeared at the end of the seventh century; it was at once in debt to the past and unique to Islam. The impression produced upon the Arabs by Christian building in Syria was the catalyst; from it they learnt, but they sought to surpass it, for believers should, they were sure, have places of worship better and more beautiful than the Christians' churches. Moreover, a distinctive architectural style could visibly serve as a separating force in the non-Muslim world which surrounded the first Arab conquerors of Egypt and Syria.

The Arabs borrowed Roman techniques and Hellenistic ideas of internal space, but what resulted was distinctive. The oldest architectural monument of Islam is the Dome of the Rock built at Jerusalem in 691. Stylistically, it is a landmark in architectural history, the first Islamic building with a dome. It appears to have been built as a monument to victory over Jewish and Christian belief, but unlike the congregational mosques which were to be the great buildings of the next three centuries, the Dome of the Rock was a shrine glorifying and sheltering one of the most sacred places of Jew and Muslim alike; men believed that on the hill-top it covered Abraham had offered up his son Isaac in sacrifice and that from it Muhammad was taken up into heaven.

Soon afterwards came the Umayyad mosque at Damascus, the greatest of the

classical mosques of a new tradition. As so often in this new Arab world, it embodied much of the past; a Christian basilica (which had itself replaced a temple of Jupiter) formerly stood on its site, and it was itself decorated with Byzantine mosaics. Its novelty was that it established a design derived from the pattern of worship initiated by the Prophet in his house at Medina; its essential was the *mihrab*, or alcove in the wall of the place of worship, which indicated the direction of Mecca.

THE ARTS

Architecture and sculpture, like literature, continued to flourish and to draw upon elements culled from traditions all over the Near East and Asia. Potters strove to achieve the style and finish of the Chinese porcelain which came to them down the Silk Road. The

Built on the site of the Christian basilica of St Vicente, the Great Mosque in Córdoba is one of the most magnificent edifices of western Islamic architecture. The mosque was begun by Abd-ar-Rahman I in 785 and was enlarged over the following two centuries. Its most striking feature is this prayer hall – a forest of marble columns supporting superimposed arches.

The Dome of the Rock in Jerusalem was built during the caliphate of Abd-al-Malik (685–705). He had several motives for its construction. Rebellions in Medina and Mecca, where an "anti-caliph" had ruled for a decade, had prevented Muslims from making their pilgrimages to those cities' holy sites. A great Islamic shrine in Jerusalem, which was firmly in the control of the Damascus-based caliphate, could provide a secure focus for Muslim pilgrims. Abd-al-Malik also knew that, by attracting Muslim pilgrims as well as Jews and Christians, Jerusalem would grow in status and wealth. Perhaps most importantly, however, the caliph wanted to create an Islamic building that would rival any Christian church in splendour and size.

performing arts were less cultivated and seem to have drawn little on other traditions, whether Mediterranean or Indian. There was no Arab theatre, though the storyteller, the poet, the singer and the dancer were esteemed. Arabic musical art is commemorated in European languages through the names of lute, guitar, and rebec; its achievements, too, have been seen as among the greatest of Arabic culture, though they remain less accessible to Western sensibility than those of the plastic and visual arts.

Many of the greatest names of this civilization were writing and teaching when its political framework was already in decay, even visibly collapsing. In part this was a matter of the gradual displacement of Arabs within the caliphate's élites, but the Abbasids in their turn lost control of their empire, first of the peripheral provinces and then of Iraq itself. As an international force they peaked early; in 782 an Arab army appeared for the last time before Constantinople. They were never to get so far again. Haroun-al-Raschid might have been treated with respect by Charlemagne but the first signs of an eventually irresistible tendency to fragmentation were already there in his day.

UMAYYAD SPAIN

In Spain, in 756, an Umayyad prince who had not accepted the fate of his house had proclaimed himself emir, or governor, of Córdoba, the first breach of its unity. Others were to follow in Morocco and Tunisia. Meanwhile, El-Andalus acquired its own caliph only in the tenth century (until then its rulers remained emirs) but long before that was independent de facto. This did not mean that Umayyad Spain was untroubled. Islam had never conquered the whole peninsula and the Franks recovered the northeast by the

El-Andalus: Islamic Spain

In 711 the Muslim armies' invasion of Visigoth Spain marked the beginning of one of the most important eras in the history of the Iberian peninsula. For almost eight centuries, until 1492, El-Andalus (the name given to Muslim Spain by Arab writers) was a cultural centre of great importance – its Islamic inheritance has had a deep and lasting effect on the Western world. Muslim Spain enjoyed a level of urban civilization unequalled in the Christian world. It boasted a society with an original and enriching culture that was both polyglot (Arabic, Romance and Hebrew) and tolerant (the Muslims granted Christians and Jews the freedom to practise their religions openly).

During the early years of Muslim rule El-Andalus was the most westerly province of the Islamic Abbasid Empire and was governed by a representative sent from Damascus. This period came to an end in 756 when Abd-ar-Rahman I, an Umayyad prince who was the only member of his family to have avoided assassination, set up the Umayyad emirate of Córdoba, with the aim of turning the city into the new Damascus. In 929 the Córdoba caliphate was established: Abd-ar-Rahman III was declared caliph and prince of the faithful, making way for the era of greatest political, economic and cultural development that El-Andalus was ever to see.

However, the caliphs' authority slowly diminished. During the 11th century, increasing political fragmentation led to the foundation of "cantons", also known as *taifas*, which were governed by various local dynasties. On two occasions these *taifas* came under the control of African warriors – the Almoravids and the Almohads – who attempted to impose a fierce, centralized power. Their failure resulted in the reduction of Muslim Spain to the small kingdom of Granada, which survived until 1492, when it was conquered by the Catholic Monarchs, thus putting an end to a unique period in the history of Spain.

An aerial view of the ruins of the 10th-century caliphate palace of Madinat-al-Zahara, in the province of Córdoba.

tenth century. There were by then Christian kingdoms in northern Iberia and they were always willing to help stir the pot of dissidence within Arab Spain where a fairly tolerant policy towards Christians did not end the danger of revolt.

Yet El-Andalus prospered. The Umayyads developed their sea-power and contemplated imperial expansion not towards the north, at the expense of the Christians, but into Africa, at the expense of Muslim powers, even negotiating for alliance with Byzantium in the process. It was not until the eleventh and twelfth centuries, when the caliphate of Córdoba was in decline, that Spain's Islamic civilization reached its greatest beauty and maturity in a golden age of creativity which rivalled that of Abbasid Baghdad. This left behind great monuments as well as producing great learning and philosophy. The seven hundred mosques of tenth-century Córdoba numbered among them one which can still be thought the most beautiful building in the world. Arab Spain was of enormous importance to Europe, a door to the learning and science of the East, but one through which were also to pass more material goods as well: through it Christendom received knowledge of agricultural and irrigation techniques, oranges and lemons, sugar. As for Spain itself, the Arab stamp went very deep, as many students of the later, Christian, Spain have pointed out, and can still be observed in language, manners and art.

THE DECLINE OF THE CALIPHS' POWER

Another important breakaway within the Arab world came when the Fatimids from Tunisia set up their own caliph and moved their capital to Cairo in 973. The Fatimids were Shi'ites and maintained their government of Egypt

Islamic Iberia

In the middle of the 11th century there were two quite distinct political entities in the Iberian peninsula. One – the Christians – continually advancing towards the south, was comprised of the kingdoms of Castile and León, Navarre, Aragon and the county of Barcelona. The other – the Muslim world – suffered a gradual break-up, until the arrival in 1086 of the Almoravids, who halted the Christian "conquest".

This chess piece dates from the Fatimid era. The Fatimids, who were named after Muhammad's daughter Fatima, founded a new caliphate in Tunisia. In 973 they moved the capital to Cairo, making the city one of the period's most important economic centres. Unlike other believers, who maintained that Allah was the one and only god, the Fatimids deified Fatima and her husband Ali.

until a new Arab invasion destroyed it in the twelfth century. Less conspicuous examples could be found elsewhere in the Abbasid dominions as local governors began to term themselves emir and sultan. The power base of the caliphs narrowed more and more rapidly; they were unable to reverse the trend. Civil wars among the sons of Haroun led to a loss of the support by the religious teachers and the devout. Bureaucratic corruption and embezzlement alienated the subject populations. Recourse to tax-farming as a way round these ills only created new examples of oppression. The army was increasingly recruited from foreign mercenaries and slaves; even by the death of Haroun's successor it was virtually Turkish. Thus, barbarians were

A Muslim man may cast out his wife, and then wait three months for the dissolution of the marriage to be definitive. This 13th-century picture shows a *qadi* (judge) listening to a man whose wife is standing behind him.

incorporated within the structure of the caliphates as had been the western barbarians within the Roman Empire. As time went by they took on a praetorian look and increasingly dominated the caliphs. And all the time popular opposition was exploited by the Shi'ites and other mystical sects. Meanwhile, the former economic prosperity waned. The wealth of Arab merchants was not to crystallize in a vigorous city life such as that of the late medieval West.

Abbasid rule effectively ended in 946 when a Persian general and his men deposed a caliph and installed a new one. Theoretically, the line of Abbasids continued, but in fact the change was revolutionary; the new Buwayhid dynasty lived henceforth in Persia. Arab Islam had fragmented; the unity of the Near East was once more at an end. No empire remained to resist the centuries of invasion which followed, although it was not until 1258 that the last Abbasid was slaughtered by the Mongols. Before that, Islamic unity had another revival in response to the crusades, but the great days of Islamic empire were over.

"The Women" from the Koran

"O believers, it is not lawful for you
to inherit women against their will;
neither debar them, that you may go off
with part of what you have given them,
except when they commit a flagrant indecency.
Consort with them honourably; or if
you are averse to them, it is possible
you may be averse to a thing, and God see
in it much good.
And if you desire to exchange a wife
in place of another, and you have given
to one a hundredweight, take of it nothing.
What, will you take it by way of calumny
and manifest sin?
How shall you take it, when each of you has been
privily with the other, and they have taken from
you a solemn compact?
And do not marry women that your fathers
married, unless it be a thing of the past;
surely that is indecent and hateful, an evil way."

An extract from Book IV ("The Women") of the Koran, translated by Arthur J. Arberry.

THE ISLAMIC REVOLUTION

The peculiar nature of Islam meant that religious authority could not long be separated from political supremacy; the caliphate was eventually to pass to the Ottoman Turks, therefore, when they became the makers of Near Eastern history. They would carry the frontier of Islam still farther afield and once again deep into Europe. But their Arab predecessors' work was awe-inspiringly vast for all its ultimate collapse. They had destroyed both the old Roman Near East and Sassanid Persia, hemming Byzantium in to Anatolia. In the end, though, this would call Western Europeans back into the Levant. The Arabs had also implanted Islam ineradicably from Morocco to Afghanistan. Its coming was in many ways revolutionary. It kept women, for example, in an inferior position, but gave them legal rights over property not available to women in many European countries until the nineteenth century. Even the slave had rights and inside the community of the believers there were no castes nor inherited status. This revolution was rooted in a religion which – like that of the Jews – was not distinct from other sides of life, but embraced them all; no words exist in Islam to express the distinctions of sacred and profane, spiritual and temporal, which our own tradition takes for granted. Religion *is* society for the Muslims, and the unity this has provided has outlasted centuries of political division. It was a unity both of law and of a certain attitude; Islam is not a religion of miracles (though it claims some), but of practice and intellectual belief.

THE DISPERSION OF ISLAM WORLDWIDE

Besides having a great intellectual impact on Christendom, Islam also spread far beyond the world of Arab hegemony, to Central Asia in the tenth century, India between the eighth and eleventh, and in the eleventh beyond the Sudan and to the Niger. Between the twelfth and sixteenth centuries still more of Africa would become Muslim; Islam remains today the fastest-growing faith of that continent. Thanks to the conversion of Mongols in the thirteenth century, Islam would also reach China. In the fifteenth and sixteenth centuries it spread across the Indian Ocean to Malaya and Indonesia. Missionaries, migrants and merchants carried it with them, the Arabs above all, whether they moved in caravans into Africa or took their dhows from the

Islam beyond the Arabic world until 1800

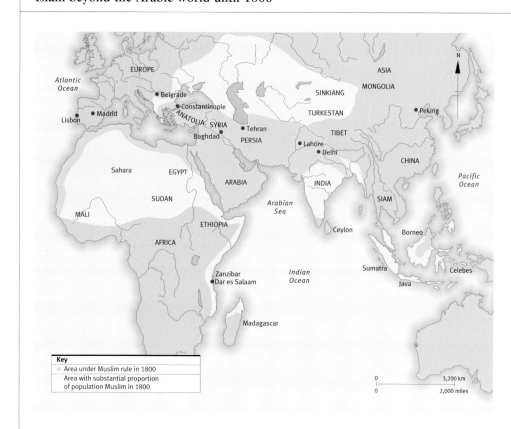

Over the centuries since the death of the prophet Muhammad, Islam has spread through most parts of the world. Regions in which the Islamic religion was already particularly well established in 1800 include the Middle East, a large part of Asia and much of northern Africa, as this map shows.

Key
Area under Muslim rule in 1800
Area with substantial proportion of population Muslim in 1800

Persian Gulf and Red Sea to the Bay of Bengal. There would even be a last, final, extension of the faith in southeastern Europe in the sixteenth and seventeenth centuries. It was a remarkable achievement for an idea at whose service there had been in the beginning no resources except those of a handful of Semitic tribes. But in spite of its majestic record no Arab state was ever again to provide unity for Islam after the tenth century. Even Arab unity was to remain only a dream, though one cherished still today.

The *mihrab* is a highly decorated arched niche oriented towards Mecca, indicating the direction in which worshippers must face when praying. It is usually situated in the centre of the main part of the mosque and was first seen in Islamic architecture in the mosque at Medina, which dates from the beginning of the 8th century. Decorated with beautiful mosaics, this example is from the Great Mosque in Córdoba, Spain.

3 BYZANTIUM AND ITS SPHERE

IN 1453, NINE HUNDRED YEARS after Justinian, Constantinople fell to an infidel army. "There has never been and there never will be a more dreadful happening," wrote one Greek scribe. It was indeed a great event. No one in the West was prepared; the whole Christian world was shocked. More than a state, Rome itself was at an end. The direct descent from the classical Mediterranean civilization had been snapped at last; if few saw this in quite so deep a perspective as the literary enthusiasts who detected in it retribution for the Greek sack of Troy, it was still the end of two thousand years' tradition. And if the pagan world of Hellenistic culture and

The troops of the Ottoman sultan Mehmet II, who is depicted in this portrait, took Constantinople by storm on 29 May 1453. The last Byzantine emperor, Constantine XI, died defending his capital. This event marked the end of the Eastern Roman Empire.

ancient Greece were set aside, a thousand years of Christian empire at Byzantium itself was impressive enough for its passing to seem an earthquake.

This is one of those subjects where it helps to know the end of the story before beginning it. Even in their decline Byzantine prestige and traditions had amazed strangers who felt through them the weight of an imperial past. To the end its emperors were *augusti* and its citizens called themselves "Romans". For centuries, St Sophia had been the greatest of Christian churches, the Orthodox religion it enshrined needing to make even fewer concessions to religious pluralism as previously troublesome provinces were swallowed by the Muslims. Though in retrospect it is easy to see the inevitability of decline and fall, this was not how the people who lived under it saw the Eastern Empire. They knew, consciously or unconsciously, that it had great powers of evolution. It was a great conservative *tour de force* which had survived many extremities and its archaic style was almost to the end able to cloak important changes.

THE IMPERIAL OFFICE

A THOUSAND YEARS brought great upheavals in both East and West; history played upon Byzantium, modifying some elements in its heritage, stressing others, obliterating others, so that the empire was in the end very different from Justinian's while never becoming wholly distinct from it. There is no clear dividing line between antiquity and Byzantium. The centre of gravity of the

In this 6th-century mosaic from the church of St Vitale in Ravenna, the empress Theodora is depicted with her entourage. Theodora's head is encircled by a nimbus – a pagan solar symbol adapted to serve the purposes of Byzantine imperial ambition.

empire had begun to shift eastwards before Constantine and when his city became the seat of world empire it was the inheritor of the pretensions of Rome. The office of the emperors showed particularly sharply how evolution and conservatism could combine. Until 800 there was no formal challenge to the theory that the emperor was the secular ruler of all humanity. When a Western ruler was hailed as an "emperor" in Rome that year, the uniqueness of the imperial purple of Byzantium was challenged, whatever might be thought and said in the East about the exact status of the new régime. Yet Byzantium continued to cherish the fantasy of universal empire; there would be emperors right to the end and their office was one of awe-inspiring grandeur. Still theoretically chosen by Senate, army and people, they had none the less an absolute authority. While the realities of his accession might determine for any particular emperor the actual extent of his power – and

Time chart (330–1453)

	330 Constantine moves the capital of the Roman Empire to Byzantium and renames it Constantinople	726–843 The Iconoclast era		c.1200 The Venetians monopolize Byzantine trade with Europe	
300	600	900	1200	1500	
	527–565 The reign of Justinian I	551 The Byzantines seize southern Spain from the Visigoths	1014 The Byzantine emperor Basil II defeats the Bulgars	1453 Constantinople is conquered by the Turks	

The Byzantine emperors, unlike their Western counterparts, had absolute political and religious power – they saw themselves as God's representatives on earth. This is clearly illustrated in this mosaic from the church of St Sophia (now a mosque) in Constantinople (now Istanbul): the figure on the left represents the emperor Justinian, who is holding a model of a church in his hands, while the figure on the right is that of the emperor Constantine holding a model of a city – no doubt symbolizing Constantinople, which he founded.

sometimes the dynastic succession broke under the strains – he was *autocrat* as a Western emperor never was. Respect for legal principle and the vested interests of bureaucracy might muffle the emperor's will in action, but it was always supreme in theory. The heads of the great departments of state were responsible to no one but him. This authority explains the intensity with which Byzantine politics focused at the imperial court, for it was there, and not through corporate and representative institutions such as evolved slowly in the West, that authority could be influenced.

RELIGION AND EMPERORS

Autocracy had its harsh side. The *curiosi* or secret police informers who swarmed through

the empire were not there for nothing. But the nature of the imperial office also laid obligations on the emperor. Crowned by the Patriarch of Constantinople, the emperor had the enormous authority, but also the responsibilities, of God's representative upon earth. The line between lay and ecclesiastical was always blurred in the East where there was nothing like the Western opposition of Church and State as a continuing challenge to unchecked power. Yet in the Byzantine scheme of things there was a continuing pressure upon God's vice-regent to act appropriately, to show *philanthropia*, a love of humanity, in his acts. The purpose of the autocratic power was the preservation of the human race and of the conduits by which it drew the water of life – orthodoxy and the Church. Appropriately most of the early Christian emperors were canonized – just as pagan emperors had been deified. Other traditions than the Christian also affected the office, as this suggested. Byzantine emperors were to receive the ritual prostrations of oriental tradition and the images of them which look down from their mosaics show their heads surrounded by the nimbus in which the last pre-Christian emperors were depicted, for it was part of the cult of the sun god. (Some representations of Sassanid rulers have it, too.) It was, none the less, above all as a Christian ruler that the emperor justified his authority.

ORTHODOX TRADITION

The imperial office itself thus embodied much of the Christian heritage of Byzantium. That heritage also marked the Eastern Empire off sharply from the West at many other levels. There were, in the first place, the ecclesiastical peculiarities of what came to be called the Orthodox Church. Islam, for example, was sometimes seen by the Eastern clergy less as a pagan religion than a heresy. Other differences lay in the Orthodox view of the relationship of clergy to society; the coalescence of spiritual and lay was important at many levels below the throne. One symbol of it was the retention of a married clergy; the Orthodox priest, for all his presumed holiness, was never to be quite the man apart his Western and Catholic colleague became. This suggests the great role of the Orthodox Church as a cementing force in society down to modern times. Above all, no sacerdotal authority as great as that of the papacy would

Byzantium – the great empire of the East

By the early 4th century, the Romans were desperate to ensure the protection of their eastern border against Slav and Persian attack. This was one of the factors that motivated Constantine to transfer the capital of the Eastern half of the Roman Empire to the small city of Byzantium, which the emperor officially named Constantinople in the year 330. As the capital of the Eastern Roman Empire, Constantinople was to become the only power that could claim the title of Roman Empire after the collapse of the West in 476. The most important of the early Byzantine emperors was Justinian I (527–565), who reconquered the western Mediterranean basin, built the magnificent church of St Sophia in Constantinople and published the legal code that took his name.

The beginning of the end for Byzantium came in 1204 when the crusaders conquered Constantinople. The empire was lost in 1453, conquered by the Ottoman Turks, although the Greek Orthodox Trebizond Empire, the last bastion of Byzantium, survived until 1461.

Justinian I is depicted in this mosaic in St Vitale, Ravenna.

emerge. The focus of authority was the emperor, whose office and responsibility towered above the equally ranked bishops. Of course, so far as social regulation went, this did not mean that Orthodoxy was more tolerant than the Church of the medieval West. Bad times were always liable to be interpreted as evidence that the emperor had not been doing his Christian duty – which included the harrying of such familiar scapegoats as Jews, heretics and homosexuals.

EAST AND WEST GROW APART

Distinction from the West was in part a product of political history, of the gradual loosening of contact after the division of the empires, in part a matter of an original distinction of style. The Catholic and Orthodox traditions were on divergent courses from early times, even if at first the divergence was only slight. At an early date Latin Christianity was somewhat estranged by the concessions the Greeks had to make to Syrian and Egyptian practice. Yet such concessions had also kept alive a certain polycentrism within Christendom. When Jerusalem, Antioch and Alexandria, the other three great patriarchates of the East, fell into Arab hands, the polarization of Rome and Constantinople was accentuated. Gradually, the Christian world was ceasing to be bilingual; a Latin West came to face a Greek East. It was at the beginning of the seventh century that Latin finally ceased to be the official language of the army and of justice, the two departments where it had longest resisted Greek. That the bureaucracy was Greek-speaking was to be very important. When the Eastern Church failed among Muslims, it opened a new missionary field and won much ground among the pagans to the north. Eventually, southeastern Europe and Russia were to owe their

evangelizing to Constantinople. The outcome – among many other things – was that the Slav peoples would take from their teachers not only a written language based on Greek, but many of their most fundamental political ideas. And because the West was Catholic, its relations with the Slav world were sometimes hostile, so that the Slav peoples came to view the Western half of Christendom with deep reservations. This lay far in the future and takes us further afield than we need to go for the present.

The distinctiveness of the Eastern Christian tradition 'could be illustrated in

Constantinople's cathedral of St Sophia is probably the most impressive surviving example of Byzantine architecture. Its design is attributed to Anthemius of Tralles and Isidore of Miletus and work on its construction began in 532 by order of the emperor Justinian I. St Sophia was consecrated in 537. On the night of 28–29 May 1453 – the last night of Byzantium – a final Christian service was held in the great cathedral, attended by a congregation of thousands. Four days later, having converted the building into a mosque, the Turkish conquerors held the first Muslim service there. The four minarets seen in this picture are later Islamic additions.

many ways. Monasticism, for example, remained closer to its original forms in the East and the importance of the Holy Man has always been greater there than in the more hierarchically aware Roman Church. The Greeks, too, seem to have been more disputatious than the Latins; the Hellenistic background of the early Church had always favoured speculation and the Eastern Churches were open to oriental trends, always susceptible to the pressures of many traditional influences. Yet this did not prevent the imposition of dogmatic solutions to religious quarrels.

THEOLOGICAL DISPUTES

Some religious quarrels were about issues which now seem trivial or even meaningless. Inevitably, a secular age such as our own finds even the greatest of them difficult to fathom simply because we lack a sense of the mental world lying behind them. It requires an effort to recall that behind the exquisite definitions and logic-chopping of the Fathers lay a concern of appalling importance, nothing less than that humanity should be saved from damnation. A further obstacle to understanding arises for the diametrically opposed reason that theological differences in Eastern Christianity often provided symbols and debating forms for questions about politics and society, about the relationship of national and cultural groups to authority, much as hair-splitting about the secular theology of Marxist-Leninism was to mask practical differences between twentieth-century communists. There is more to these questions than appears

The image of Christ Pantocrator was common in the iconography of Byzantine coins such as this one.

at first sight and much of it affected world history just as powerfully as the movements of armies or even peoples. The slow divergence of the two main Christian traditions is of enormous importance; it may not have originated in any sense in theological division, but theological disputes propelled divergent traditions yet further apart. They created circumstances which make it more and more difficult to envisage an alternative course of events.

THE ISSUE OF MONOPHYSITISM

One episode provides an outstanding example, the debate on Monophysitism, a doctrine which divided Christian theologians from about the middle of the fifth century. The significance of the theological issue is at first sight obscure to our post-religious age. It originated in an assertion that Christ's nature while on earth was single; it was wholly divine, instead of dual (that is, both divine and human), as had generally been taught in the early Church. The delicious subtleties of the long debates which this view provoked must, perhaps regrettably, be bypassed here. It is sufficient only to notice that there was an important non-theological setting of the uproar of Aphthartodocetists, Corrupticolists

and Theopaschitists (to name a few of the contesting schools). One element in it was the slow crystallization of three Monophysite Churches separated from Eastern Orthodoxy and Roman Catholicism. These were the Coptic Church of Egypt and Ethiopia, and the Syrian Jacobite and the Armenian Churches; they became, in a sense, national Churches in their countries. It was in an endeavour to reconcile such groups and consolidate the unity of the empire in the face of first the Persian and then the Arab threat that the emperors were drawn into theological dispute; there was more to it, that is to say, than the special responsibility of the office first revealed by Constantine's presiding at the Council of Nicaea. The emperor Heraclius, for example, did his best in the early seventh century to produce a compromise formula to reconcile the disputants over Monophysitism. It took the form of a new theological definition soon called Monothelitism, and on it, for a time, agreement seemed likely, though it was in the end condemned as Monophysitism under a new name.

Meanwhile, the issue had pushed East and West still further apart in practice. Though, ironically, the final theological outcome was agreement in 681, Monophysitism had produced a forty-year schism between Latins and Greeks as early as the end of the fifth century. This was healed, but then came the further trouble under Heraclius. The empire had to leave Italy to its own devices when threatened by the Arab onslaught but both pope and emperor were now anxious to show a common front. This partly explains the pope's endorsement of Monothelitism (on which Heraclius had asked his view so as to quieten the theological misgivings of the Patriarch of

Unlike Nestorianism and Arianism, in which the human nature of Christ is of foremost importance, the Monophysitic doctrine emphasizes the divine nature of Christ. Monophysitism had many followers in Egypt within the early Coptic Church. This Monophysitic marble plaque shows Christ being taken down from the cross.

Jerusalem). Pope Honorius, successor of Gregory the Great, supported Heraclius and so enraged the anti-Monophysites that almost half a century later he achieved the distinction (unusual among popes) of being condemned by an ecumenical council at which even the Western representatives at the council joined in the decision. At a crucial moment of danger Honorius had done much damage. The sympathies of many Eastern churchmen in the early seventh century had been alienated still further from Rome by his imprudent action.

In the many naval battles they fought against the Arabs, the Byzantines deployed a highly effective secret weapon. Known as "Greek fire" (a compound of petroleum, saltpetre, quicklime and sulphur), it was a substance that ignited on impact and could be sprayed or shot in projectiles at enemy vessels, as depicted in this 11th-century manuscript illustration.

BYZANTIUM AND ASIA

The Byzantine inheritance was not only imperial and Christian. It also owed debts to Asia. These were not merely a matter of the direct contacts with alien civilizations symbolized by the arrival of Chinese merchandise along the Silk Road, but also of the complex cultural inheritance of the Hellenistic East. Naturally, Byzantium preserved the prejudice which confused the idea of "barbarians" with that of peoples who did not speak Greek, and many of its intellectual leaders felt they stood in the tradition of Hellas. Yet the Hellas of which they spoke was one from which the world had long been cut off except through the channels of the Hellenistic East. When we look at that area it is hard to be sure how deep Greek roots went there and how much nourishment they owed to Asiatic sources. The Greek language, for example, seems in Asia Minor to have been used mainly by the few who were city-dwellers. Another sign comes from the imperial bureaucracy and leading families, which reveal more and more Asian names as the centuries go by. Asia was bound to count for more after the losses of territory the empire suffered in the fifth and sixth centuries, for these pinned it increasingly into only a strip of mainland Europe around the capital. Then the Arabs hemmed it in to Asia Minor, bounded in the north by the Caucasus and in the south by the Taurus. On the edges of this, too, ran a border always permeable to Muslim culture. The people who lived on it naturally lived in a sort of marcher world, but sometimes there are indications of deeper external influence than this upon Byzantium. The greatest of all the Byzantine ecclesiastical disputes, that over Iconoclasm, had its parallels almost contemporaneously within Islam.

MEDIEVAL BYZANTIUM

The most characteristic features of a complicated inheritance were set in the seventh and eighth centuries: an autocratic tradition of government, the Roman myth, the guardianship of Eastern Christianity and practical confinement to the East. There had by then begun to emerge from the late Roman Empire the medieval state which was sketched under Justinian. Yet of these crucial centuries we know little. Some say that no adequate history of Byzantium in that era can be written, so poor are the sources and so skimpy the present state of archaeological knowledge. At the start of this disturbed period the empire's assets are clear enough. It had at its disposal a great accumulation of diplomatic and bureaucratic skills, a military tradition and enormous prestige. Once its commitments could be reduced in proportion, its potential tax resources were considerable and so were its reserves of manpower. Asia Minor was a recruiting ground which relieved the Eastern Empire of the need to rely upon Germanic barbarians as had been necessary in the West. It had a notable war-making technology; the "Greek fire", which was its secret weapon, was used powerfully against ships which might attack the capital. The situation of Constantinople, too, was a military asset. Its great walls, built in the fifth century, made it hard to attack by land without heavy weapons unlikely to be available to barbarians; at sea the fleet could prevent a landing.

What was less secure in the long run was the social basis of the empire. It was always to be difficult to maintain the smallholding peasantry and prevent powerful provincial landlords from encroaching on their properties. The law courts would not always protect the small man. He was, too, under economic pressure from the steady expansion of church estates. These forces could not easily be offset by the imperial practice of making grants to smallholders on condition that they supplied military service. But this was a problem whose dimensions were only to be revealed with the passage of centuries; the short-term prospects gave the emperors of the seventh and eighth centuries quite enough to think about.

Umayyad Arabs laid siege to the city walls of Constantinople between 674 and 678. This illustration shows the Persian attack on the Byzantine capital.

To create mosaics, small cubes of glass or stone, known as *tesserae*, were set into a plaster surface. It was in the Byzantine Empire, mainly during the 10th and 11th centuries, that mosaic decoration reached the height of technical and artistic perfection. The famous "Entourage of Virgins" is one of a number of mosaics that embellish the church of St Apollinare the New in Ravenna.

THE PROBLEMS OF EMPIRE

The emperors' resources were over-extended. In 600 the empire still included the North African coast, Egypt, the Levant, Syria, Asia Minor, the far coast of the Black Sea beyond Trebizond, the Crimean coast and that from Byzantium up to the mouths of the Danube. In Europe there were Thessaly, Macedonia and the Adriatic coast, a belt of territory across central Italy, enclaves in the toe and heel of the peninsula, and finally the islands of Sicily, Corsica and Sardinia. Given the empire's potential enemies and the location of its resources, this was a strategist's nightmare. The story of the next two centuries was to be of the return again and again of waves of invaders. Persians, Avars, Arabs, Bulgars and Slavs were to harry the main body of the empire, while in the West the territories won back by the generals of Justinian were almost all soon taken away again by Arabs and Lombards. Eventually, the West, too, was to reveal itself as a predator; that the Eastern Empire for centuries absorbed much of the punishment which might otherwise have fallen on the West, would not save it. The result of this was that the Eastern Empire faced continual warfare. In Europe it meant fighting up to the very walls of Constantinople; in Asia it meant wearisome campaigning to dispute the marches of Asia Minor.

Such challenges from the outside world were offered to a state which, even at the beginning of the seventh century, already had only a very loose control over its domain and depended for much of its power on a penumbra of influence, diplomacy, Christianity and military prestige. Its relations to its neighbours might be seen in more than one way; what looks to a later eye like blackmail paid by every emperor from Justinian to Basil II to menacing barbarians was in the Roman

This detail from an illustration in the 15th-century "Madrid Bible" represents a Jewish menorah (sacred candelabrum) housed in a Khazar tent. In spite of the Byzantines' attempts to convert them to Christianity, the Khazars turned to Judaism.

a huge, but loose, state founded by nomads who by 600 dominated the other peoples of the Don and Volga valleys. This established them across the Caucasus, the strategic land bridge which they thus barred to Persians and Arabs for two centuries. At its widest the Khazar state ran round the Black Sea coast to the Dniester and northwards to include the Upper Volga and Don. Byzantium made great efforts to keep the goodwill of the Khazars and seems to have tried, but failed, to convert them to Christianity. What exactly happened is a mystery, but the Khazar leaders, while tolerating Christianity and several other cults, were apparently converted to Judaism in about 740, possibly as a result of Jewish immigration from Persia after the Arab conquest and probably as a conscious act of diplomacy. As Jews they were not likely to be sucked either into the spiritual and political orbit of the Christian empire, or into that of the caliphs. Instead they enjoyed diplomatic relations and trade with both.

A SHRINKING EMPIRE

The first great hero of the Byzantine struggle for survival was Heraclius, who strove to balance the threats in Europe with alliances and concessions so that he could campaign vigorously against the Persians. Successful though he eventually was, the Persians had by then done appalling damage to the empire in the Levant and Asia Minor before their expulsion. They have been believed by some scholars to be the real destroyers of the Hellenistic world of great cities; the archaeology is mysterious still, but after Heraclius' victory there are signs that once-great cities lay in ruins, that some were reduced to little more than the acropolis which was their core and that population fell sharply. It was, then, on a structure much of which was already badly

tradition bounty to subject allies and *foederati*. Its diversity of peoples and religions was masked by official ideology. Its Hellenization was often superficial. The reality was expressed in the willingness with which many of the Christian communities of Syria welcomed the Arab, as, later, many of those in Anatolia were to welcome the Turk. Here, religious persecution came home to roost. Moreover, Byzantium numbered no great power among her allies. In the troubled seventh and eighth centuries the most important friendly power was the Khanate of Khazaria,

The Byzantine Empire

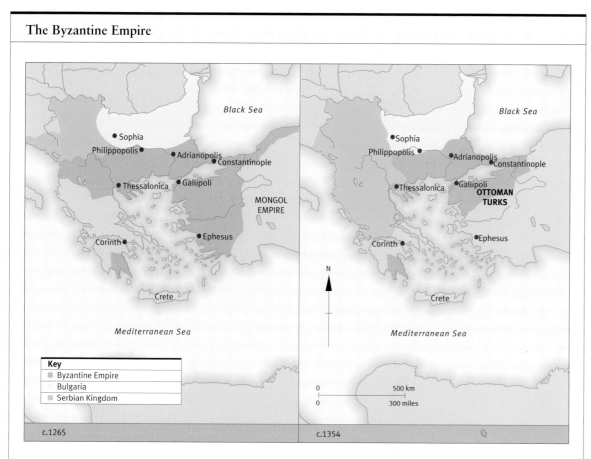

External pressures always threatened Byzantium. By the 13th and 14th centuries, these had resulted in the significant loss of territory shown in these maps of the empire's extent in 1265 and 1354 respectively.

shaken that the Arab onslaughts fell – and they were to continue for two centuries. Before Heraclius died in 641 virtually all his military achievements had been overturned. Some of the emperors of his line were men of ability, but they could do little more than fight doggedly against a tide flowing strongly against them. In 643 Alexandria fell to the Arabs and that was the end of Greek rule in Egypt. Within a few years they had lost North Africa and Cyprus. Armenia, that old battleground, went in the next decade and finally the high-water mark of Arab success came with the five years of attacks on Constantinople (673–678); it may have been Greek fire that saved the capital from the Arab fleet. Before this, in spite of a personal visit by the emperor to Italy, no progress had been made in recovering the Italian and Sicilian territories taken by Arabs and Lombards. And so the century went on, with yet another menace appearing in its last quarter as Slavs pressed down into Macedonia and Thrace and another race, the Bulgars, themselves one day to be Slavicized, crossed the Danube.

THE ISAURIAN RECOVERY

The seventh century ended with a revolt in the army and the replacement of one emperor by another. All the symptoms suggested that the Eastern Empire would undergo the fate of the West, the imperial office becoming the prize of the soldiers. A succession of beastly or incompetent emperors at the beginning of the eighth century let the Bulgars come to the gates of Constantinople and finally brought about a second siege of the capital by the Arabs in 717. But this was a true turning-point, though it was not to be the last Arab appearance in the Bosphorus. In 717 there had already come to the throne one of the greatest Byzantine emperors, the Anatolian Leo III. He was a provincial official who had successfully resisted Arab attacks on his territory and who had come to the capital to defend it and force the emperor's abdication. His own elevation to the purple followed and was both popular and warmly welcomed by

the clergy. This was the foundation of the Isaurian Dynasty, so-called from their place of origin; it was an indication of the way in which the élites of the Eastern Roman Empire were gradually transformed into those of Byzantium, an oriental monarchy.

The eighth century brought the beginning of a period of recovery, though with setbacks. Leo himself cleared Anatolia of the Arabs and his son pushed back the frontiers to those of Syria, Mesopotamia and Armenia. From this time, the frontiers with the caliphate had rather more stability than hitherto, although each campaigning season brought border raids and skirmishes. From this achievement – in part attributable, of course, to the relative decline in Arab power – opened out a new period of progress and expansion which lasted until the early eleventh century. In the West little could be done. Ravenna was lost and only a few toeholds remained in Italy and Sicily. But in the East the empire expanded again from the base of Thrace and Asia Minor which was its heart. A chain of "themes", or administrative districts, was established along the fringe of the Balkan peninsula; apart from them, the empire had no foothold there for two centuries. In the tenth century Cyprus, Crete and Antioch were all recovered. Byzantine forces at one time crossed the Euphrates and the struggle for northern Syria and the Taurus continued. The position in Georgia and Armenia was improved.

This miniature portrays Basil II (976–1025) as a triumphant emperor with defeated Bulgarian princes grovelling at his feet. During Basil's reign, the Byzantine Empire enjoyed a period of great wealth and power, following the conquest of Bulgaria in 1014 and victory over the Arabs.

BULGAROCTONOS AND THE LATE ISAURIAN DYNASTY

In eastern Europe the Bulgar threat was finally contained after reaching its peak at the beginning of the tenth century, when the Bulgars had already been converted to Christianity. Basil II, who has gone down in history as *Bulgaroctonos*, the "slayer of Bulgars", finally destroyed their power at a great battle in 1014 which he followed up by blinding 15,000 of his prisoners and sending them home to encourage their countrymen. The Bulgar ruler is said to have died of shock. Within a few years Bulgaria was a Byzantine province, though it was never to be successfully absorbed. Shortly afterwards the last conquests of Byzantium were made when Armenia passed under its rule.

The overall story of these centuries is therefore one of advance and recovery. It was also one of the great periods of Byzantine culture. Politically there was an improvement in domestic affairs in that, by and large, the dynastic principle was observed between 820 and 1025. The Isaurian Dynasty had ended badly in an empress who was followed by another series of short reigns and irregular successions until Michael II, the founder of the Phrygian Dynasty, succeeded a murdered emperor in 820. His house was replaced in 867 by the Macedonian Dynasty, under whom Byzantium reached its summit of success. Where there were minorities the device of a

co-emperor was adopted to preserve the dynastic principle.

ICONOCLASM

ONE MAJOR SOURCE OF DIVISION and difficulty for the empire in the earlier part of this period was, as so often before, religion. This plagued the empire and held back its recovery because it was so often tangled with political and local issues. The outstanding example was a controversy which embittered feelings for over a century, the campaign of the Iconoclasts.

The depicting of the saints, the Blessed Virgin and God Himself had come to be one of the great devices of Orthodox Christianity for focusing devotion and teaching. In late antiquity such images, or icons, had a place in the West, too, but to this day they occupy a special place in Orthodox churches, where they are displayed in shrines and on special screens to be venerated and contemplated by the believer. They are much more than mere decoration, for their arrangement conveys the teachings of the Church and (as one authority has said) provides "a point of meeting between heaven and earth", where the faithful amid the icons can feel surrounded by the whole invisible Church, by the departed, the saints and angels, and Christ and His mother themselves. It is hardly surprising that something concentrating religious emotion so intensely should have led in paint or mosaic to some of the highest achievements of Byzantine (and, later, Slav) art.

Icons had become prominent in Eastern churches by the sixth century. There followed two centuries of respect for them and in many places growing popular devotion to them, but then their use came to be questioned. Interestingly, this happened just after the caliphate had mounted a campaign against

The Iconoclast Byzantine emperor Constantine V (741 and 743–775), who is depicted on this coin, launched a bloody campaign of persecution against the Iconophiles.

The consecration of icons

Ever since the Byzantine era, priests in Orthodox churches around the world have conducted the same ceremony for the consecration of icons. During the ceremony, the priest, after singing the *Hymn to the Holy Trinity* and the *Kyrie Eleison*, recites:

"Lord, God, you have created Man in your image, which has been blemished by the fall, but by the incarnation of your Christ made Man, you have restored it and thus have restored your saints to their original dignity. Worshipping them, we worship your image and your likeness, and through them, we glorify your Archetype."

This 11th- or 12th-century plaque is probably part of an ornate cover for a religious manuscript. It is dedicated to St Michael and the materials used in its decoration include enamels, precious stones, pearls and gold.

the use of images in Islam, but it cannot be inferred that the Iconoclasts took their ideas from Muslims. The critics of the icons claimed that they were idols, perverting the worship due to God to the creations of human beings. They demanded their destruction or expunging and set to work with a will with whitewash, brush and hammer.

THE PERSECUTION OF THE ICONOPHILES

Leo III favoured the Iconoclasts. There is still much that is mysterious about the reason why imperial authority was thrown behind them, but he acted on the advice of bishops and other ecclesiastes, and Arab invasions and volcanic eruptions were no doubt held to indicate God's disfavour. In 730, therefore, an edict forbade the use of images in public worship. A persecution of those who resisted followed; enforcement was always more marked at Constantinople than in the provinces. The movement reached its peak under Constantine V and was ratified by a council of bishops in 754. Persecution became fiercer, and there were martyrs, particularly among monks, who usually defended icons more vigorously than did the secular clergy. But Iconoclasm was always dependent on imperial support; there were ebbings and flowings in the next century. Under Leo IV and Irene, his widow, persecution was relaxed and the "Iconophiles" (lovers of icons) recovered ground, though this was followed by renewed persecution. Only in 843, on the first Sunday of Lent, a day still celebrated as a feast of Orthodoxy in the Eastern Church, were the icons finally restored.

THE SOURCES OF ICONOCLASM

What was the meaning of this strange episode? There was a practical justification, in that the conversion of Jews and Muslims was said to be made more difficult by Christian respect for images, but this does not take us very far. Once again, a religious dispute cannot be separated from factors external to religion, but the ultimate explanation probably lies in a sense of religious precaution, and given the passion often shown in theological controversy in the

These plaques depict soldiers from the Byzantine army, an institution in which Iconoclasm was held in high regard.

The two figures who most clearly personified the disagreement over image worship are depicted in this manuscript illustration: the Iconoclast emperor Leo V (813–820) is shown receiving the anti-Iconoclast patriarch Nicephorus I at court, while on the right an icon is being coated in whitewash.

suited the mentalities of a faith which felt itself at bay. It was notable that Iconoclasm was particularly strong in the army. Another fact which is suggestive is that icons had often represented local saints and holy men; they were replaced by the uniting, simplifying symbols of eucharist and cross, and this says something about a new, monolithic quality in Byzantine religion and society from the eighth century onwards. Finally, Iconoclasm was also in part an angry response to a tide which had long flowed in favour of the monks who gave such prominence to icons in their teaching. As well as a prudent step towards placating an angry God, therefore, Iconoclasm represented a reaction of centralized authority, that of emperor and bishops, against local pieties, the independence of cities and monasteries, and the cults of holy men.

THE INCREASING DIVISIONS BETWEEN EAST AND WEST

Iconoclasm offended many in the Western Church but it showed more clearly than anything yet how far Orthodoxy now was from Latin Christianity. The Western Church had been moving, too; as Latin culture was taken over by the Germanic peoples, it drifted away in spirit from the churches of the Greek East. The Iconoclast synod of bishops had been an affront to the papacy, which had already condemned Leo's supporters. Rome viewed with alarm the emperor's pretensions to act in spiritual matters. Thus Iconoclasm drove deeper the division between the two halves of Christendom. Cultural differentiation had now gone very far – not surprisingly when it could take two months by sea to go from Byzantium to Italy and by land a wedge of Slav peoples soon stood between two languages.

During the 7th and 8th centuries, some icons, such as the above image of the Virgin and Child, were created using the encaustic technique. The use of a combination of colour pigment and molten wax meant that the icon had to be painted while the mixture was still warm.

Eastern Empire, it is easy to understand how the debate became embittered. No question of art or artistic merit arose: Byzantium was not like that. What was at stake was the feeling of reformers that the Greeks were falling into idolatry in the extremity of their (relatively recent) devotion to icons and that the Arab disasters were the first rumblings of God's thunder; a pious king, as in the Israel of the Old Testament, could yet save the people from the consequences of sin by breaking the idols. This was easier in that the process

The Iconoclast movement

In Byzantium, representations of Christ, the Virgin, certain saints or scenes from the Bible were used as subjects for icons. Iconoclasm, the movement for the prohibition of this type of image, had a significant impact on the principal trends of European thought. According to some specialists, the movement's origins can be found in Muslim Iconoclasm, which spread through the army and the Byzantine clergy based in Asia Minor, although other historians of Byzantium believe that the prohibition of images was part of an anti-monastic movement or an attempt to strengthen the emperor's absolute power.

Iconoclasm was at its most ferocious and pervasive during the reign of Constantine V, when hundreds of religious icons and mosaics were destroyed. However, the Iconophiles never gave up the fight to keep their holy images and by the 9th century icons were once more at the centre of Byzantine religious life.

Long before Iconoclasm reached its height, Byzantine artists used emblematic designs in religious mosaics, often incorporating images of plants and animals as Christian symbols alongside portraits of saints and emperors, as in the decoration of the 6th-century church of St Vitale in Ravenna. This style became the only one acceptable during the Iconoclastic period. After the ravages of Iconoclasm, artists showed a greater tendency than before to concentrate on imperial and holy figures.

This Byzantine icon represents the archangels Michael and Gabriel and dates from the 10th or 11th century – the early post-Iconoclastic period.

Contact between East and West could not be altogether extinguished at the official level. But here, too, history created new divisions, notably when the Pope crowned a Frankish king "emperor" in 800. This was a challenge to the Byzantine claim to be the legatee of Rome. Distinctions within the Western world did not much matter in Constantinople; the

Byzantine art and architecture

During the 7th and 8th centuries, wars against the Muslims and Slavs were a constant drain on the resources of the Byzantine Empire. This in turn meant that Byzantine art suffered a serious decline, which worsened during the Iconoclastic period.

When the Macedonian Dynasty came to power, all the fine arts underwent a renaissance, principally due to the patronage of Basil II (976–1025). Architecture also enjoyed a period of great splendour. The origins of the architectural style that was to become characteristic of this era can be seen in the monasteries of Mount Athos, particularly in the beauty of the Grand Lavra Monastery.

During the 13th century, Byzantine artists produced a large number of outstanding mosaics and paintings – the mosaics of Pammakaristos (Constantinople) and the paintings of Mistra form part of the legacy of this brilliant creative period. Another centre of artistic interest was the Greek city of Trebizond, where the dome of St Eugene's church is considered by many to be of great note.

Byzantine art had a remarkable influence on cultures far beyond the empire's political borders. Byzantium's distinct style left a lasting mark in states such as Armenia, Georgia and Serbia, as this detail from a 13th-century fresco in a Belgrade church demonstrates.

Byzantine officials identified a challenger in the Frankish realm and thereafter indiscriminately called all westerners "Franks", a usage which was to spread as far as China. The two states failed to cooperate against the Arab and offended one another's susceptibilities. The Roman coronation may itself have been in part a response to the assumption of the title of emperor at Constantinople by a woman, Irene, an unattractive mother who had blinded her own son. But the Frankish title was only briefly recognized in Byzantium; later emperors in the West were regarded there only as kings. Italy divided the two Christian empires, too, for the remaining Byzantine lands there came to be threatened by Frank and Saxon as much as they had ever been by Lombards. In the tenth century

Byzantine coins often depict two or more people. The emperors Heraclius, Constantine and Heraclonas appear on this *solidus*.

the manipulation of the papacy by Saxon emperors made matters worse.

THE SPLENDOUR OF BYZANTIUM

Of course the two Christian worlds could not altogether lose touch. One German emperor of the tenth century had a Byzantine bride and German art of the tenth century was much influenced by Byzantine themes and techniques. But it was just the difference of two cultural worlds that made such contacts fruitful, and, as the centuries went by, the difference became more and more palpable. The old aristocratic families of Byzantium were replaced gradually by others drawn from Anatolian and Armenian stocks. Above all, there was the unique splendour and complication of the life of the imperial city itself, where religious and secular worlds seemed completely to interpenetrate one another. The calendar of the Christian year was inseparable from that of the court; together they set the rhythms of an immense theatrical spectacle in which the rituals of both Church and State displayed to the people the majesty of the empire. There was some secular art, but the art constantly before the people's eyes was overwhelmingly religious. Even in the worst times it had a continuing vigour, expressing the greatness and omnipresence of God, whose vice-regent was the emperor. Ritualism sustained the rigid etiquette of the court about which there proliferated the characteristic evils of intrigue and conspiracy. The public

This clasp belonged to a lady from the Visigoth aristocracy and was found in a tomb in Tureñuelo in Spain. The fact that the clasp is clearly Eastern in style – it appears to have Syrian influences – has caused speculation about its origin. One theory is that the lady may have brought the jewel back to the Iberian peninsula as a souvenir of a trip to the holy sites of Jerusalem.

appearance of even the Christian emperor could be like that of the deity in a mystery cult, preceded by the raising of several curtains from behind which he dramatically emerged. This was the apex of an astonishing civilization which showed half the world for perhaps half a millennium what true empire was. When a mission of pagan Russians came to Byzantium in the tenth century to examine its version of the Christian religion as they had examined others, they could only report that what they had seen in Hagia Sophia had amazed them. "There God dwells among men," they said.

THE BYZANTINE ECONOMY

What was happening at the base of the empire is not easy to say. There are strong indications that population fell in the seventh and eighth centuries; this may be connected both with the disruptions of war and with plague. At the same time there was little new building in the provincial cities and the circulation of the coinage diminished. All these things suggest a flagging economy, as does more and more interference with it by the state. Imperial officials sought to ensure that its primary needs would be met by arranging for direct levies of produce, setting up special organs to feed the cities and by organizing artisans and tradesmen bureaucratically in guilds and corporations. Only one city of the empire retained its economic importance throughout, and that was the capital itself, where the spectacle of Byzantium was played out at its height. Trade never dried up altogether in the empire and right down to the twelfth century there was still an important transit commerce in luxury goods from Asia to the West; its position alone guaranteed Byzantium a great commercial role and stimulation for the artisan industries which

Representing St Gregory, this miniature is one of the most important surviving examples of Byzantine art. It was commissioned by the emperor Basil I the Macedonian (867–886).

The style of this buckle, which originates from the Byzantine city of Trebizond, was much copied in workshops throughout western Europe.

provided other luxuries to the West. Finally, there is evidence across the whole period of the continuing growth in power and wealth of the great landowners. The peasants were more and more tied to their estates and the later years of the empire see something like the appearance of important local economic units based on the big landholdings.

INTERNAL POWER STRUGGLES

The economy was able to support both the magnificence of Byzantine civilization at its height and the military effort of recovery under the ninth-century emperors. Two centuries later an unfavourable conjuncture once more overtaxed the empire's strength and opened a long era of decline. It began with a fresh burst of internal and personal troubles. Two empresses and a number of short-lived emperors of poor quality weakened control at

During most of the 11th century, the Normans and the Arabs were a constant source of problems for the Byzantine Empire. This manuscript illustration depicts a battle between Byzantine and Arab armies.

the centre. The rivalries of two important groups within the Byzantine ruling class got out of hand; an aristocratic party at court whose roots lay in the provinces was entangled in struggles with the permanent officials, the higher bureaucracy. In part this reflected also a struggle of a military with an intellectual élite. Unfortunately, the result was that the army and navy were starved of the funds they needed by the civil servants and were left incapable of dealing with new problems.

NEW ENEMIES

At one end of the empire new problems were provided by the last barbarian migrants of the West, the Christian Normans, now moving into south Italy and Sicily. In Asia Minor they arose from Turkish pressure. Already in the eleventh century a Turkish sultanate of Rum was established inside imperial territory (hence its name, for "Rum" signified "Rome"), where Abbasid control had slipped into the hands of local chieftains. After a shattering defeat by the Turks at Manzikert in 1071 Asia Minor was virtually lost, and this was a terrible blow to Byzantine fiscal and manpower resources. The caliphates with which the emperors had learnt to live were giving way to fiercer enemies. Within the empire there was a succession of Bulgarian revolts in the eleventh and twelfth centuries and there spread widely in that province the most powerful of the dissenting movements of medieval Orthodoxy, the Bogomil heresy, a popular movement drawing upon hatred of the Greek higher clergy and their Byzantinizing ways.

A new dynasty, the Comneni, once again rallied the empire and managed to hold the line for another century (1081–1185). They pushed back the Normans from Greece and they fought off a new nomadic threat from

mperor John II Comnenus (1118–1143) is portrayed in this mosaic in St Sophia in Constantinople. The Comneni Dynasty's policies concentrated on finding the solutions to three major problems: the control of the Slav peoples in the Balkans, the expulsion of the Normans and the halting of the onslaught of the Seljuk Turks.

south Russia, the Pechenegs, but could not crack the Bulgars or win back Asia Minor and had to make important concessions to do what they did. Some concessions were to their own magnates; some were to allies who would in turn prove dangerous.

THE GROWTH OF VENETIAN POWER

To one of Byzantium's allies, the Republic of Venice, once a satellite of the empire, concessions were especially ominous, for her whole

The growth of Venice as a Mediterranean power

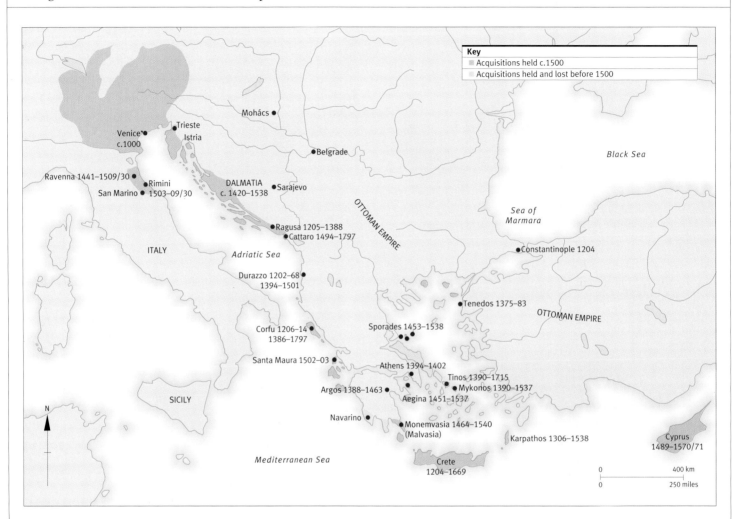

Key
- Acquisitions held c.1500
- Acquisitions held and lost before 1500

The city of Venice was formally a Byzantine dependency and run by a *magister militum* appointed by Constantinople. From the 11th century, however, it was virtually independent and came to almost monopolize trade between East and West. In 1082 the emperor Alexius I Comnenus (1081–1118) conceded considerable commercial privileges to Venice. Together with the freedom of trade with Germany, this led to the city's enormous growth. After taking part in the Fourth Crusade and the storming of Constantinople in 1204, the Venetians were also able to take control of most of the Greek islands, as well as part of Thrace and the Peloponnese.

Venice's greatest rival was Genoa. The two cities fought for the domination of eastern Mediterranean trade for most of the 13th and 14th centuries, including the "War of Chioggia" (1378–1381), which ended in defeat for Genoa. The commercial supremacy of Venice was now undeniable: for three centuries the Venetian ducat was the standard monetary unit for the eastern Mediterranean world.

raison d'être had come to be aggrandizement in the eastern Mediterranean. She was the major beneficiary of Europe's trade with the East and at an early time had developed a specially favoured position. In return for help against the Normans in the eleventh century, the Venetians were given the right to trade freely throughout the empire; they were to be treated as subjects of the emperor, not as foreigners. Venetian naval power grew rapidly and, as the Byzantine fleet fell into decline, it was more and more dominant. In 1123 the Venetians destroyed the Egyptian fleet and thereafter were uncontrollable by their former suzerain. One war was fought with Byzantium, but Venice did better from supporting the empire against the Normans and from the pickings of the crusades. Upon these successes followed commercial concessions and territorial gains and the former mattered most; Venice, it may be said, was built on the decline of the empire, which was an economic host of huge potential for the Adriatic parasite – in the middle of the twelfth century there were said to be 10,000 Venetians living at Constantinople, so important was their trade there. By 1204 the Cyclades, many of the other Aegean islands, and much of the Black Sea coasts belonged to them: hundreds of communities were to be added to those and Venetianized in the next three centuries. The first commercial and maritime empire since ancient Athens had been created.

THE CRUSADERS' THREAT TO THE BYZANTINE EMPIRE

The appearance of the Venetian challenge and the persistence of old ones would have been embarrassing enough for the Byzantine emperors had they not also faced new trouble at home. In the twelfth century revolt became more common. This was doubly dangerous when the West was entering upon enterprise in the East in the great and complex movement which is famous as the crusades. The Western view of the crusades need not detain us here; from Byzantium these irruptions from the West looked more and more like new barbarian invasions. In the twelfth century they left behind four crusading states in the former Byzantine Levant as a reminder that there was now another rival in the field in the Near East. When the Muslim forces rallied under Saladin, and there was a resurgence of Bulgarian independence at the end of the twelfth century, the great days of Byzantium were finally over.

THE "FRANKS" SACK CONSTANTINOPLE

The fatal blow came in 1204, when Constantinople was at last taken and sacked, but by Christians, not by the pagans who had threatened it so often. A Christian army which had gone east to fight the infidel in a fourth crusade was turned against the empire by the Venetians. It terrorized and pillaged the city (this was when the bronze horses of the Hippodrome were carried off to stand, as they still do, in front of St Mark's Cathedral in Venice), and enthroned a prostitute in the patriarch's seat in St Sophia. East and West could not have been more brutally distinguished; the act was to live in Orthodox memory as one of infamy. The "Franks", as the Greeks called them, did not see Byzantium as a part of their civilization, nor, perhaps, as even a part of Christendom, for a schism had existed in effect for a century and a half. Though they were to abandon Constantinople and the emperors would be restored in 1261 the Franks would not again be cleared from the old Byzantine territories until a new conqueror came along, the Ottoman

St Mark's in Venice, the domes of which are visible here behind the city's waterfront buildings, was inspired by the Byzantine churches of St Irene in Constantinople and St John in Ephesus. Work on St Mark's began in 829. It is constructed in the shape of a Greek cross and is crowned by four Byzantine domes surrounding a larger dome.

In 1204 the crusaders entered Constantinople and created the new Latin Empire of the East, which lasted until 1261. The event is portrayed in this painting by Delacroix, which dates from 1840.

Turk. Meanwhile, the heart had gone out of Byzantium, though it had still two centuries in which to die. The immediate beneficiaries were the Venetians and Genoese to whose history the wealth and commerce of Byzantium was now annexed.

THE SLAVS

THE LEGACY OF BYZANTIUM – or a great part of it – was on the other hand already secured to the future, though not, perhaps, in a form in which the Eastern Roman would have felt much confidence or pride. It lay in the rooting of Orthodox Christianity among the Slav peoples. This was to have huge consequences, with many

of which we still live. The Russian state and the other modern Slav nations would not have been incorporated into Europe and would not now be reckoned as part of it, if they had not been converted to Christianity in the first place.

Much of the story of how this happened is still obscure, and what is known about the Slavs before Christian times is even more debatable. Though the ground-plan of the Slav peoples of today was established at roughly the same time as that of western Europe, geography makes for confusion. Slav Europe covers a zone where nomadic invasions and the nearness of Asia still left things very fluid long after barbarian society had settled down in the west. Much of the central and southeastern European landmass

The political situation in western Europe during the 12th and 13th centuries

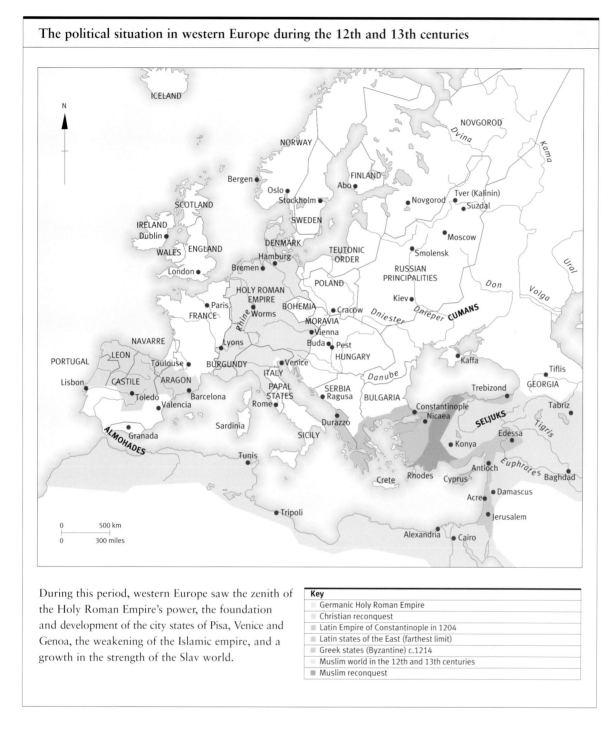

During this period, western Europe saw the zenith of the Holy Roman Empire's power, the foundation and development of the city states of Pisa, Venice and Genoa, the weakening of the Islamic empire, and a growth in the strength of the Slav world.

Key
Germanic Holy Roman Empire
Christian reconquest
Latin Empire of Constantinople in 1204
Latin states of the East (farthest limit)
Greek states (Byzantine) c.1214
Muslim world in the 12th and 13th centuries
Muslim reconquest

is mountainous. There, river valleys channelled the distribution of stocks. Most of modern Poland and European Russia, on the other hand, is a vast plain. Though for a long time covered in forests, it provided neither obvious natural lodgements nor insuperable barriers to settlements. In its huge spaces, rights were disputed for many centuries. By the end of

the process, at the beginning of the thirteenth century, there had emerged in the East a number of Slav peoples who would have independent historical futures. The pattern thus set has persisted down to our own day.

There had also come into existence a characteristic Slav civilization, though not all Slavs belonged wholly to it and in the end the peoples of Poland and modern Slovakia and the Czech Republic were to be more closely tied by culture to the West than to the East. The state structures of the Slav world would come and go, but two of them, those evolved by the Polish and Russian nations, proved particularly tenacious and capable of survival in organized form. They would have much to survive, for the Slav world was at times – notably in the thirteenth and twentieth centuries – under pressure as much from the West as from the East. Western aggressiveness is another reason why the Slavs retained a strong identity of their own.

SLAV ORIGINS

The story of the Slavs has been traced back at least as far as 2000 BCE when this ethnic group appears to have been established in the eastern Carpathians. For two thousand years they spread slowly both west and east, but especially to the east, into modern Russia. From the fifth to the seventh century CE Slavs from both the western and eastern groups began to move south into the Balkans.

Perhaps their direction reflects the power of the Avars, the Asiatic people who, after the ebbing of the Hun invasions, lay like a great barrier across the Don, Dnieper and Dniester valleys, controlling south Russia as far as the Danube and courted by Byzantine diplomacy.

Throughout their whole history the Slavs have shown remarkable powers of survival. Harried in Russia by Scythians and Goths, in Poland by Avars and Huns, they none the less stuck to their lands and expanded them; they must have been tenacious agriculturists. Their early art shows a willingness to absorb the culture and techniques of others; they learnt from masters whom they outlasted. It was important, therefore, that in the seventh century there stood between them and the dynamic power of Islam a barrier of two peoples, the Khazars and the Bulgars. These strong peoples also helped to channel the gradual movement of Slavs into the Balkans and down to the Aegean. Later it was to run up the Adriatic coast and was to reach Moravia and central Europe, Croatia, Slovenia and Serbia. By the tenth century Slavs must have been numerically dominant throughout the Balkans.

This illustration from an 11th-century historical manuscript portrays a scene from the Bulgar siege of Thessaloniki. Deleanos, the Bulgar leader, is about to receive one of his army commanders, while some of his soldiers watch from their tented encampment.

THE BULGARS

THE FIRST SLAV STATE to emerge was Bulgaria, though the Bulgars were not Slavs, but stemmed from tribes left behind by the Huns. Some of them gradually became Slavicized by intermarriage and contact with Slavs; these were the western Bulgars, who were established in the seventh century on the Danube. They cooperated with the Slav peoples in a series of great raids on Byzantium; in 559 they had penetrated the defences of Constantinople and camped in the suburbs. Like their allies, they were pagans. Byzantium exploited differences between Bulgar tribes and a ruler from one of them was baptized in Constantinople, the Emperor Heraclius standing godfather. He used the Byzantine alliance to drive out the Avars from what was to be Bulgaria. Gradually, the Bulgars were diluted by Slav blood and influence. When a Bulgar state finally appears at the end of the century we can regard it as Slav. In 716 Byzantium recognized its independence; now an alien body existed on territory long taken for granted as part of the empire. Though there were alliances, this was a thorn in the side of Byzantium which helped to cripple her attempts at recovery in the West. At the beginning of the ninth century the Bulgars killed an emperor in battle (and made a cup for their king from his skull); no emperor had died on campaign against the barbarians since 378.

THE BULGARS CONVERT TO CHRISTIANITY

A turning-point – though not the end of conflict – was reached when the Bulgars were converted to Christianity. After a brief period during which, significantly, he dallied with Rome and the possibility of playing her off

against Constantinople, another Bulgarian prince accepted baptism in 865. There was opposition among his people, but from this time Bulgaria was Christian. Whatever diplomatic gain Byzantine statesmen may have hoped for, it was far from the end of their Bulgarian problem. None the less, it is a landmark, a momentous step in a great process, the Christianizing of the Slav peoples. It was also an indication of how this would happen: from the top downwards, by the conversion of their rulers.

The Bulgars could prove formidable enemies for Byzantium. Here, the skull of the Byzantine emperor Nicephorus I (802–811) – turned into a bowl or cup – is shown being offered to the Bulgar king Krum by his subjects.

THE CYRILLIC ALPHABET

What was at stake was a great prize, the nature of the future Slav civilization. Two great names dominate the beginning of its

The brothers Cyril and Methodius, who set out to Christianize the Slav territories during the 9th century, are represented in this fresco from the church of St Clement in Rome. The two saints are just visible kneeling before the figure of Christ, who is accompanied by angels and by saints Andrew and Clement.

shaping, those of the brothers St Cyril and St Methodius, priests still held in honour in the Orthodox communion. Cyril had earlier been on a mission to Khazaria and their work must be set in the overall context of the ideological diplomacy of Byzantium; Orthodox missionaries cannot neatly be distinguished from Byzantine diplomatic envoys, and these churchmen would have been hard put to recognize such a distinction. But they did much more than convert a dangerous neighbour. Cyril's name is commemorated still in the name of the Cyrillic alphabet which he devised. It was rapidly diffused through the Slav peoples, soon reaching Russia, and it made possible not only the radiation of Christianity but the crystallization of Slav culture. That culture was potentially open to other influences, for Byzantium was not its only neighbour, but Eastern Orthodoxy was in the end the deepest single influence upon it.

KIEV AND BYZANTIUM

From the Byzantine point of view a still more important conversion than that of the Bulgars was to follow, though not for more than a century. In 860 an expedition with 200 ships raided Byzantium. The citizens were terrified. They listened tremblingly in St Sophia to the prayers of the patriarch: "A people has crept down from the north ... the people is fierce and has no mercy, its voice is as the roaring sea ... a fierce and savage tribe ... destroying everything, sparing nothing." It might have been the voice of a Western monk invoking divine protection from the sinister longships of the Vikings, and understandably so, for Vikings in essence these raiders were. But they were known to the Byzantines as Rus (or Rhos) and the raid marks the tiny beginnings of Russia's military power.

As yet, there was hardly anything that could be called a state behind it. Russia was still in the making. Its origins lay in an amalgam to which the Slav contribution was basic. The east Slavs had over the centuries dispersed over much of the upper reaches of the river valleys which flow down to the Black Sea. This was probably because of their agricultural practice, a primitive matter of cutting and burning, exhausting the soil in two or three years and then moving on. By the eighth century there were enough of them for there to be signs of relatively dense inhabitation, perhaps of something that could be called town life, on the hills near Kiev. They lived in tribes whose economic and social arrangements remain obscure, but this was the basis of future Russia. We do not know who their native rulers were, but they seem to have lived in the defended stockades which were the first towns, exacting tribute from the surrounding countryside.

VIKING RUSSIA

On to the Slav tribes in the Kiev hills fell the impact of Norsemen who became their overlords or sold them as slaves in the south. These Scandinavians combined trade, piracy and colonization, stimulated by land-hunger. They brought with them important commercial techniques, great skills in navigation and the management of their longships, formidable fighting power and, it seems, no women. As

This ceramic icon from the Patleina Monastery, close to Preslav, is the oldest surviving Bulgarian icon. It dates from the end of the 9th century, around the time that Bulgaria adopted Christianity as its official religion.

in the Humber and the Seine, they used the Russian rivers, much longer and deeper, to penetrate the country which was their prey. Some went right on; by 846 we hear of the "Varangians", as they were called, at Baghdad. One of their many sallies in the Black Sea was that to Constantinople in 860. They had to contend with the Khazars to the east and may have first established themselves in Kiev, one of the Khazar tributary districts, but Russian traditional history begins with their establishment in Novgorod, the Holmgardr of Nordic saga. Here, it was said, a prince called Rurik had established himself with his brothers in about 860. By the end of the century another Varangian prince had taken Kiev and transferred the capital of a new state to that town.

The appearance of a new power caused consternation but provoked action in Byzantium. Characteristically, its response to a new diplomatic problem was cast in ideological terms; there seems to have been an attempt to convert some Rus to Christianity and one ruler may have succumbed. But the Varangians retained their northern

The Vikings made their much-feared raids by boat, crossing oceans and navigating rivers for thousands of miles. This detail from a mythological scene, taken from an 8th-century Norse picture stone, shows men at sea and gives an impression of the form of the Viking longboat with its large, square sail.

paganism – their gods were Thor and Odin – while their Slav subjects, with whom they were increasingly mingled, had their own gods, possibly of very ancient Indo-European origins; in any case, these deities tended to merge as time passed. Soon there were

renewed hostilities with Byzantium. Oleg, a prince of the early tenth century, again attacked Constantinople while the fleet was away. He is said to have brought his fleet ashore and to have put it on wheels to outflank the blocked entrance to the Golden

Viking mythology

The Vikings worshipped a pantheon of gods who had their origins in Indo-European culture. The most significant of these gods was Odin, the All-Father and Lord of Magic. He was associated with the underworld and the dead and his followers were called Berserks. Odin is sometimes portrayed accompanied by two ravens and mounted on an eight-legged horse known as Sleipnir.

Odin's son, Thor, although less powerful than his father, was more popular. He was usually portrayed carrying a hammer and travelling across the skies in a chariot pulled by two goats. Thor was known for his enormous appetite, his fearful temper and his extra-ordinary strength.

The Scandinavian god of fertility and plenty was Freyr, who was the son of Njörd, god of ships and the sea. Freyr and Njörd belonged to the Vanir – a group of gods associated with the land and water, symbolized by a golden boar and a ship. The Vanir were in direct opposition to the Aesir, the gods of the sky.

A 19th-century painting by M. Ewinge, in which the Nordic god Thor, whose name means "thunder", is depicted fighting giants.

Horn. However he did it, he was successful in extracting a highly favourable treaty from Byzantium in 911. This gave the Russians unusually favourable trading privileges and made clear the enormous importance of trade in the life of the new principality. Half a century or so after the legendary Rurik, it was a reality, a sort of river-federation centred on Kiev and linking the Baltic to the Black Sea. It was pagan, but when civilization and Christianity came to it, it would be because of the easy access to Byzantium which water gave to the young principality, which was first designated as Rus in 945. Its unity was still very loose. An incoherent structure was made even less rigid by the Vikings' adoption of a Slav principle which divided an inheritance. Rus princes tended to move around as rulers among the centres, of which Kiev and Novgorod were the main ones. Nevertheless, the family of Kiev became the most important.

CONFLICT AND DIPLOMACY

During the first half of the tenth century the relation between Byzantium and Kiev Rus was slowly ripening. Below the level of politics and trade a more fundamental re-orientation was taking place as Kiev relaxed its links with Scandinavia and looked more and more to the south. Varangian pressure seems to have been diminishing, and this may have had something to do with the success of Norsemen in the West, where one of their

A rt in Christian Russia was strongly influenced by its Byzantine inheritance, as this 12th-century gold Gospel cover demonstrates.

Khazars and more trouble could be expected there. Nor did Varangian raids come to an end, though there was something of a turning-point when the Rus fleet was driven off by Greek fire in 941. A treaty followed which significantly reduced the trading privileges granted thirty years earlier. But the reciprocity of interests was emerging more clearly as Khazaria declined and the Byzantines realized that Kiev might prove to be a valuable ally against Bulgaria. Signs of contact multiplied; Varangians appeared in the royal guard at Constantinople and Rus merchants came there more frequently. Some are believed to have been baptized.

EARLY RUSSIAN CHRISTIANITY

Christianity, though sometimes despising the merchant, has often followed the trader's wares. There was already a church in Kiev in 882, and it may have been there for foreign merchants. But nothing seems to have followed from this. There is little evidence of Russian Christianity until the middle of the next century. Then, in 945, the widow of a Kievan prince assumed the regency on behalf of his successor, her son. This was Olga. Her son was Sviatoslav, the first prince of Kiev to bear a Slav and not a Scandinavian name. Later, Olga made a state visit to Constantinople. She may have been secretly baptized a Christian before this, but she was publicly and officially converted on this visit in 957, the emperor himself attending the ceremonies in St Sophia. Because of its diplomatic overtones it is difficult to be sure exactly how to understand this event. Olga had, after all, also sent to the West for a bishop, to see what Rome had to offer. Furthermore, there was no immediate practical sequel. Sviatoslav, who reigned from 962 to 972, turned out to be a militant pagan, like

rulers, Rollo, had been granted in 911 land later to be known as the duchy of Normandy. Yet it was a long time before there were closer ties between Kiev and Byzantium. One obstacle was the caution of Byzantine diplomacy, still quite as concerned in the early tenth century to fish in troubled waters by negotiating with the wild tribes of the Pechenegs as to placate the Rus whose territories they harried. The Pechenegs had already driven to the west the Magyar tribes which had previously formed a buffer between the Rus and the

ПРАСНОЕ ИСЦЕЛЕНИЕ И ПРОСЛАВИ БГА РЕ ТИ ПЕРВОД ВЕД ЕБА

This miniature from a 15th-century Russian manuscript, the Radziwill Chronicle, depicts a momentous event for Russia – the baptism of Vladimir. The ceremony took place in 988 in Cherson, a Byzantine outpost in the Crimea, and immediately preceded Vladimir's marriage to a Byzantine princess.

other Viking military aristocrats of his time. He clung to the gods of the north and was doubtless confirmed in his belief by his success in raiding Khazar lands. He did less well against the Bulgars, though, and was finally killed by the Pechenegs.

This was a crucial moment. Russia existed but was still Viking, poised between Eastern and Western Christianity. Islam had been held back at the crucial period by Khazaria, but Russia might have turned to the Latin West. Already the Slavs of Poland had been converted to Rome and German bishoprics had been pushed forward to the east in the Baltic coastlands and Bohemia. The separation, even hostility, of the two great Christian Churches was already a fact, and Russia was a great prize waiting for one of them.

VLADIMIR

In 980 a series of dynastic struggles ended with the victorious emergence of the prince who made Russia Christian, Vladimir. It

seems possible that he had been brought up as a Christian, but at first he showed the ostentatious paganism which became a Viking warlord. Then he began to enquire of other religions. Legend says that he had their

During the 11th century, Kiev was one of the most important cities in Europe. The Cathedral of St Sophia, the interior of which is shown here, was built in Kiev between 1018 and 1037. It was one of the first of many great Russian churches to have clear Byzantine features.

Several artistic schools for the production of icons were founded in Russia from the beginning of the 12th century. However, the most revered icon of all, the "Virgin of Vladimir" (so-called because it was housed in a church in the city of Vladimir for a while) was made in Constantinople in the early 12th century. It is one of the earliest examples of the exaltation of the Virgin Mary as the Mother of God and it inspired countless copies by Russian artists, who sought to recapture the tenderness of the image.

different merits debated before him; Russians treasure the story that Islam was rejected by him because it forbade alcoholic drink. A commission was sent to visit the Christian Churches. The Bulgarians, they reported, smelt. The Germans had nothing to offer. But Constantinople had won their hearts. There, they said in words often to be quoted, "we knew not whether we were in heaven or earth, for on earth there is no such vision nor beauty, and we do not know how to describe it; we know only that there God dwells among men". The choice was accordingly made. Around about 986–8 Vladimir accepted Orthodox Christianity for himself and his people.

It was a turning-point in Russian history and culture, as Orthodox churchmen have recognized ever since. "Then the darkness of idolatry began to leave us, and the dawn of orthodoxy arose," said one, eulogizing Vladimir a half-century or so later. Yet for all the zeal Vladimir showed in imposing baptism on his subjects (by physical force if necessary), it was not only enthusiasm which influenced him. There were diplomatic dimensions to the choice, too. Vladimir had been giving military help to the emperor and now he was promised a Byzantine princess as a bride. This was an unprecedented acknowledgment of the standing of a prince of Kiev. The emperor's sister was available because Byzantium needed the Rus alliance against the Bulgars. When things did not go smoothly, Vladimir put on the pressure by occupying Byzantine possessions in the Crimea. The marriage then soon took place. Kiev was worth a nuptial mass to Byzantium, though Vladimir's choice was decisive of much more than diplomacy. Two hundred years later his countrymen acknowledged this: Vladimir was canonized. He had made the single decision which, more than any other, determined Russia's future.

SOCIETY IN KIEV RUS

Probably tenth-century Kiev Rus had in many ways a richer culture than most of western Europe could offer. Its towns were great trading centres, channelling goods into the Near East where Russian furs and beeswax were prized. This commercial emphasis reflects another difference: in western Europe the self-contained, subsistence economy of the manor had emerged as the institution bearing the strain of the collapse of the classical economic world. Without the western manor, Russia would also be without the western feudal nobleman. A territorial aristocracy would take longer to emerge in Russia than in Catholic Europe; Russian nobles were for a long time to remain very much the companions and followers of a war-leader. Some of them opposed Christianity and paganism hung on in the north for decades. As in Bulgaria, the adoption of Christianity was a political act with internal as well as external dimensions and though the capital of a Christian principality, Kiev was not yet the

Russia's conversion to Orthodox Christianity, at the end of the 10th century, resulted in an influx of artistic influences from Byzantium, although Russian Orthodox art and architecture also developed their own characteristics. The Cathedral of St Sophia in Novgorod, pictured here, was built during the reign of Yaroslav the Wise (1019–1054).

centre of a Christian nation. The monarchy had to assert itself against a conservative alliance of aristocracy and paganism. Lower down the social scale, in the towns, the new faith gradually took root, at first thanks to Bulgarian priests, who brought with them the liturgy of the south Slav Church and the Cyrillic alphabet which created Russian as a literary language. Ecclesiastically, the influence of Byzantium was strong and the Metropolitan of Kiev was usually appointed by the Patriarch of Constantinople.

From 1157, Vladimir became the centre of the Russian principality of Vladimir-Suzdal. It was later to become an important religious centre – the church of St Dmitri (shown here) was built there between 1193 and 1197.

THE APOGEE OF KIEV RUS

Kiev became famous for the magnificence of its churches; it was a great time of building in a style showing Greek influence. Unhappily, being of wood, few of them survive. But the repute of this artistic primacy reflects Kiev's wealth. Its apogee came under Yaroslav "the Wise", when one western visitor thought she rivalled Constantinople. Russia was then culturally as open to the outside world as it was ever to be for centuries. In part this reflected Yaroslav's military and diplomatic standing. He exchanged diplomatic missions with Rome while Novgorod received the merchants of the German Hanse. Having himself married a Swedish princess, he found husbands for the womenfolk of his family in kings of Poland, France and Norway. A harried Anglo-Saxon royal family took refuge at his court. Links with western courts were never to be so close again. Culturally, too, the first fruits of the Byzantine implantation on Slav culture were being gathered. Educational foundation and legal creation reflected this. From this reign comes also one of the first great Russian works of literature, *The Primary Chronicle*, an interpretation of Russian history with a political purpose. Like much other early Christian history, it sought to provide a Christian and historical argument for what had already been done by Christian princes, in this case the unification of Russia under Kiev. It stressed the Slav heritage and offered an account of Russian history in Christian terms.

THE NORTHERN PRINCEDOMS

The weaknesses of Kiev Rus lay in the persistence of a rule of succession which almost guaranteed division and dispute at the death of the major prince. Though one other

Kiev Rus

According to Russian legend, Rurik arrived in eastern Europe in around 860 and established himself in Novgorod as a "Varangian" prince (the name that the Russians and Greeks gave to the Vikings). During the 9th century, the name Rus or Rhos came to denote all the eastern Slavs. Rurik's descendants gradually became Slavicized, although they maintained some contact with their place of origin, Scandinavia, until the 12th century. The above map shows Viking trade routes into Russia and the territory that belonged to Kiev at the height of the principality's power in the 11th century.

eleventh-century prince managed to assert his authority and hold foreign enemies at bay, the Kiev supremacy waned after Yaroslav. The northern princedoms showed greater autonomy; Moscow and Novgorod were, eventually, the two most important among them, though another "grand" princedom to match Kiev's was established at Vladimir in the second half of the thirteenth century. In part this shift of the centre of gravity of Russia's history reflects a new threat to the south in the pressure of the Pechenegs, now

Long after the apogee of Kiev Rus and after the conquest of Constantinople by the Ottoman Turks in the mid-15th century, icons continued to be venerated in the Slav countries that had converted to Orthodox Christianity. This Bulgarian icon depicting the crucifixion dates from 1541.

This early 14th-century Byzantine icon, from the church of St Saviour in Constantinople's Chora Monastery, portrays the "Fathers of the Eastern Church": St Basil, St Gregory and St Cyril. All three are holding copies of the Gospels.

reaching its peak.

This was a momentous change. In these northern states, the beginnings of future trends in Russian government and society can be discerned. Slowly, grants from the princes were transforming the old followers and boon-companions of the warlord kings into a territorial nobility. Even settled peasants began to acquire rights of ownership and inheritance. Many of those who worked the land were slaves, but there was no such pyramid of obligations as constituted the territorial society of the medieval West. Yet these changes unrolled within a culture whose major direction had been settled by the Kiev period of Russian history.

THE EMERGENCE OF POLAND

Another enduring national entity which began to crystallize at about the same time as Russia was Poland. Its origins lay in a group of Slav tribes who appear at the outset, in the tenth century, struggling against pressure from the Germans in the west. It may well have been politics, therefore, that dictated the choice of Christianity as a religion by Poland's first historically recorded ruler, Mieszko I. The choice was not, as in Russia's case, the Eastern Orthodox Church. Mieszko plumped for Rome. Poland, therefore, would be linked throughout her history to the West as would be Russia to the East. This

The name Bohemia comes from the Boios, early occupants of this central European region. Later the area was inhabited by various Slav tribes. According to legend, the founder of the first Bohemian dynasty was Premysl. This statue portrays Premysl's grandson, Ottokar I, and was made in around 1373 for his tomb in the cathedral of St Vitus in Prague.

conversion, in 966, opened a half-century of rapid consolidation for the new state. A vigorous successor began the creation of an administrative system and extended his lands to the Baltic in the north and through Silesia, Moravia and Cracow in the west. One German emperor recognized his sovereignty in 1000 and in 1025 he was crowned King of Poland as Boleslav I. Political setbacks and pagan reactions dissipated much of what he had done and there were grim times to come, but Poland was henceforth a historical reality. Moreover, three of the dominating themes of her history had also made their appearance: the struggle against German encroachment from the west, the identification with the interests of the Roman Church, and the factiousness and independence of the nobles towards the Crown. The first two of these do much to account for Poland's unhappy history, for they tugged her in different directions. As Slavs, Poles guarded the glacis of the Slav world; they formed a breakwater against the tides of Teutonic immigration. As Catholics, they were the outposts of Western culture in its confrontation with the Orthodox East.

RELIGIOUS DIFFERENCES BETWEEN SLAV PEOPLES

During these confused centuries other branches of the Slav peoples had been pushing on up the Adriatic and into central Europe. From them emerged other nations with important futures. The Slavs of Bohemia and Moravia had in the ninth century been converted by Cyril and Methodius, but were then reconverted by Germans to Latin Christianity. The conflict of faiths was important, too, in Croatia and Serbia, where another branch settled and established states separated from the eastern Slav stocks first by Avars, and then by Germans and Magyars, whose invasions from the ninth century were especially important in cutting off central European Orthodoxy from Byzantine support.

SLAV EUROPE UNDER STRAIN

A Slav Europe therefore existed at the start of the twelfth century. It was divided, it is true, by religion and into distinct areas of settlement. One of the peoples settled in it, the

Yaroslav the Wise, who is shown in this fresco with his family, carried out a policy of expansion that extended the Russian territories as far as the Baltic. He also tried to strengthen Christianity through an extensive building programme. The churches of St Sophia in Kiev and Novgorod are among the many that were constructed during his reign.

Magyars, who had crossed the Carpathians from south Russia, were not Slav at all. The whole of the area was under growing pressure from the west, where politics, crusading zeal and land-hunger all made a drive to the east irresistibly attractive to Germans. The greatest Slav power, Kievan Russia, developed less than its full potential; it was handicapped by political fragmentation after the eleventh century and harried in the next by the Cumans. By 1200 it had lost its control of the Black Sea river route; Russia had retreated to the north and was becoming Muscovy. Bad times for the Slavs lay ahead. A hurricane of disasters was about to fall upon Slav Europe, and for that matter on Byzantium. It was in 1204 that the crusaders sacked Constantinople and the world power which had sustained Orthodoxy was eclipsed. Worse still was to come. Thirty-six years later the Christian city of Kiev fell to a terrible nomadic people. These were the Mongols.

Russian icons, although clearly influenced by the style of Byzantium, gained renown across the Christian East for their great beauty and spirituality. This 12th-century icon, known as *The Annunciation of Ustjug*, was painted by a Russian artist of the Novgorod school.

4 THE DISPUTED LEGACIES OF THE NEAR EAST

BYZANTIUM WAS NOT the only temptation to the predators prowling about the Near East; indeed, she survived their attentions longer than her old enemy the Abbasid caliphate. The Arab empire slipped into decline and disintegration and from the tenth century we enter an age of confusion which makes any brief summary of what happened a despairing exercise. There was no take-off into sustained growth such as the flowering of commerce and the emergence of moneyed men outside the ruling and military hierarchies might have seemed to promise.

Rapacious and arbitrary expectations by government may be the basic explanation. In the end, for all the comings and goings of rulers and raiders, nothing disturbed the foundations of Islamic society. The whole area from the Levant to the Hindu Kush was pervaded for the first time in history by a single culture and it was to endure. Within that zone, the Christian inheritance of Rome hung on as a major cultural force only until the eleventh century, bottled up beyond the Taurus in Asia Minor. After that, Christianity declined in the Near East to become only a matter of the communities tolerated by Islam.

THE CALIPHATE DYNASTIES

The stability and deep-rootedness of Islamic social and cultural institutions were enormously important. They far transcended the weaknesses – which were mainly political and administrative – of the semi-autonomous states which emerged to exercise power under the formal supremacy of the caliphate in its decadent period. About them little need be said. Interesting to Arabists though they are, they need be noted here rather as convenient landmarks than for their own sake. The most important and strongest of them was ruled by the Fatimid Dynasty which controlled Egypt, most of Syria and the Levant, and the Red Sea coast. This territory included the great shrines of Mecca and Medina and therefore the profitable and important pilgrim trade. On the borders of Anatolia and northern Syria another dynasty, the Hamdanid, stood between the

This carved ivory casket, known as the Jar of Zamora, dates from 964 – the era of the Umayyad Córdoba caliphate. It bears the following inscription: "God's blessing for Iman Abd-Allah al-Hakim al-Mustansir Billah, Prince of the Faithful. This was ordered to be made by the Lady Mother of Abd-ar-Rahman III and given to the care of Durri the Boy."

The famous mosque of al-Azhar in Cairo was built by the Fatimid caliph al-Muizz (953–975). Its construction, begun in 970, took just two years to complete. During the reign of the next caliph, al-Aziz (975–996), a school was installed in the mosque and took its name. Part of the building still serves as an Islamic university today.

Fatimids and the Byzantine Empire, while the heartland of the caliphate, Iraq and western Iran, together with Azerbaijan, was ruled by the Buwayhid. Finally, the northeastern provinces of Khurasan, Sijistan and Transoxiana had passed to the Samanids. Listing these four groupings of power far from exhausts the complications of the unsettled Arab world of the tenth century, but it provides all the background now needed to narrate the unrolling of the process by which two new empires appeared within Islam, one based on Anatolia and one on Persia.

THE TURKISH PEOPLES

THE THREAD is provided by a Central Asian people already introduced into this story, the Turks. Some of them had been granted a home by the Sassanids in their last years in

Time chart (909–1453)						
909 Founding of the Fatimid Dynasty	1055 The Seljuk Turks take Baghdad	1096–1099 The First Crusade		1250 Founding of the Mameluke Sultanate		
900	1000	1100	1200	1300	1400	1500
	1071 The Seljuk Turks destroy Byzantine power in Asia Minor	1099 The crusades establish the Latin kingdom of Jerusalem	1237 Chinghis Khan's Mongol armies enter Europe			1453 Constantinople is conquered by the Turks

ولعارض وهو في يده السري وعمر على وسط خط الميدان حتى يصلوا الى وسط الموكب ثم يتناول العنان مع الدرء بشماله ويضرب بقايم السيف قبة الورقة ويثني عليها بالدبابة ويرد فرسك يمنة ويذرق بالدرقة يسار عن كهل الفرس ويرجح على خط الداس

الكسين وجرى الخلفه يفعل كفعل الاول ويرد فرسته شمالا على خط الدارج خط الكسين وجرى الثالث يفعل كفعل صاحبه ويرد فرسته يمنة وجرى الاول فيفعل كما فعل الاول ولاورد

The Mamelukes, four of whom are shown in this 13th-century illustration, were famed for their courage and horse-manship and were much in demand as mercenaries.

had fallen the great Arab onslaught. In 667 the Arabs invaded Transoxiana and in the next century they finally shattered the remains of the Turkish empire in western Asia. They were only stopped at last in the eighth century by the Khazars, another Turkish people. Before this the eastern Turkish confederation had broken up.

In spite of this collapse what had happened was very important. For the first time a nomadic polity of sorts had spanned Asia and it had lasted for more than a century. All four of the great contemporary civilizations, China, India, Byzantium, and Persia, had felt bound to undertake relations with the Turkish khans, whose subjects had learned much from these contacts. Among other things, they acquired the art of writing; the first surviving Turkish inscription dates from the early eighth century. Yet in spite of this, for long stretches of Turkish history we must rely upon other people's accounts and records, for no Turkish authority seems to go back beyond the fifteenth century and the archaeological record is sporadic.

THE MUSLIM TURKS

This lack of documentary evidence, combined with the fragmentation of the Turkish tribes, makes for obscurity until the tenth century. Then came the collapse of the T'ang Dynasty in China, a great event which offered important opportunities to the eastern and Sinicized Turks, just at the moment when signs of weakness were multiplying in the Islamic world. One was the emergency of the Abbasid successor states. Turkish slaves or "Mamelukes" had long served in the caliphates' armies; now they were employed as mercenaries by the dynasties which tried to fill their vacuum of power. But the Turkish peoples themselves were again on the move by the tenth century.

return for help. In those days the Turkish "empire", if that is the right word for their tribal confederation, ran right across Asia; it was their first great era. Like that of other nomadic peoples, this ascendancy soon proved to be transient. The Turks faced at the same time inter-tribal divisions and a resurgence of Chinese power and it was on a divided and disheartened people that there

In the middle of it a new dynasty re-established Chinese power and unity; perhaps it was this which provided the decisive impetus for another of the long shunting operations by which Central Asian peoples jostled one another forward to other lands. Whatever the cause, a people called the Oghuz Turks were in the van of those who pressed into the northeastern lands of the old caliphate and set up their own new states there. One clan among them were the Seljuks. They were notable because they were already Muslim. In 960 they had been converted by the assiduous missionary efforts of the Samanids, when still in Transoxiana.

Many of the leaders of the new Turkish régimes were former slave soldiers of the Arab-Persians; one such group were the Ghaznavids, a dynasty who briefly built a huge dominion which stretched into India (this was also the first post-Abbasid régime to choose its generals as sultans, or heads of state). But they were in their turn pushed aside as new nomadic invaders arrived. The

During the Seljuk era a restoration of Islamic culture took place, particularly in the field of architecture. The style that developed during that time – of which the famous 12th-century Friday Mosque in Isfahan, Iran, pictured here, is an example – is still influential today.

The Seljuk poet Khoja Dehhani wrote, "In describing your lips, my poetry ... is sweet, because pure distilled sugar sweetens the water." This 17th-century painting of lovers is by Riza-i Abbasi of Isfahan.

Oghuz came in sufficient numbers to produce a major change in the ethnic composition of Iran and also in its economy. In another way, too, their arrival means a deeper change than any preceding one and opened a new phase of Islamic history. Because of what the Samanids had done, some of the Oghuz Turks were already Muslim and respected what they found. There now began the translation into Turkish of the major works of Arabic and Persian scholarship which was to give the Turkish peoples access to Arab civilization as never before.

THE SELJUK EMPIRE

Early in the eleventh century the Seljuks crossed the Oxus, too. This was to lead to the creation of a second Turkish empire, which lasted until 1194, and, in Anatolia, to 1243. After evicting the Ghaznavids from eastern Iran, the Seljuks turned on the Buwayhids and seized Iraq, thus becoming the first Central Asian invaders of historical times to penetrate further than the Iranian plateau. Perhaps because they were Sunnites they seem to have been readily welcomed by many of the former subjects of the Shi'ite Buwayhid. They went on, though, to much greater deeds than this. After occupying Syria and Palestine they invaded Asia Minor, where they inflicted on the Byzantines one of the worst defeats of their history at Manzikert in 1071. Significantly, the Seljuks called the sultanate they set up there the Sultanate of Rum, for they saw themselves henceforth as the inheritors of the old Roman territories. That Islam should have a foothold inside the old Roman Empire touched off crusading zeal in the West; it also opened Asia Minor to the settlement of Turks.

In many ways, then, the Seljuks played an outstanding historic role. Not only did they begin the conversion of Asia Minor from Christianity to Islam, but they provoked the crusades and long bore the brunt of resisting them, too. This cost them heavily on other fronts. By the mid-twelfth century Seljuk power was already dwindling in the Iranian lands. Nevertheless, the Seljuk Empire lasted long enough to make possible a final crystallization over the whole Islamic heartlands of a common culture and of institutions which this time included Turkish peoples.

THE STRUCTURE OF THE SELJUK EMPIRE

A kind of Islamic hegemony was achieved, less because Seljuk government innovated than because it recognized social (and in Islam that meant religious) realities. The essence of the Seljuk structure was tribute rather than administrative activity. It was something of a confederation of tribes and localities and was no more capable of standing up to long-term stress than its predecessors. The central apparatus of the empire was its armies and what was necessary to maintain them; locally, the notables of the *ulema*, the teachers and religious leaders of Islam, ruled. They provided a consolidation of authority and social custom which would survive the caliphates and become the cement of Islamic society all over the Middle East. They would run things until the coming of nationalism in the twentieth century. For all the divisions of schools within the *ulema*, it provided at local levels a common cultural and social system which ensured that the loyalty of the masses would be available to new régimes which replaced one another at the top and might have alien origins. It provided political spokesmen who could assure satisfaction at the local level and legitimize new régimes by their support.

This produced one of the most striking differences between Islamic and Christian society. Religious élites were the key factor in the *ulema*; they organized the locally, religiously based community, so that bureaucracy, in the Western sense, was not needed. Within the political divisions of the Islamic world in the age of the caliphates' decadence these élites provided its social unity. The Seljuk

pattern spread over the Arabic world, and was maintained under the successor empires. Another basic institution was the use of slaves, a few as administrators, but many in the armies. Though the Seljuks granted some great fiefs in return for military service, it was the slaves – often Turkish – who provided the real force on which the régime rested, its armies. Finally, it relied also on the maintenance, where possible, of the local grandee, Persian or Arab.

In the late 11th century, the Seljuk Empire split into three parts from which the Sultanate of Rum, or Iconium (the name given to the Byzantine territories), was formed. The mosque of Ala-al-Din, completed in 1220, was built in Konya, the capital of the new sultanate.

THE THREAT OF THE CRUSADES

The declining years of the Seljuk régime exposed the weaknesses in this structure. It depended heavily for its direction upon the availability of able individuals supported by tribal loyalties. But the Turks were thin on the ground and could not keep their subjects' loyalties if they did not succeed. When the first wave of Muslim settlement in Anatolia was spent, that area was still only superficially Turkish, and Muslim towns stood in the middle of a countryside linguistically distinct; local language was not Arabized as it was further south and the submergence of the Greek culture of the area was only very slowly achieved. Further east, the first Muslim lands to be lost were lost to pagans in the twelfth century; a nomad ruler (widely supposed in the West to be a Christian king, Prester John, on his way from Central Asia to help the crusaders) took Transoxiana from the Seljuks.

The crusading movement was in part a response to the establishment of Seljuk power. The Turks, perhaps because of their late conversion to Islam, were less tolerant than the Arabs. They began to trouble Christian pilgrims going to the holy places. The other causes which promoted the crusades belong rather to European than to Islamic history and can be dealt with elsewhere, but by 1100 the Islamic world felt itself on the defensive even though the Frankish threat was not yet grave. Still, the reconquest of Spain had begun, and the Arabs had already lost Sicily. The First Crusade (1096–9) was favoured by Muslim divisions which enabled the invaders to establish four Latin states in the Levant: the kingdom of Jerusalem, and its three fiefs, the county of Edessa, the principality of Antioch and the county of Tripoli. They were not to have much of a future, but in the early twelfth century their presence seemed ominous to Islam. The crusaders' success provoked Muslim reaction and a Seljuk general seized Mosul as a centre from which he built up a new state in northern Mesopotamia and Syria. He recaptured Edessa (1144); his son saw the possibilities of exploiting the Christians' alienation of the local Muslim population by bad treatment. It was a nephew of this prince, Saladin, who seized power in Egypt in 1171, declaring the Fatimid caliphate at an end.

On 4 July 1187 the battle of the Horns of Hattin took place between the armies of Saladin and those of Guy de Lusignan, the king of Jerusalem. This manuscript illustration depicts a scene from the battle in which the victorious Saladin is smashing a reliquary carried by King Guy.

SALADIN

Saladin was a Kurd. He came to be seen as the hero of the Muslim reconquest of the Levant and he remains a captivating figure even after strenuous efforts by unromantic and sceptical scholars to cut through the image of the *beau idéal* of Saracenic chivalry. The fascination he exercised over the minds of his Christian contemporaries was rooted in paradoxes which must have had real educational force. He was indisputably a pagan, yet he was good, a man of his word and just in his dealings; he was chivalrous, yet of a world that did not know the knightly ideal. (This puzzled some Frenchmen so much that they were forced to believe he had in fact been knighted by a Christian captive and that he baptized himself on his deathbed.) On a more mundane level, Saladin's first great triumph was the recapture of Jerusalem (1187), which provoked a new, and third, crusade (1189–92). This could achieve little against him, though it further intensified the irritation of Muslims who now began to show a quite new and unprecedented bitterness and ideological hostility towards Christianity. Persecution of Christians followed and with it began the slow but irreversible decline of the formerly large Christian populations of the Muslim lands.

Saladin founded a dynasty, the Abbuyid sultans, which ruled the Levant (outside the crusader enclaves), Egypt and the Red Sea coast. It lasted until it was replaced by rulers drawn from its own palace guards, the Turkish Mamelukes. These were to be the destroyers of the remaining crusader conquests in Palestine. The revival of the caliphate which followed at Cairo (it was given to a member of the Abbasid house) is of small significance in comparison with this. It registered, nevertheless, that so far as Islam still had a preponderant power and a cultural focus, both were now to be found in Egypt. Baghdad was never to recover.

THE MONGOLS AND TATARS

THE MAMELUKES were to have another, greater, achievement to their credit in the thirteenth century. It was they who finally halted the tide of a conquest far more threatening than that of the Franks, when it had been rising for more than half a century. This was the onslaught of the Mongols. Their history makes nonsense of chronological and

The confrontation between Richard the Lionheart, king of England (1189–1199), and Saladin, sultan of Egypt and Syria (1174–1193), has been a recurrent theme in the iconography dedicated to the crusades.

attention of Chinese governments then lived there. Generally, China played off one of them against another in the interests of its own security. They were barbarians, not much different in their cultural level from others who have already crossed these pages. Two tribes among them, the Tatars and that which became known as the Mongols, competed and on the whole the Tatars had the best of it. They drove one young Mongol to extremes of bitterness and self-assertion. The date of his birth is uncertain, but in the 1190s he became khan to his people. A few years later he was supreme among the Mongol tribes and was acknowledged as such by being given the title of Chinghis Khan. By an Arabic corruption of this name he was to become known in Europe as Genghis Khan. He extended his power over other peoples in Central Asia and in 1215 defeated (though he did not overthrow) the Chin state in northern China and Manchuria. This was only the beginning. By the time of his death, in 1227, he had become the greatest conqueror the world has ever known.

This miniature depicts Chinghis Khan sitting in his tent. He is shown giving arrows to his sons, who are accompanied by a male servant.

territorial divisions. In an astonishingly short time this nomadic people drew into their orbit China, India, the Near East and Europe and left ineffaceable marks behind them. Yet there is no physical focus for their history except the felt tents of their ruler's encampment; they blew up like a hurricane to terrify half a dozen civilizations, slaughtered and destroyed on a scale the twentieth century alone has emulated, and then disappeared almost as suddenly as they came. They demand to be considered alone as the last and most terrible of the nomadic conquerors.

Twelfth-century Mongolia is as far back as a search for their origins need go. A group of peoples speaking the languages of the family called Mongol who had long demanded the

CHINGHIS KHAN

Chinghis Khan seems unlike all earlier nomad warlords. He genuinely believed he had a mission to conquer the world. Conquest, not booty or settlement, was his aim and what he conquered he often set about organizing in a systematic way. This led to a structure which deserves the name "empire" more than do most of the nomadic polities. He was superstitious, tolerant of religions other than his own paganism, and, said a Persian historian, "used to hold in esteem beloved and respected sages and hermits of every tribe, considering this a procedure to please God". Indeed, he seems to have held that he was himself the recipient of a divine mission.

The Great Khan of the Mongols

Chinghis Khan, the Mongols' first "Great Khan", is one of the most important historical figures of all time. Probably born in 1162 or 1167, he unified all of the Mongol and Turkish-Mongol tribes who, after having defeated the Merkit clan, proclaimed him king in 1196. Chinghis proclaimed himself *jagan* (supreme khan or universal sovereign) in a popular assembly held in 1206, following which he embarked on a campaign of conquests. In order to maximize the efficiency of the troops, he carried out a number of military reforms and strong discipline, based on the *yasa* (strict law), became one of the Mongol army's most important features.

The first Mongol incursion into China was carried out against the Chin Dynasty. This was settled with the conquest of Peking in 1215, which opened the way to Bokhara and Samarkand. Seven years later, Chinghis Khan's troops penetrated southern Russia, defeating the Prince of Kiev on 31 May 1223. To these conquests he added Burma (now known as Myanmar), Central Asia, Iran and the Near East, forming an enormous Mongol empire.

Chinghis Khan also carried out reforms of the civil service, creating a series of institutions to render it more efficient, including a postal service. In spite of his intransigence in many respects, the Mongol leader showed a great tolerance of other religions, with the exception of Islam. He became a legendary figure in medieval Europe where, at one time, he was identified with the mysterious Prester John.

Chinghis Khan's power lay in his remarkable ability to bring together under his control the diverse Mongol tribes, who led nomadic lives between northern China and southern Siberia.

Chinghis Khan died on 18 August 1227, leaving his three heirs, Ogoday (1229–1241), Güyük (1246–1248) and Möngke (1251–1259), with the task of continuing his conquests. However, rivalry amongst the Great Khan's descendants eventually led to the empire's division into khanates.

This religious eclecticism was of the first importance, as was the fact that he and his followers (except for some Turks who joined them) were not Muslim, as the Seljuks had been when they arrived in the Near East. Not only was this a matter of moment to Christians and Buddhists – there were both Nestorians and Buddhists among the Mongols – but it meant that the Mongols were not identified with the religion of the majority in the Near East.

In 1218 Chinghis Khan turned to the west and the era of Mongol invasions opened in Transoxiana and northern Iran. He never acted carelessly, capriciously, or without premeditation, but it may well be that the attack was provoked by the folly of a Muslim prince who killed his envoys. From there Chinghis went on to a devastating raid into Persia followed by a swing northward through the Caucasus into southern Russia, and returned, having made a complete circuit of the Caspian.

All this was accomplished by 1223. Bokhara and Samarkand were sacked with massacres of the townspeople which were meant to terrify others who contemplated resistance. (Surrender was always the safest course with the Mongols and several minor peoples were to survive with nothing worse

Chinghis Khan's Mongol Empire

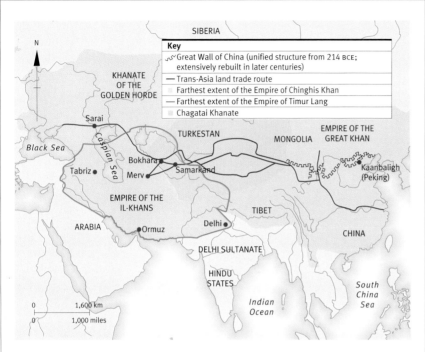

Throughout its history, the Mongol Empire experienced a series of major political and geographical transformations. Continual expansion occurred during the reign of Chinghis Khan as his conquests accumulated. In the second half of the 13th century, however, the empire broke up into khanates, which soon became mutual enemies. In the 14th century Timur Lang tried, although unsuccessfully, to rebuild Chinghis Khan's empire.

than the payment of tribute and the arrival of a Mongol governor.) Transoxiana never recovered its place in the life of Islamic Iran after this. Christian civilization was given a taste of Mongol prowess by the defeat of the Georgians in 1221 and of the southern Russian princes two years later. Even these alarming events were only the overture to what was to follow.

THE MONGOLS IN EUROPE

Chinghis died in the East in 1227, but his son and successor returned to the West after completing the conquest of northern China. In 1236 his armies poured into Russia. They took Kiev and settled on the lower Volga, from which they organized a tributary system for the Russian principalities they had not occupied. Meanwhile they raided Catholic Europe. The Teutonic knights, the Poles and the Hungarians all went down before them. Cracow was burnt and Moravia devastated. A Mongol patrol crossed into Austria, while the pursuers of the king of Hungary chased him through Croatia and finally reached Albania before they were recalled.

The Mongols left Europe because of dissensions of their leaders and the arrival of the news of the death of the khan. A new one was not chosen until 1246. A Franciscan friar attended the ceremony (he was there as an emissary of the pope); so did a Russian grand duke, a Seljuk sultan, the brother of the Abbuyid sultan of Egypt, an envoy from the Abbasid caliph, a representative of the king of Armenia, and two claimants to the Christian throne of Georgia. The election did not solve the problems posed by dissension among the Mongols and it was not until another Great Khan was chosen (after his predecessor's death had ended a short reign) that the stage was set for another Mongol attack.

THE MONGOL ONSLAUGHT ON ISLAM

This time the force of Mongol aggression fell almost entirely upon Islam, and provoked unwarranted optimism among Christians who noted also the rise of Nestorian influence at the Mongol court. The area nominally still subject to the caliphate had been in a state of disorder since Chinghis Khan's campaign. The Seljuks of Rum had been defeated in 1243 and were not capable of asserting authority. In this vacuum, relatively small and local Mongol forces could be effective and the Mongol Empire relied mainly upon vassals among numerous local rulers.

The campaign was entrusted to the younger brother of the Great Khan and began with the crossing of the Oxus on New Year's Day 1256. After destroying the notorious sect of the Assassins en route, he moved on Baghdad, summoning the caliph to surrender. The city was stormed and sacked and the last Abbasid caliph murdered – because there were superstitions about shedding his blood he is supposed to have been rolled up in a carpet and trampled to death by horses. It was a black moment in the history of Islam as, everywhere, Christians took heart and anticipated the overthrow of their Muslim overlords. When, the following year, the Mongol offensive was launched against Syria, Muslims were forced to bow to the cross in the streets of a surrendered Damascus and a mosque was turned into a Christian church. The Mamelukes of Egypt were next on the list for conquest when the Great Khan died. The Mongol commander in the West favoured the succession of his younger brother, Kubilai, far away in China. But he was distracted and withdrew many of his men to Azerbaijan to wait on events. It was on a weakened army that the Mamelukes fell at the Goliath Spring near Nazareth on 3 September 1260. The Mongol general was killed, the legend of Mongol invincibility was shattered and a turning-point in world history was reached. For the Mongols the age of conquest was over and that of consolidation had begun.

THE KHANATES

The unity of Chinghis Khan's empire was at an end. After civil war the legacy was divided among the princes of his house, under the nominal supremacy of his grandson Kubilai, Khan of China, who was to be the last of the Great Khans. The Russian khanate was divided into

three: the khanate of the Golden Horde ran from the Danube to the Caucasus and to the east of it lay the "Cheibanid" khanate in the north (it was named after its first khan) and that of the White Horde in the south. The khanate of Persia included much of Asia Minor, and stretched across Iraq and Iran to the Oxus. Beyond that lay the khanate of Turkestan. The quarrels of these states left the Mamelukes free to mop up the crusader enclaves and to take revenge upon the Christians who had compromised themselves by collaboration with the Mongols.

In retrospect it is still far from easy to understand why the Mongols were so successful for so long. In the west they had the advantage that there was no single great power such as Persia or the Eastern Roman Empire had been, to stand up to them, but in

An illustration from a later era portrays a scene from the Mongol court, in which two dancers are depicted entertaining the khan while he dines. The painting gives an impression of the great opulence that was perceived to have been at the heart of the Mongol Empire.

This illustration is taken from a 15th-century edition of Marco Polo's *The Book of the Wonders of the World*, in which the Venetian traveller described Kubilai Khan's palace in Peking. The building, he wrote, was made of marble, the interior walls were covered in gold and silver and the dining halls could seat 6,000 people.

the east they defeated China, undeniably a great imperial state. It helped, too, that they faced divided enemies; Christian rulers toyed with the hope of using Mongol power against the Muslim and even against one another, while any combination of the civilizations of the West with China against the Mongols was inconceivable given Mongol control of communication between the two. Their tolerance of religious diversity, except during the period of implacable hatred of Islam, also favoured the Mongols; those who submitted peacefully had little to fear. Would-be resisters could contemplate the ruins of Bokhara or Kiev, or the pyramids of skulls where there had been Persian cities; much of the Mongol success must have been a result of the sheer terror which defeated many of their enemies before

they ever came to battle. In the last resort, though, simple military skill explained their victories. The Mongol soldier was tough, well-trained and led by generals who exploited all the advantages which a fast-moving cavalry arm could give them. Their movement was in part the outcome of the care with which reconnaissance and intelligence work was carried out before a campaign. The discipline of their cavalry and their mastery of the techniques of siege warfare (which, none the less, the Mongols preferred to avoid) made them much more formidable than a horde of nomadic freebooters. As conquests continued, too, the Mongol army was recruited by specialists among its captives; by the middle of the thirteenth century there were many Turks in its ranks.

MONGOL RULE

Though his army's needs were simple, the empire of Chinghis Khan and, in somewhat less degree, of his successors was an administrative reality over a vast area. One of the first innovations of Chinghis was the reduction of Mongol language to writing, using the Turkish script. This was done by a captive. Mongol rule always drew willingly upon the skills made available to it by its conquests. Chinese civil servants organized the conquered territories for revenue purposes; the Chinese device of paper money, when introduced by the Mongols into the Persian economy in the thirteenth century, brought about a disastrous collapse of trade, but the failure does not make the example of the use of alien techniques less striking.

In so great an empire, communications were the key to power. A network of post-houses along the main roads looked after rapidly moving messengers and agents. The roads helped trade, too, and for all their ruthlessness to the cities which resisted them, the Mongols usually encouraged rebuilding and the revival of commerce, from the taxation of which they sought revenue. Asia knew a sort of *Pax Mongolica*. Caravans were protected against nomadic bandits by the policing of the Mongols, poachers turned gamekeepers. The most successful nomads of all, they were not going to let other nomads spoil their game. Land trade was as easy between China and Europe during the Mongol era as at any time; Marco Polo is the most famous of Europe's travellers to the Far East in the thirteenth century and by the time he went there the Mongols had conquered China, but before he was born his father and uncle had begun travels in Asia which were to last years. They were both Venetian merchants and were sufficiently successful to set off again almost as soon as they got back, taking the young Marco with them. By sea, too, China's trade was linked with Europe, through the port of Ormuz on the Persian Gulf, but it was the land-routes to the Crimea and Trebizond which carried most of the silks and spices westward and provided the bulk of Byzantine

In this 14th-century Mongol illustration a wealthy nobleman, who is seated on the right, waits for his servants to bring his meal.

Marco Polo's travels

Marco Polo was born in 1254 to a family of Venetian nobles. In 1271 his merchant father Niccolò and his uncle Mafio, who had already visited the court of Kubilai Khan (1259–1294), decided to return to China. Taking Marco with them, they passed through Armenia, Tabriz and Keman, reaching Ormuz in the Persian Gulf. From Ormuz they followed a dangerous route through Persia, Pamir and the Gobi desert, finally arriving in Peking in 1275. Marco Polo stayed in the Far East for two decades, in the service of Kubilai Khan. He was put in charge of Mongol embassies in Yunan, Cochin China, Tibet and India.

In 1291 the Polos were requested to accompany an imperial princess to Persia. They then returned to Europe via Sumatra and the southern coasts of Asia, as far as the Persian Gulf and, from there, across Persia and Armenia. They reached Constantinople and later their home port of Venice, where they were received with great honours. They had made their fortunes in the East and returned as very wealthy men.

In 1298, during the war between Venice and Genoa, Marco Polo was imprisoned by the Genoese. Upon his returned to Venice in 1299 he was made a member of the Great Council. He remained in the city until his death in 1324.

Marco Polo's memoirs, which he entitled *The Book of Marco*, gained international renown. Later editions were called *The Book of the Wonders of the World* and *The Discovery of the World*.

Marco Polo is depicted kneeling before an idealized Kubilai Khan in this illustration from a 15th-century edition of his memoirs. The khan's servant is handing the Venetian a passport to enable him to travel to distant Mongolia.

trade in its last centuries. The land-routes depended on the khans, and, significantly, the merchants were always strong supporters of the Mongol régime.

MONGOL ARROGANCE

In its relations with the rest of the world, the Mongol Empire came to show the influence of China in its fundamental presuppositions. The khans were the representatives on earth of the one sky god, Tengri; his supremacy had to be acknowledged, though this did not mean that the practice of other religions would not be tolerated. But it did mean that diplomacy in the Western sense was inconceivable. Like the Chinese emperors whom they were to replace, the khans saw themselves as the upholders of a universal monarchy;

Mongol armies are shown besieging a fortress defended by archers in this illustration from *The History of the Conquest of the World* by Ala-al-din.

those who came to it had to come as suppliants. Ambassadors were the bearers of tribute, not the representatives of powers of equal standing. When in 1246 emissaries from Rome conveyed papal protests against the Mongol treatment of Christian Europe and a recommendation that he should be baptized, the new Great Khan's reply was blunt: "If you do not observe God's command, and if you ignore my command, I shall know you as my enemy. Likewise I shall make you understand." As for baptism, the pope was told to come in person to serve the khan. It was not an isolated message, for another pope had the same reply from the Mongol governor of Persia a year later: "If you wish to keep your land, you must come to us in person and thence go on to him who is master of the earth. If you do not, we know not what will happen: only God knows."

MONGOL CULTURE

The cultural influences playing upon the Mongol rulers and their circle were not only

Marco Polo in the East

"In that region there were many monks dedicated to the worship of idols. There is a large monastery there, which because of its size seems more like a small city, in which nearly two thousand monks live and worship idols. In contrast to the custom of the layman they shave their heads and beards and wear clothes more in tune with their religious role. They sing great canticles in the celebration of their gods and light an incredible number of candles in their temple."

An extract describing a Buddhist temple in Nepal, from the *The Book of the Wonders of the World* by Marco Polo.

Chinese. There is much evidence of the importance of Nestorian Christianity at the Mongol court and it encouraged European hopes of a rapprochement with the khans. One of the most remarkable Western visitors to the khan, the Franciscan William of Roebruck, was told just after New Year 1254, by an Armenian monk, that the Great Khan would be baptized a few days later, but nothing came of it. William went on, however, to win a debate before him, defending the Christian faith against Muslim and Buddhist representatives and coming off best. This was, in fact, just the moment at which Mongol strength was being gathered for the double assault on world power, against Sung China and the Muslims, which was finally checked in Syria by the Mamelukes in 1260.

PERSIA UNDER THE IL-KHANS

Their defeat in Syria did not put an end to Mongol attempts to conquer the Levant. None was successful, though; the Mongols' quarrels among themselves had given the Mamelukes a clear field for too long. Logically, Christians regretted the death of Hulugu, the last khan to pose a real threat to the Near East for decades. After him a succession of Il-khans, or subordinate khans, ruled in Persia, preoccupied with their quarrels with the Golden and White Hordes. Gradually Persia recovered under them from the invasions it had suffered earlier in the century. As in the east, the Mongols ruled through locally recruited administrators and were tolerant of Christians and Buddhists, though not, at first, of Muslims. There was a clear sign of a change in the relative positions of Mongol and European when the Il-khans began to suggest to the pope that they should join in an alliance against the Mamelukes.

The mausoleum of Oljeyetu (1302–1317) stands close to the city of Sultaniya (in present-day Iran), which was founded by the Mongol king Arghun in 1290. Oljeyetu was the successor of Ghazan, the first Mongol ruler to convert to Islam.

PERSIA TURNS TO ISLAM

When Kubilai Khan died in China in 1294 one of the few remaining links that held together the Mongol Empire had gone. In the following year an Il-khan called Ghazan made a momentous break with the Mongol tradition; he became a Muslim. Since then the rulers of Persia have always been Muslim. But this did not do all that might have been hoped and the Il-khan died young, with many problems unsolved. To embrace Islam had been a bold stroke, but it was not enough. It had offended many Mongols and in the last resort the khans depended upon their captains. Nevertheless, the contest with the Mamelukes was not yet abandoned. Though in the end unsuccessful, Ghazan's armies took Aleppo in 1299; he was prayed for in the Umayyad mosque at Damascus the next year. He was the last khan to attempt to realize the plan of Mongol conquest of the Near East set out a half-century before, but was frustrated in the end when the Mamelukes defeated the last Mongol invasion of Syria in 1303. The Il-khan died the following year.

As in China, it soon appeared in Persia that Mongol rule had enjoyed only a brief Indian summer of consolidation before it began to crumble. Ghazan was the last Il-khan of stature. Outside their own lands, his successors could exercise little influence; the

Mamelukes terrorized the old allies of the Mongols, the Christian Armenians, and Anatolia was disputed between different Turkish princes. There was little to hope for from Europe, where the illusion of the crusading dream had been dissipated. As Mongol states crumbled, one last flash of the old terror in the west came with a conqueror who rivalled even Chinghis.

TIMUR LANG

In 1369 Timur Lang, or Timur the lame, became ruler of Samarkand. For thirty years the history of the Il-khans had been one of civil strife and succession disputes; Persia was conquered by Timur in 1379. Timur (who has passed into English literature, thanks to Marlowe, as Tamberlane) aspired to rival Chinghis. In the extent of his conquests and the ferocity of his behaviour he did; he may even have been as great a leader of men. None the less, he lacked the statesmanship of his predecessors. Of creative art he was barren. Though he ravaged India and sacked Delhi (he was as hard on his fellow-Muslims as on Christians), thrashed the khans of the Golden Horde, defeated Mameluke and Turk alike and incorporated Mesopotamia as well as Persia in his own domains, he left little behind. His historic role was, except in two respects, almost insignificant. One negative achievement was the almost complete extinction of Asiatic Christianity in its Nestorian and Jacobite form. This was hardly in the Mongol tradition, but Timur was as much a Turk by blood as a Mongol and knew nothing of the nomadic life of Central Asia from which Chinghis came, with its willingness to indulge Christian clergy. His sole positive achievement was unintentional and temporary: briefly, he prolonged the life of Byzantium. By a great defeat of an Anatolian Turkish people,

the Ottomans, in 1402, he prevented them for a while from going in to the kill against the Eastern Empire.

This was the direction in which Near Eastern history had been moving ever since the Mongols had been unable to keep their grip on Seljuk Anatolia. The spectacular stretch of Mongol campaigning – from Albania to Java – makes it hard to sense this until Timur's death, but then it was obvious. Before that, the Mongols had already been overthrown in China. Timur's own legacy crumbled, Mesopotamia eventually becoming the emirate of the attractively named Black Sheep Turks, while his successors for a while still hung on to Persia and Transoxiana. By the middle of the fifteenth century, the Golden Horde was well advanced in its break-up. Though it could still terrorize Russia, the Mongol threat to Europe was long over.

THE LAST PHASE OF BYZANTIUM

BY THE FIFTEENTH CENTURY, Byzantium was at her last gasp. For more than two centuries she fought a losing battle for survival, and not merely with powerful Islamic neighbours. It was the West which had first reduced Byzantium to a tiny patch of territory and had sacked her capital. After the mortal wound of 1204 she was only a small Balkan state. A Bulgarian king had seized the opportunity of that year to assure his country's independence and this was one of several ephemeral successor states which made their appearance. Furthermore, on the ruins of Byzantine rule there was established a new western European maritime empire, that of Venice, the cuckoo in the nest which had been in the first place bribed to enter it. This former client, though having to sustain a bitter

ΖΜΕΤΑC
ΑΘΕCΑΜΠⲰ
ΚΑⲨΚⲞ

Having occupied the Byzantine throne for seven years, John VI Cantacuzenus abdicated in 1354 to become a monk. He spent the remaining 29 years of his life in a remote monastery, where he wrote *Histories*, an account of his reign, and studied theology. His dual roles, as an emperor and as a monk, are represented in this manuscript illustration, which dates from 1347–1354.

During the era of the Palaeologus Dynasty, Byzantine art, particularly fresco painting and mosaics, reached new heights, rarely surpassed since. This 14th-century mosaic, entitled *The Dormition of the Virgin*, is from the church of the Chora Monastery in Istanbul. The Virgin lies surrounded by the apostles. In the centre, Christ is depicted with an infant in his arms, representing the rebirth of Mary's soul in heaven.

commercial and political rivalry with another Italian city-state, Genoa, had by the middle of the fourteenth century taken for herself from the Byzantine heritage the whole Aegean complex of islands, with Rhodes, Crete, Corfu and Chios.

In 1261 the Byzantines had regained possession of their own capital from the Franks. They did so with the help of a Turkish power in Anatolia, the Osmanlis. Two factors might still benefit the empire; the crucial phase of Mongol aggression was past (though this could hardly have been known and Mongol attacks continued to fall on peoples who cushioned her from them), and in Russia there existed a great Orthodox power which was a source of help and money. But there were also new threats and these outweighed the positive factors. Byzantine recovery in Europe in the later thirteenth century was soon challenged by a Serbian prince with aspirations to empire. He died before he could take Constantinople, but he left the empire with little but the hinterland of the capital and a fragment of Thrace. Against the Serbs, the empire once more called on Osmanli help. Already firmly established on the Asian shores of the Bosphorus, the Turks took a toehold in Europe at Gallipoli in 1333.

THE SHRINKING EMPIRE

The best that the last eleven emperors, the Palaeologi, could manage in these circumstances was a rearguard action. They lost what was left of Asia Minor to the Osmanlis in 1326 and it was there that the fatal danger lay. In the eastern Black Sea they had an ally in the Greek empire of Trebizond, a great trading state which was just to outlive Byzantium itself, but in Europe they could hope for little. The ambitions of the Venetians and Genoese (who by now dominated even

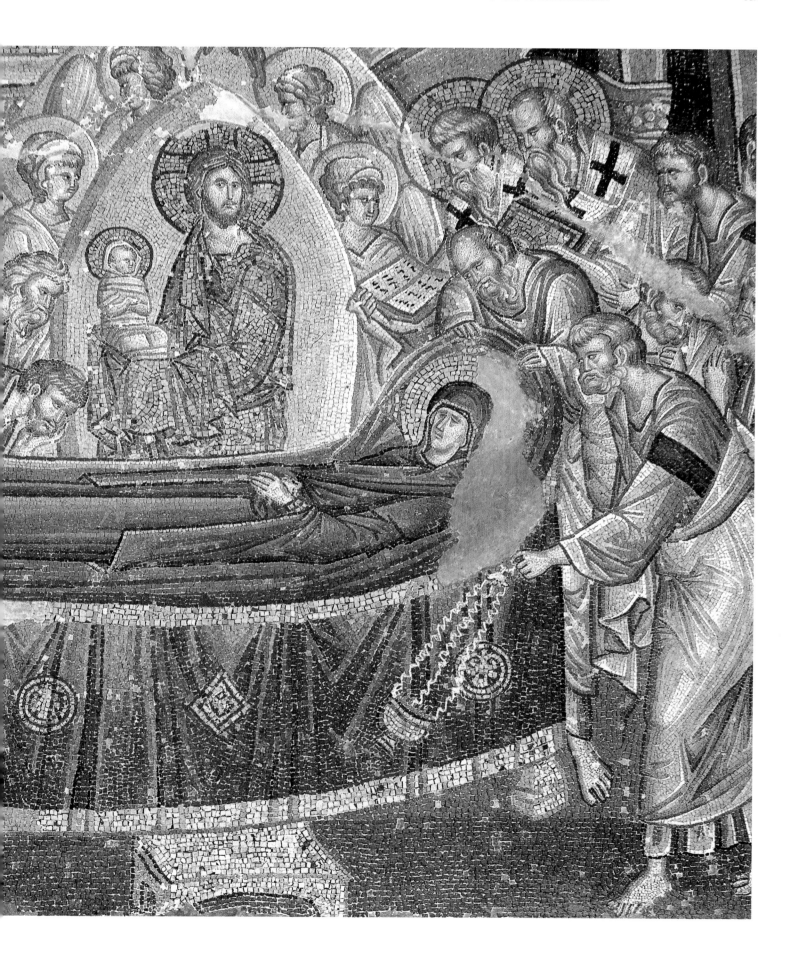

This 15th-century manuscript illustration depicts the troops of John II Kalojan, King of Bulgaria (1197–1207), defeating the army of Baldwin I (1171–1205), Count of Flanders and Latin Emperor of the East, near Adrianopolis in 1205.

to use Western mercenaries from Catalonia only led to their attacking Constantinople and setting up yet another breakaway state, the Catalan duchy of Athens, in 1311. Occasional victories when an island or a province was retaken did not offset the general tendency of these events, nor the debilitating effect of occasional civil war within the empire. True to their traditions, the Greeks managed even in this extremity to invest some of these struggles with a theological dimension. On top of all this, the plague in 1347 wiped out a third of what was left of the empire's population.

CHRISTIANITY DIVIDED

In 1400, when the emperor travelled the courts of western Europe to drum up help (a little money was all he got) he ruled only Constantinople, Salonica and the Morea. Many in the West now spoke of him, significantly, as "emperor of the Greeks", forgetting he was still titular emperor of the Romans. The Turks surrounded the capital on all sides, and had already carried out their first attack on it. There was a second in 1422. John VIII made a last attempt to overcome the strongest barrier to cooperation with the West. He went in 1439 to an ecumenical council sitting in Florence and there accepted papal primacy and union with Rome. Western Christendom rejoiced; the bells were rung in all the parish churches of England. But the Orthodox East scowled. The council's formula ran headlong against its tradition; too much stood in the way – papal authority, the equality of bishops, ritual and doctrine. The most influential Greek clergy had refused to attend the council; the large number who did all signed the formula of union except one (he, significantly, was later canonized) but many of them recanted when they went home. "Better," said one

the trade of the capital city itself), and the King of Naples, gave Byzantium little respite. One emperor desperately accepted papal primacy and reunion with the Roman Church; this policy did little except antagonize his own clergy and his successor abandoned it. Religion still divided Christendom.

As the fourteenth century wore on, the Byzantines had a deepening sense of isolation. They felt abandoned to the infidel. An attempt

Byzantine dignitary, "to see in the city the power of the Turkish turban than that of the Latin tiara." Submission to the pope was for most Greeks a renegade act; they were denying the true Church, whose tradition Orthodoxy had conserved. In Constantinople itself priests known to accept the council were shunned; the emperors were loyal to the agreement but thirteen years passed before they dared to proclaim the union publicly at Constantinople. The only benefit from the submission was the pope's support for a last crusade (which ended in disaster in 1441). In the end the West and East could not make common cause. The infidel was, as yet, battering only at the West's outermost defences. France and Germany were absorbed in their own affairs; Venice and Genoa saw their interest might lie as much in conciliation of the Turk as in opposition to him. Even the Russians, harried by Tatars, could do little to help Byzantium, cut off as they were from direct contact with it. The imperial city, and little else, was left alone and divided within itself to face the Ottomans' final effort.

THE OTTOMANS

WHO WERE THE OSMANLIS, or, as they became known in Europe, the Ottomans? They were one of the Turkish peoples who had emerged from the collapse of the sultanate of Rum. When the Seljuks arrived they found on the borderlands between the dissolved Abbasid caliphate and the Byzantine Empire a number of Muslim marcher lords, petty princes called *ghazis*, sometimes Turkish by race, lawless, independent and the inevitable beneficiaries of the ebbing of paramount power. Their existence was precarious, and the Byzantine Empire had absorbed some of them in its tenth-century recovery, but they were hard to eliminate.

Many survived the Seljuk era and benefited from the Mongol destruction of the Seljuks at a time when Constantinople was in the hands of the Latins. One of these *ghazis* was Osman, a Turk who may have been an Oghuz. But his appeal lay in his leadership and enterprise, and men gathered to him. His quality is shown by the transformation of the world *ghazi*: it came to mean "warrior of the faith". Fanatical frontiersmen, his followers seem to have been distinguished by a certain spiritual *élan*. Some of them were influenced by a particular mystical tradition within Islam. They also developed highly characteristic institutions of their own. They had a military organization somewhat like that of merchant guilds or religious orders in medieval Europe and it has been suggested that the West learnt in these matters from the Ottomans. Their situation on a curious borderland of cultures, half-Christian, half-Islamic, must also have been provoking. Whatever its ultimate source, their staggering record of conquest rivals that of Arab and

After its conquest by the sultan Orkhan (1326–1359), son of the founder of the Ottoman Dynasty, Bursa (Turkey) became the Ottoman Empire's first capital. Most of the sultans are buried there. The Green Mausoleum, pictured here, was built in 1421 and houses the remains of the sultan Mehmet I.

Mongol. They were in the end to reassemble under one ruler the territory of the old Eastern Roman Empire and more.

THE OTTOMAN SULTANS

The first Ottoman to take the title of Sultan did so in the early fourteenth century. This was Orkhan, Osman's son. Under him began the settlement of conquered lands which was eventually to be the basis of Ottoman military power. Like his foundation of the "Janissaries", the "New Army" of infantry which he needed to fight in Europe, the change marked an important stage in the evolution of Ottoman empire away from the institutions of a nomadic people of natural cavalrymen. Another sign that things were settling down was Orkhan's issue of the first Ottoman coinage. At his death he ruled the strongest of the post-Seljuk states of Asia Minor as well as some European lands. Orkhan was important enough to be three times called upon by the Byzantine emperor for help and he married one of the emperor's daughters.

His two successors steadily ate up the Balkans, conquering Serbia and Bulgaria. They defeated another "crusade" against them in 1396 and went on to take Greece. In 1391 they began their first siege of Constantinople, which they maintained successfully for six years. Meanwhile, Anatolia was absorbed by war and diplomacy. There was only one bad setback, the defeat by Timur which brought on a succession crisis and almost dissolved the Ottoman Empire. The advance was then resumed and the Venetian Empire now began to suffer, too. But for Byzantine and Turk alike, the struggle was essentially a religious one and its heart was the possession of the thousand-year-old Christian capital, Constantinople.

THE FALL OF CONSTANTINOPLE

It was under Mehmet II, named the Conqueror, that in 1453 Constantinople fell to the Turks and the Western world shuddered. It was a great feat of arms, depleted though the resources of Byzantium were, and supremely Mehmet's achievement, for he had persisted against all obstacles. The age of gunpowder was now well under way and he had a Hungarian engineer build him a gigantic cannon whose operation was so cumbersome that it could only be moved by a hundred oxen and fired only seven times a day (the Hungarian's assistance had been turned down by the Christians though the fee he asked was a quarter of what Mehmet gave him). It was a failure. Mehmet did better with orthodox methods, driving his soldiers forward ruthlessly, cutting them down if they flinched from the assault. Finally, he carried seventy ships overland to get them behind the imperial squadron guarding the Horn.

The last attack began early in April 1453. After nearly two months, on the evening of 28 May, Roman Catholics and Orthodox alike gathered in St Sophia and the fiction of the religious reunion was given its last parade. The emperor Constantine XI, eightieth in succession since his namesake, the great first Constantine, took communion and then went out to die worthily, fighting. Soon afterwards, it was all over. Mehmet entered the city, went straight to St Sophia and there set up a triumphant throne. The church which had been the heart of Orthodoxy was made a mosque.

OTTOMAN EXPANSION INTO EUROPE

The conquest of Constantinople was only a step, great as it was; the banner of Ottoman

During the mandate of Sultan Orkhan, the Janissaries, an élite body of soldiers, was formed. Its ranks were initially made up of Christians who were abducted from their families as children and brought up as Muslims. From the 17th century, recruitment to the Janissaries was carried out from amongst the Turks themselves.

success was to be raised yet higher. The invasion of Serbia in 1459 was almost at once followed by the conquest of Trebizond. Unpleasant though this may have been for the inhabitants, it would merit only a foot-note to the roll of Turkish conquest were it not also the end of Hellenism. At this remote spot on the southeastern coast of the Black Sea in 1461 the world of Greek cities made possible by the conquest of Alexander the Great gave its last gasp. It marked an epoch as decisively as the fall of Constantinople, which a humanist pope bewailed as "the second death of Homer and Plato". From

Trebizond, Turkish conquest rolled on. In the same year the Turks occupied the Peloponnese. Two years later they took Bosnia and Herzegovina. Albania and the Ionian islands followed in the next twenty years. In 1480 they captured the Italian port of Otranto and held it for nearly a year. In 1517 Syria and Egypt were conquered. They took longer to pick up the remainder of the Venetian Empire, but at the beginning of the sixteenth century Turkish cavalry were near Vicenza. In 1526 at Mohács they wiped out the army of the Hungarian king in a defeat which is remembered still as the black day of Hungarian history. Three years later they besieged Vienna for the first time. In 1571 Cyprus fell to them and nearly a century later

Crete. By this time they were deep into Europe. They again besieged Vienna in the seventeenth century; their second failure to take it was the high-water mark of Turkish conquest. But they were still conquering new territory in the Mediterranean as late as 1715. Meanwhile, they had taken Kurdistan from Persia, with whom they had hardly ceased to quarrel since the appearance of a new dynasty there in 1501, and had sent an army as far south as Aden.

THE CONSEQUENCES OF OTTOMAN VICTORY

The Ottoman Empire was of unique importance to Europe. It is one of the big differences marking off the history of its eastern from that of its western half. It was crucial that the Church survived and was tolerated in the Ottoman Empire. That preserved the heritage of Byzantium for its Slav subjects (and, indeed, ended any threat to the supremacy of the patriarch at Constantinople either from the Catholics or from national Orthodox churches in the Balkans). Outside the former empire, only one important focus of Orthodoxy remained; it was crucial that the Orthodox Church was now the heritage of Russia. The establishment of the Ottoman Empire for a time sealed off Europe from the Near East and the Black Sea and, therefore, in large measure from the land routes to Asia. The Europeans had really only themselves to blame; they had never been (and were never to be) able to unite effectively against the Turks. Byzantium had been left to her fate. "Who will make the English love the French? Who will unite Genoese and Aragonese?" asked a fifteenth-century pope despairingly; not long after, one of his successors was sounding out the possibilities of Turkish help against France. Yet the challenge

Ottoman expansion in the 14th and 15th centuries

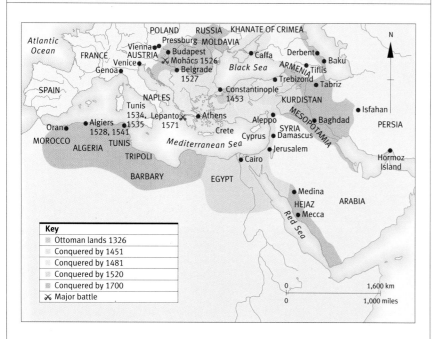

The above map shows the expansion and decline of the Ottoman Empire and gives the dates of its major campaigns. The Ottomans first entered Europe in 1345; by 1520 they controlled most of southeastern Europe, as well as parts of the Middle East and North Africa. The tide of conquest was largely stemmed in Europe with the Turkish defeat at Lepanto in 1571. Tunis was successfully captured in 1574, but the Ottoman army's second siege of Vienna in 1683 was a disaster for the Turks – the days of great Ottoman expansion were over, although there were still conquests to come.

had awoken another sort of response, for even before the fall of Constantinople Portuguese ships were picking their way southwards down the African coast to look for a new route to the spices of the East and, possibly, an African ally to take the Turk in the flank from the south. People had mused over finding a way round the Islamic barrier since the thirteenth century, but the means had long been inadequate. By one of history's ironies they were just about to become available as Ottoman power reached its menacing peak.

RELIGIOUS TOLERANCE UNDER MEHMET

Behind the Ottoman frontiers a new multi-racial policy was organized. Mehmet was a man of wide, if volatile, sympathies and later Turks found it hard to understand his forbearance to the infidel. He was a man who could slaughter a boy, the godson of the emperor, because his sexual advances were refused, but he allowed a band of Cretans who would not surrender to sail away after the fall of Constantinople because he admired their courage. He seems to have wanted a multi-religious society. He brought back Greeks to Constantinople from Trebizond and appointed a new patriarch under whom the Greeks were eventually given a kind of self-government. The Turkish record towards Jew and Christian was better than that of Spanish Christians towards Jew and Muslim.

Thus the Ottomans reconstructed a great power in the eastern Mediterranean. While they rebuilt something like the Byzantine Empire, another power was emerging in

The Sulaimaniye Mosque in Istanbul was built between 1550 and 1557, during the reign of Sulaiman the Magnificent. The famous Ottoman architect, Sinan, based the design of the mosque on that of the former church of St Sophia. The new mosque, however, was intended to surpass its rival in size and beauty and thus assert the superiority of Islam over Christianity.

This view of the interior of the great Byzantine church of St Sophia, which now houses a museum, shows one of the two half-domed apses. From the Ottoman conquest of Constantinople in 1453, when it was converted into a mosque, the building's interior was gradually Islamicized. Additions have included a *mihrab*, Koranic inscriptions, chandeliers and railings. In 1623, the original baptistry was transformed into a mausoleum to the sultan Mustafa I; and under Ahmed III (1703–1730), a pulpit, or *minbar*, was erected.

The origins of the Persian Safavid Dynasty can be traced to the members of a ruling Turkish family who were natives of Ardabil. This bowl was produced during the Safavid era.

Persia which was also reminiscent of the past, this time of the empire of the Sassanids.

SAFAVID PERSIA

BETWEEN 1501 AND 1736 the Safavid Dynasty ruled Persia. Like their predecessors, the Safavids were not themselves Persian. Since the days of the Sassanids, conquerors had come and gone. The continuities of Persian history were meanwhile provided by culture and religion. Persia was defined by geography, by its language and by Islam, not by the maintenance of national dynasties. The Safavids were originally Turk, *ghazis* like the Osmanlis, and succeeded, like them, in distancing possible rivals. The first ruler they gave to Persia was Ismail, a descendant of the fourteenth-century tribal ruler who had given his name to the line.

At first, Ismail was only the most successful leader of a group of warring Turkish tribes rather like those further west, exploiting similar opportunities. The Timurid inheritance had been in dissolution since the middle of the fifteenth century. In 1501 Ismail defeated the people known as the White Sheep Turks, entered Tabriz and proclaimed himself shah. Within twenty years he had carved out an enduring state and had also embarked upon a long rivalry with the Ottomans.

This rivalry had a religious dimension, for the Safavids were Shi'ites. When in the early sixteenth century the caliphate passed to the Ottomans they became the leaders of Sunnite Muslims who saw the caliphs as the proper interpreters and governors of the faith. The Shi'ites were therefore automatically anti-Ottoman. Ismail's establishment of the sect in Persia thus gave a new distinctiveness to Persia's civilization and this was to prove of great importance in preserving it.

SHAH ABBAS THE GREAT

Ismail's immediate successors had to fight off the Turks several times before a peace was made in 1555 which left Persia intact

Under the Safavids, Isfahan regained the splendour it had enjoyed during the 11th and 12th centuries when it had been ruled by the Seljuk Dynasty. Shah Abbas the Great instigated an ambitious building programme designed to convert Isfahan into a great imperial capital. Here, a view from the Royal Mosque towards the dome of the Lutfullah Mosque takes in the Maidan – a rectangular public space that served both as a marketplace and as a sportsfield.

This Persian bathing scene is taken from a 15th-century Safavid miniature.

and opened Mecca and Medina to Persian pilgrims. There were domestic troubles, too, and fighting for the throne, but in 1587 there came to it one of the most able of Persian rulers, Shah Abbas the Great. Under his rule the Safavid Dynasty was at its zenith. Politically and militarily he was very successful, defeating the Uzbeks and the Turks and taming the old tribal loyalties which had weakened his predecessors. He had important advantages: the Ottomans were distracted in the west, the potential of Russia was sterilized by internal troubles and Moghul India was past its peak. He was clever enough to see that Europe could be enrolled against the Turk. Yet a favourable conjuncture of international forces did not lead to schemes of world conquest. The Safavids did not follow the Sassanid example. They never took the offensive against Turkey except to recover earlier loss and they did not push north through the Caucasus to Russia, or beyond Transoxiana.

Persian culture enjoyed a spectacular flowering under Shah Abbas, who built a new capital at Isfahan. Its beauty and luxury astounded European visitors. Literature flourished. The only ominous note was religious. The shah insisted on abandoning the religious toleration which had until now characterized Safavid rule and imposed conversion to Shi'ite views. This did not at once mean the imposition of an intolerant system; that would only come later. But it did mean that Safavid Persia had taken a significant step towards decline and towards the devolution of power into the hands of religious officials.

The Safavid ruler Shah Abbas the Great (1587–1629) lowered taxes, improved the road network, encouraged the development of trade and supported craftsmen and artists. This brazier dates from the Safavid era.

SAFAVID DECLINE

After Shah Abbas' death in 1629 events rapidly took a turn for the worse. His unworthy successor did little about this, preferring to withdraw to the seclusion of the harem and its pleasures, while the traditional splendour of the Safavid inheritance cloaked its actual collapse. The Turks took Baghdad again in 1638. In 1664 came the first portents of a new threat: Cossack raids began to harry the Caucasus and the first Russian mission arrived in Isfahan. Western Europeans had already long been familiar with Persia. In 1507 the Portuguese had established themselves in the port of Ormuz where Ismail levied tribute on them. In 1561 an English merchant reached Persia overland from Russia and opened up Anglo-Persian trade.

In the early seventeenth century his connexion was well established and by then Shah Abbas had Englishmen in his service. This was the result of his encouragement of relations with the West, where he hoped to find support against the Turk.

The growing English presence was not well received by the Portuguese. When the East India Company opened operations they attacked its agents, but unsuccessfully. A little later the English and Persians joined forces to eject the Portuguese from Ormuz. By this time other European countries were becoming interested, too. In the second half of the seventeenth century the French, Dutch and Spanish all tried to penetrate the Persian trade. The shahs did not rise to the opportunity of playing off one set of

Safavid poetry

"I have made my grandparents glorious by my own hand!
If I should ever flee, cut short my life if it is long!
May my grandparents put the envious to shame by my hand.
Do not allow them to spit in my face, but rather only over my dead body!
Make my adversaries thirty thousand heroes, and may each one of them be a Rustam!
I will go to the battlefield when I feel inclined and then they will see I will fight all of them!
I will put them all to the edge of my sword.
They will neither be able to agree or to attack.
And do heroes worry about dying?
Should I let a sack of bran rot?"

A poem by Ismail I (1486–1524), the founder of the Persian Safavid Dynasty.

foreigners against another.

At the beginning of the eighteenth century Persia was suddenly exposed to a double onslaught. The Afghans revolted and established an independent Sunnite state; religious antagonism had done much to feed their sedition. From 1719 to 1722 the Afghans were at war with the last Safavid shah. He abdicated in that year and an Afghan, Mahmud, took the throne, thus ending Shi'ite rule in Persia. The story must none the less be taken a little further forward, for the Russians had been watching with interest the progress of Safavid decline. The Russian ruler had sent embassies to Isfahan in 1708 and 1718. Then, in 1723, on the pretext of intervention in the succession, the Russians seized Derbent and Baku and obtained from the defeated Shi'ites promises of much more. The Turks decided not to be left out and, having seized Tiflis, agreed in 1724 with the Russians upon a dismemberment of Persia. That once great state seemed to be ending in nightmare. In Isfahan a massacre of possible Safavid sympathizers was carried out by orders of a shah who had now gone mad. There was, before long, to be a last Persian recovery by the last great Asiatic conqueror, Nadir Kali. But though he might restore Persian empire, the days when the Iranian plateau was the seat of a power which could shape events far beyond its borders were over until the twentieth century, and then it would not be armies which gave Iran its leverage.

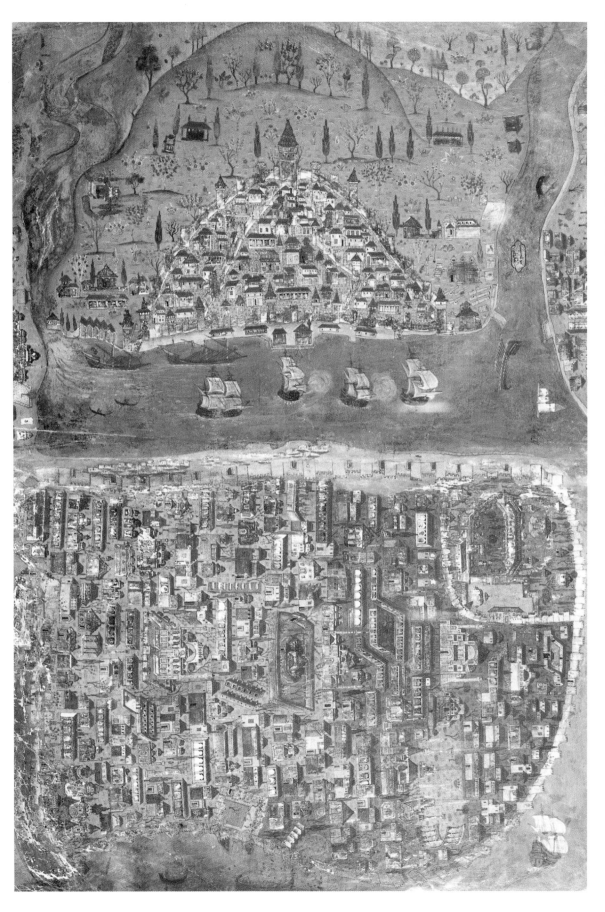

The arrival of the Ottoman Turks in Constantinople was to radically change the appearance of the ancient Christian city. Building fever gripped successive sultans – the personal ambitions of each one live on in an array of mosques and minarets. Many of the city's new Islamic buildings can be seen in this illustration, dated 1537.

5 THE MAKING OF EUROPE

During the 11th century, Saragossa was one of the most important Islamic centres in the Western world. This frieze embellishes the so-called Marble Room in the city's enormous Aljaferia Palace, which was built during the reign of al-Muqtadir.

IN COMPARISON WITH BYZANTIUM or the caliphate, Europe west of the Elbe was for centuries after the Roman collapse an almost insignificant backwater. Its boundaries were soon far narrower than had been those of Western Christianity. Its inhabitants felt themselves a beleaguered remnant and in a sense so they were. Islam cut them off from Africa and the Near East and Arab raids tormented their southern coasts. From the eighth century the

seemingly inexplicable violence of the Norse peoples we call Vikings fell like a flail time and time again on the northern coasts, river valleys and islands. In the ninth century the eastern front was harried by the pagan Magyars. Europe was formed in a hostile, heathen world.

THE CONSOLIDATION OF EUROPE

THE FOUNDATIONS of a new civilization had to be laid in barbarism and backwardness, which only a handful of men was available to tame and cultivate. No city in the West could approach in magnificence Constantinople, Córdoba, Baghdad or Ch'ang-an. Europe would long be a cultural importer. It took centuries before its architecture could compare with that of the classical past, of Byzantium or the Asian empires, and when it emerged it did so by borrowing the style of Byzantine Italy and the pointed arch of the Arabs. For just as long, no science, no school in the West could match those of Arab Spain or Asia. Nor could the West produce an effective political unity or theoretical justification of power such as the Eastern Empire and the caliphates; for centuries even the greatest European kings were hardly more than barbarian warlords to whom the population clung for protection and in fear of something worse.

Had it come from Islam, that something might well have been better. At times, such an outcome must have seemed possible, for the Arabs established themselves not only in

Spain but in Sicily, Corsica, Sardinia and the Balearics; people long feared they might go further. They had more to offer than the Scandinavian barbarians, yet the northerners left more of a mark in the end on the kingdoms established by earlier migrants. As for Slavic Christendom and Byzantium, both were culturally sundered from the West and able to contribute little to it. Yet they were a cushion which just saved Europe from the full impact of Eastern nomads and of Islam. A Muslim Russia would have meant a very different history for the West.

The area they occupied was all but landlocked; though the Atlantic was wide open, there was almost nowhere to go in that direction once Iceland was settled by the Norwegians, while the western Mediterranean, the highway to other civilizations and their trade, was an Arab lake. Only a thin channel of seaborne communication with an increasingly alien Byzantium brought Europe some relief from its introverted, narrow existence. Its people grew used to privation rather than opportunity.

This dish is one of many similar glazed ceramic pieces that are characteristic of Islamic art. Known as "green and manganese", the technique used consists of covering plaster in varnished tin and decorating it with copper and manganese oxides.

GEOGRAPHICAL LIMITS

Roughly speaking, Western Christendom before 1000 CE meant half the Iberian peninsula, all modern France and Germany west of the Elbe, Bohemia, Austria, the Italian mainland and England. At the fringes of this area lay barbaric, but Christian, Ireland and Scotland, and, just at the end of these centuries, the Scandinavian kingdoms. To this area the word "Europe" began to be applied in the tenth century; a Spanish chronicle even spoke of the victors of 732 as "European".

Found in the medieval cemetery of St Mary's church in Llugo de Llanera, Spain, this tablet dates from between the 8th and 10th centuries. It features the ancient symbol of the tree of life, upon which two lions appear to be feeding. The tree's roots are immersed in water, represented by a line of half moons. Appropriated by Christian, and particularly Byzantine, symbolism, this motif was common all over Europe.

Time chart (711–962)

700	750	800	850	900	950	1000

711
The Muslims invade the Iberian peninsula

843
The Treaty of Verdun results in the three-way division of the Carolingian Empire

910
Foundation of the Abbey of Cluny

751
Pepin the Short founds the Carolingian Dynasty

771
Charlemagne becomes sole ruler of the Frankish kingdoms

871–899
Alfred the Great is king of Wessex

962
Otto I is crowned Holy Roman Emperor by the pope

As the end of the 1st millennium approached, many Christians believed that the Kingdom of God was about to be established on earth, freeing the poor of the world from their bonds. Others believed in the prophecy, contained in the Book of Revelation, that the Devil would be set free from his chains and rule on earth. This miniature comes from the "Apocalypse of St Sever" (a manuscript named after the French church in which it was originally housed) and depicts the "fifth plague": the Angel of Hell (Satan) watches gleefully as locusts torment human beings.

They huddled together under the rule of a warrior class whose protection they needed.

In fact, the worst was over in the tenth century. The Magyars were checked, the Arabs were beginning to be challenged at sea, and the northern barbarians were on the road to Christianity. Though, as the portentous date 1000 approached, some thought that the end of the world might be at hand, that year can serve, very approximately, as the marker of an epoch. Not only had the pressures upon Europe begun to relax, but the lineaments of a later, expanding Europe were already hardening. Her basic political and social structure was set and her Christian culture had already much of its peculiar flavour. The eleventh century was to begin an era of revolution and adventure, for which the centuries sometimes called the Dark Ages had provided raw materials. As a way to understand how this happened, a good starting-point is the map.

Down to the eleventh century, three great changes began the making of the European map we know. One was a cultural and psychological shift away from the Mediterranean, the focus of classical civilization. Between the fifth and eighth centuries, the centre of European life, in so far as there was one, moved to the valley of the Rhine and its tributaries.

The Western world in the year 1000

Key
- Holy Roman Empire under Otto III (996–1002)
- Anglo-Saxon reconquest in the 10th century
- Principality of Kiev in 912
- Expansion of the Principality of Kiev from 912 to 1054
- Byzantine Empire in the 10th century
- Western extent of Byzantine Empire on the death of Basil II in 1025
- Bulgarian Empire of Tsar Samuel in around 996
- Muslim world at the end of the 10th century
- Christian kingdoms in the Iberian peninsula

By preying on the sea-lanes to Italy and by its distraction of Byzantium in the seventh and eighth centuries, Islam, too, helped to throw back the West upon this heartland of a future Europe. The second change was more positive, a gradual advance of Christianity and settlement in the East. Though far from complete by 1000, the advance guards of Christian civilization had by then long been pushed out well beyond the old Roman frontier. The third change was the slackening of barbarian pressure. The Magyars were checked in the tenth century; the Norsemen who were eventually to provide rulers in

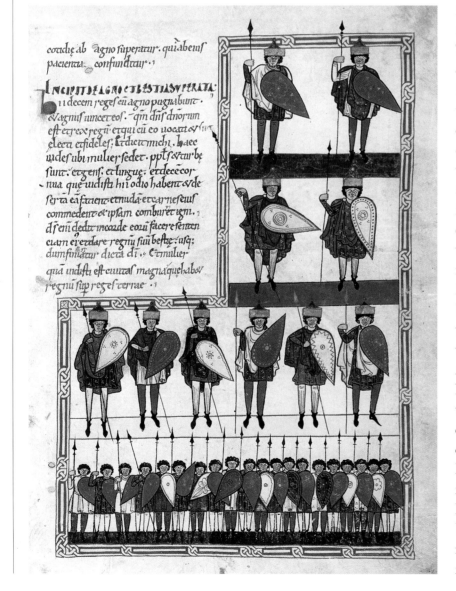

Frankish warriors, such as the ones depicted in this 11th-century miniature, rendered military service to the Romans in exchange for permission to settle on the empire's frontiers.

England, northern France, Sicily and some of the Aegean came from the last wave of Scandinavian expansion, which was in its final phase in the early eleventh century. Europe was no longer to be just a prey to others. True, even two hundred years later, when the Mongols menaced her, it must have been difficult to feel this. None the less, by 1000 she was ceasing to be wholly plastic.

WESTERN CHRISTENDOM

Western Christendom can be considered in three big divisions. In the central area built round the Rhine valley the future France and the future Germany were to emerge. Then there was a west Mediterranean littoral civilization, embracing at first Catalonia, the Languedoc and Provence. With time and the recovery of Italy from the barbarian centuries, this extended itself further to the east and south. A third Europe was the somewhat varied periphery in the west, northwest and north where there were to be found the first Christian states of northern Spain, which emerged from the Visigothic period; England, with its independent Celtic and semi-barbarous neighbours, Ireland, Wales and Scotland; and lastly the Scandinavian states. We must not be too categorical about such a picture. There were areas one might allocate to one or the other of these three regions, such as Aquitaine, Gascony and sometimes Burgundy. Nevertheless, these distinctions are real enough to be useful. Historical experience, as well as climate and race, made these regions significantly different, yet of course most people living in these areas would not have known in which one they lived; they would certainly have been more interested in differences between them and their neighbours in the next village than of those between their region and its neighbour. Dimly aware that they were a part of Christendom, very few of them would have had even an approximate conception of what lay in the awful shadows beyond that comforting idea.

THE FRANKISH HERITAGE

The origin of the heartland of the medieval West was the Frankish heritage. It had fewer towns than the south and they mattered little; a settlement like Paris was less troubled by the collapse of commerce than, say, Milan. Life centered on the soil, and aristocrats were successful warriors turned landowners. From this base, the Franks began the colonization of Germany, protected the Church and hardened and passed on a tradition of kingship whose origins lay somewhere in the magical powers of Merovingian rulers. But for centuries, state structures were fragile things, dependent on strong kings, for ruling was a personal activity.

Frankish ways and institutions did not help. After Clovis, though there was dynastic continuity, a succession of impoverished and therefore feeble kings led to more independence for landed aristocrats, who warred with one another; they had the wealth which could buy power. One family from Austrasia came to overshadow the Merovingian royal line. It produced Charles Martel, the soldier who turned the Arabs back at Tours in 732 and the supporter of St Boniface, the evangelizer of Germany. This is a considerable double mark to have left on European history (St Boniface said he could not have succeeded without Charles' support) and it confirmed the alliance of Martel's house with the Church. His second son, Pepin the Short, was chosen king by the Frankish nobles in 751. Three years later, the pope came to France and anointed him king as Samuel had anointed Saul and David.

PAPAL RECOGNITION

The papacy needed a powerful friend. The pretensions of the emperor in Constantinople were a fiction and in Roman eyes he had fallen into heresy, in any case, through taking up Iconoclasm. To confer the title of Patrician on Pepin, as Pope Stephen did, was really a usurpation of imperial authority, but the Lombards were terrorizing Rome. The papacy drew the dividend on its investment almost at once. Pepin defeated the Lombards and in 756 established the Papal States of the future by granting Ravenna "to St Peter". This was the beginning of eleven hundred years of the Temporal Power, the secular authority enjoyed by the pope over his own dominions as a ruler like any other ruler. A Romano-Frankish axis was created. From it stemmed the reform of the Frankish Church, further colonization and missionary conversion in Germany (where wars were waged against the pagan Saxons), the throwing back of the Arabs across the

The conversion to Roman Catholicism of the Merovingian monarch Clovis (this illustration shows his baptism in 496), was a political measure. It was a means of drumming up the support of the Gallo-Roman people for the Franks against other Germanic peoples such as the Visigoths, Ostrogoths and Burgundians, who advocated Arian heresy.

Pyrenees and the conquest of Septimania and Aquitaine. These were big gains for the Church. It is hardly surprising to find Pope Hadrian I no longer dating official documents by the regnal year of the emperor at Byzantium, and minting coins in his own name. The papacy had a new basis for independence. Nor did the new magic of anointing benefit only kings. Though it could replace or blur mysteriously with the old Merovingian thaumaturgy and raise kings above common men in more than their power, the pope gained the subtle implication of authority latent in the power to bestow the sacral oil.

S cenes from the life of Charlemagne (742–814) are shown in these illustrations from a 15th-century manuscript of the emperor's biography.

CHARLEMAGNE

P EPIN, LIKE ALL FRANKISH KINGS, divided his land at his death but the whole Frankish heritage was united again in 771 in his elder

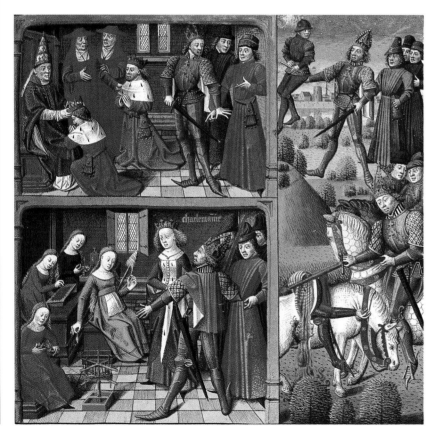

Charlemagne's churches

"With the gold that Charlemagne gave to the kings and princes of Spain, he enriched the Basilica of Santiago, in whose lands he had stayed for three years; he established a bishop and canons, according to the Order of St Isadore, bishop and confessor, and with great dignity furnished it with bells, tapestries, books and other ornaments. With the rest of the gold and the endless amount of silver that he had taken out of Spain having returned from there, he built many churches, namely: the Church of the Virgin Mary in Aquisgranum (Aachen) and the Basilica of Santiago in the same city; the Church of Santiago in Béziers; the Basilica of Santiago in Toulouse and in Gascony, between the city which is popularly known as Aix and St Jean de Sorde on the Jacobean route; the church that is in the city of Paris between the River Seine and Montmartre, and innumerable abbeys throughout the world."

An extract from Chapter V, Book IV of the "Pseudo-Turpin Chronicle", from the *Liber Santi Jacobi* or *Codex Calistinus*, thought to be the work of Turpin, Archbishop of Reims (died c.794).

son. This was Charlemagne, crowned emperor in 800. The greatest of the Carolingians, as the line came to be called, he was soon a legend. This increases the difficulties, always great in medieval history, of penetrating an individual's biography. Charlemagne's actions speak for certain continuing prepossessions. He was obviously still a traditional Frankish warrior-king; he conquered and his business was war. What was more novel was the seriousness with which he took the Christian sanctification of this role. He took his duties seriously, too, in patronizing learning and art; he wanted to magnify the grandeur and prestige of his court by filling it with evidence of Christian learning.

The achievements of Charlemagne's reign

One of the most significant figures in European history is, without a doubt, Charlemagne (also known as Charles the Great). The son of Pepin the Short and Bertha, daughter of Cariberto, Count of Lyons, Charlemagne ruled a unified Carolingian kingdom from 771 to 814.

Although Charlemagne's empire lacked centralized organization, it did achieve a remarkable ascendancy over the political and warrior class, of a kind that had not been seen in Europe since the fall of the Western Roman Empire. One of his important achievements as emperor was the enforcement throughout the imperial territories of a general code of law, issued through a series of instructions. Charlemagne also initiated a cultural renaissance and the use of Latin as the official language. He carried out monetary reform, imposing an imperial monopoly on the minting of coins. Even such cohesion as his empire achieved, however, was to be short-lived: it did not survive the reign of his son, Louis the Pious (814–831 and 835–840).

Charlemagne's dreams are depicted in this miniature from a 15th-century manuscript entitled "The Great Chronicles of France".

Territorially, Charlemagne was a great builder, overthrowing the Lombards in Italy and becoming their king; their lands, too, passed into the Frankish heritage. For thirty years he hammered away in campaigns on the Saxon March and achieved the conversion of the

Legend has it that this sword, with its elaborate hilt, once belonged to the emperor Charlemagne. It was customary for a small relic of a saint to be carried in the hilt of such swords: this was thought to render the user invincible.

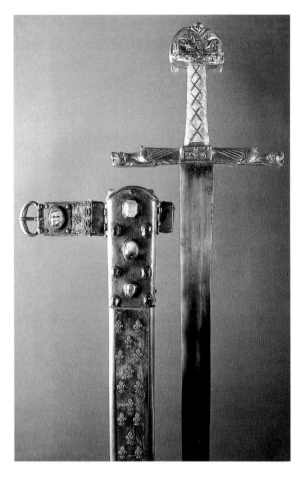

Saxon pagans by force. Fighting against the Avars, Wends and Slavs brought him Carinthia and Bohemia and, perhaps as important, the opening of a route down the Danube to Byzantium. To master the Danes, the Dane Mark (March) was set up across the Elbe. Charlemagne pushed into Spain early in the ninth century and instituted the Spanish March across the Pyrenees down to the Ebro and the Catalonian coast. But he did not put to sea; the Visigoths had been the last western European sea-power.

CHARLEMAGNE AND THE IMPERIAL TITLE

Charlemagne put together a realm bigger than anything in the West since Rome. Historians have been arguing almost ever since about what its reality was and about what Charlemagne's coronation by the pope on Christmas Day, 800, and his acclamation as emperor, actually meant. "Most pious Augustus, crowned by God, the great and peace-giving Emperor" ran the chart at the service but there already was an emperor whom everybody acknowledged to be such: he lived in Constantinople. Did a second ruler with the title mean that there were two emperors of a divided Christendom, as in later Roman times? Clearly, it was a claim to authority over many peoples; by this title, Charlemagne said he was more than just a ruler of Franks. Perhaps Italy mattered most in explaining it, for among the Italians a link with the imperial past might be a cementing factor as nowhere else. An element of papal gratitude – or expediency – was involved, too;

"La Chanson de Roland"

A number of "epic poems" – tales of heroic deeds recounted by minstrels – have survived from the Carolingian era and give us a fascinating insight into the feudal society and culture of the time. The epics appear to have been written by poets who turned certain historic or legendary deeds into "songs", to which they then added epic characteristics with a strong ethical content.

The oldest of the French songs is "La Chanson de Roland". The identity of the author is unknown, although some specialists believe that the monk Turoldus may have composed the song. Written in the early 12th century, it has 4,002 verses and tells of the death of Count Roland, Charlemagne's nephew. The poem is loosely based on real events – Roland was the warden of the Breton March. He and his troops, who had been left behind in Spain as a rearguard by Charlemagne in 778, were killed by Basques. The poem tells how Roland, having been betrayed by his stepfather Ganelon, was killed in Roncesvalles by the soldiers of Marsilius, King of Spain. It recounts how, before he died, Roland had managed to alert Charlemagne's troops, who rushed in vain to his aid. They then pursued Marsilius' armies, defeating them at Baligant and conquering Saragossa.

Leo III had just been restored to his capital by Charlemagne's soldiers. Yet Charlemagne is reported to have said that he would not have entered St Peter's had he known what the pope intended to do. He may have disliked the pope's implied arrogation of authority. He may well have foreseen the irritation the coronation would cause at Constantinople.

He must have known that to his own people, the Franks, and to many of his northern subjects he was more comprehensible as a traditional Germanic warrior-king than as the successor of Roman emperors, yet before long his Seal bore the legend *Renovatio Romani imperii*, a conscious reconnexion with a great past.

Charlemagne's Europe

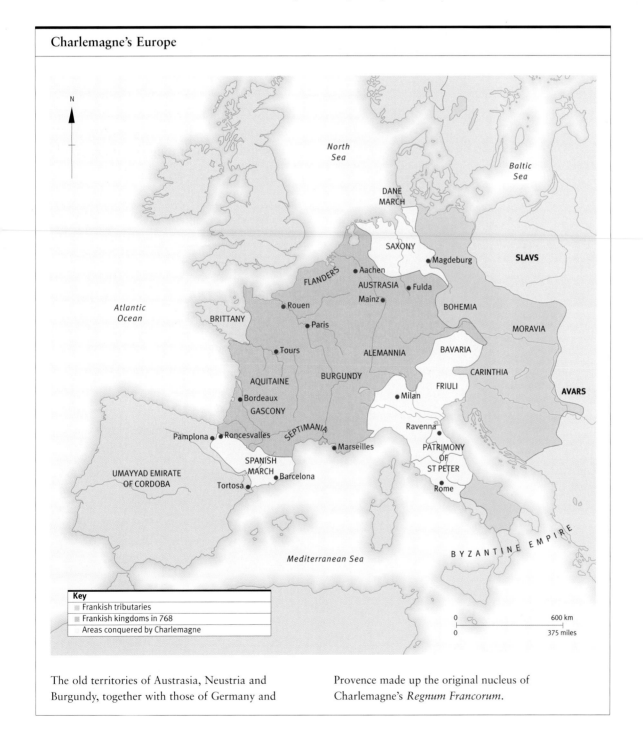

The old territories of Austrasia, Neustria and Burgundy, together with those of Germany and Provence made up the original nucleus of Charlemagne's *Regnum Francorum*.

Taken from the "Chronicle of St Denis", which was written in 1497, this illustration depicts the emperor Charlemagne surveying progress in the construction of a church he commissioned at Aachen, now Aix-la-Chapelle.

CHARLEMAGNE'S RULE

Charlemagne's relations with Byzantium were troubled, though his title was a few years later recognized as valid in the West in return for a concession to Byzantium of sovereignty over Venice, Istria and Dalmatia. With another great state, the Abbasid caliphate, Charlemagne had somewhat formal but not unfriendly relations; Haroun-al-Raschid is said to have given him a cup bearing a portrait of Khusrau I, the king under whom Sassanid power and civilization was at its height (perhaps it is significant that it is from Frankish sources that we learn of these contacts; they do not seem to have struck the Arab chroniclers as important enough to mention). The Umayyads of Spain were different; they were marked down as the

According to legend, the famous "Cup of Solomon" was given to Charlemagne by the Abbasid caliph Haroun-al-Raschid. At the centre of the cup, the Sassanid king Khusrau I is depicted.

enemies of a Christian ruler because near enough to be a threat. To protect the faith from pagans was a part of Christian kingship but in government this kingship had other expressions. For all his support and protection, the Church was firmly subordinate to Charlemagne's authority. He presided over the Frankish synods, pronouncing upon dogmatic questions as authoritatively as had Justinian, and seems to have hoped for an integrated reform of the Frankish Church and the Roman, imposing upon them both the Rule of St Benedict. In such a scheme there is the essence of the later European idea that a Christian king is responsible not only for the protection of the Church but for the quality of the religious life within his dominions. Charlemagne also used the Church as an instrument of government, ruling through bishops.

THE CAROLINGIAN RENAISSANCE

Further evidence of religion's special importance to Charlemagne lies in the tone of the life of his court at Aachen. He strove to beautify its physical setting with architecture and decorative treasures. There was, of course, much to be

The Four Evangelists are depicted in this illustration from a 9th-century manuscript called "The Coronation Gospels". The manuscript was produced at Charlemagne's court school in Aachen during the great creative period known as the "Carolingian Renaissance".

In the period of cultural splendour that occurred during Charlemagne's reign, the familiar traditions of Roman and Byzantine art were merged with characteristics from other cultures, including Celtic and Viking. This renaissance also influenced architecture – Gerona cathedral's 9th-century tower, known as "the Charlemagne Tower", dates from this period.

His relationship with the papacy played an important role in Charlemagne's politics. This illustration, dated 1499, depicts the emperor receiving Pope Leo III (795–816), who had fled to the Frankish court after being forced to leave Rome. Charlemagne's soldiers escorted Leo back to Rome, where the papacy was restored to him.

done. The ebbing of economic life and of literacy meant that a Carolingian court was a primitive thing by comparison with Byzantium and possibly even in comparison with those of some of the early barbarian kingdoms which were sometimes open to influence from a more cultivated world, as the appearance of Coptic themes in early barbarian art attests. When Charlemagne's men brought materials and ideas to beautify Aachen from Ravenna, Byzantine art, too, moved more freely into the north European tradition and classical models still influenced his artists. But it was its scholars and scribes who made Charlemagne's court most spectacular. It was an intellectual centre. From it radiated the impulse to copy texts in a new refined and reformed hand called Carolingian minuscule which was to be one of the great

instruments of culture in the West. Charlemagne had hoped to use it to supply an authentic copy of the Rule of St Benedict to every monastery in his realm, but the major expression of a new manuscript potential was first evident in the copying of the Bible. This had a more than religious aim, for the scriptural story was to be interpreted as a justification of Carolingian rule. The Jewish history of the Old Testament was full of examples of pious and anointed warrior-kings. The Bible was the major text in the monastic libraries which now began to be assembled throughout the Frankish lands.

Copying and the diffusion of texts went on for a century after the original impulse had been given at Aachen and were the core of what modern scholars have called "the Carolingian Renaissance". It had none of the pagan connotations of that word as it was used of a later revival of learning which focused attention on the classical past, for it was emphatically Christian. Its whole purpose was the training of clergy to raise the level of the Frankish Church and carry the faith further to the east. The leading men in the beginnings of this transmission of sacred knowledge were not Franks. There were several Irishmen and Anglo-Saxons in the palace school at Aachen and among them the outstanding figure was Alcuin, a cleric from York, a great centre of English learning. His most famous pupil was Charlemagne himself, but he had several others and managed the palace library. Besides writing books of his own he set up a school at Tours, where he became abbot, and began to expound Boethius and Augustine to the men who would govern the Frankish church in the next generation.

CHARLEMAGNE'S PERSONAL AUTHORITY

Alcuin's pre-eminence is as striking a piece of evidence as any of the shift in the centre of cultural gravity in Europe, away from the classical world and to the north. But others than his countrymen were involved in teaching, copying and founding the new monasteries which spread outwards into East and West Francia; there were Franks, Visigoths, Lombards and Italians among them, too. One of these, a layman called Einhard, wrote a life of the emperor from which we learn such fascinating human details as the facts that he could be garrulous, that he was a keen hunter and that he passionately loved swimming and bathing in the thermal springs, which explain his choice of Aachen as a residence. Charlemagne comes to life in Einhard's pages as an intellectual, too, speaking Latin as well, we are told, as Frankish, and understanding Greek. This is made more credible because we hear also of

his attempts to write, keeping notebooks under his pillow so that he could do so in bed, "but", Einhard says, "although he tried very hard, he had begun too late in life".

From this account and from his work a remarkably vivid picture can be formed of a dignified, majestic figure, striving to make the transition from warlord to ruler of a great Christian empire, and having remarkable success in his own lifetime in so doing. Clearly his physical presence was impressive (he probably towered over most of his entourage), and others saw in him the image of a kingly soul, gay, just and magnanimous, as well as that of the heroic paladin of whom poets and minstrels would be singing for centuries. His authority was a more majestic spectacle than anything seen to that time in barbarian lands. When his reign began, his

Although it was actually made for the coronation of Otto I the Great (936–973), the fact that this beautiful object is known as "Charlemagne's Crown" is indicative of the legendary status that the Carolingian emperor achieved in medieval Europe. The enamel plaque, one of four that decorate the crown, represents King Solomon as the symbol of wisdom.

This illustration, from the Bible of Count Vivian, dates from 851. It shows Charles the Bald (840–877), one of the three grandsons of Charlemagne who succeeded him in a partitioned empire, enthroned and surrounded by his courtiers.

court was still peripatetic, it normally ate its way from estate to estate throughout the year. When Charlemagne died, he left a palace and a treasury established at the place where he was to be buried. He had been able to reform weights and measures, and had given to Europe the division of the pound of silver into 240 pennies (*denarii*) which was to survive in the British Isles for eleven hundred years. But his power was also very personal. This may be inferred from the efforts he made to prevent his noblemen from replacing tribal rulers by settling down into hereditary positions of their own, and from the repeated issuing of "capitularies" or instructions to his servants (a sign that his wishes were not carried out). In the last resort, even a Charlemagne could only rely on personal rule, and that meant a monarchy based on his own domain and its produce and on the big men close enough to him for supervision. These vassals were bound to him by especially solemn oaths, but even they began to give trouble as he grew older.

THE SUCCESSORS

Charlemagne thought in traditional Frankish terms of his territorial legacy. He made plans to divide it and only the accident of sons dying before him ensured that the empire passed undivided to the youngest, Louis the Pious, in 814. With it came the imperial title (which Charlemagne gave to his son) and the alliance of monarchy and papacy; two years after his succession the pope crowned Louis at a second coronation. Partition was only delayed by this. Charlemagne's successors had neither his authority nor his experience, nor perhaps an interest in controlling fissiparous forces. Regional loyalties were forming around individuals and a series of partitions finally culminated in one between

three of Charlemagne's grandsons, the Treaty of Verdun of 843, which had great consequences. It gave a core kingdom of Frankish lands centred on the western side of the Rhine valley and containing Charlemagne's capital, Aachen, to Lothair, the reigning emperor (thus it was called Lotharingia) and added to this the kingdom of Italy. North of the Alps, this united Provence, Burgundy, Lorraine and the lands between the Scheldt, Meuse, Saône and Rhône. To the east lay a second block of lands of Teutonic speech between the Rhine and the German Marches; it went to Louis

Louis the Pious, who is pictured here, was Charlemagne's sole heir. Dethroned by his son Lothair in 831, he was reinstated as emperor by his other sons in 835, but died five years later.

The Eastern Frankish kingdom came to be made up of a mixture of peoples, including the Saxons, Bavarians, Swabians and Franconians. This initial, framed by images of the Four Evangelists, is from a 9th-century Franco-Saxon gospel.

the German. Finally, in the west, a tract of territory including Gascony, Septimania and Aquitaine, and roughly the equal of the rest of modern France, went to a half-brother of these two, Charles the Bald.

THE WEST AND EAST FRANKS

The Treaty of Verdun settlement was not long untroubled, but it was decisive in a broad and important way; it effectively founded the political distinction of France and Germany, whose roots lay in West and East Francia. Between them it set up a third unit with much less linguistic, ethnic, geographical and economic unity. Lotharingia was there in part because

three sons had to be provided for. Much future Franco-German history was going to be about the way in which it could be divided between neighbours bound to covet it and therefore likely to grow apart from one another in rivalry.

CAROLINGIAN DECLINE

No royal house could guarantee a constant flow of able kings, nor could they for ever buy loyalty from their supporters by giving away lands. Gradually, and like their predecessors, the Carolingians declined in power. The signs of break-up multiplied, an independent kingdom of Burgundy appeared and people began to dwell on the great days of Charlemagne, a significant symptom of decay and dissatisfaction. The histories of West and East Franks diverged more and more.

In West Francia the Carolingians lasted just over a century after Charles the Bald. By the end of his reign Brittany, Flanders, and Aquitaine were to all intents and purposes independent. The West Frankish monarchy thus started the tenth century in a weak position and it had the attacks of Vikings to deal with as well. In 911 Charles III, unable to expel the Norsemen, conceded lands in what was later Normandy to their leader, Rollo. Baptized the following year, Rollo set to work to build the duchy for which he did homage to the Carolingians; his Scandinavian countrymen continued to arrive and settle there until the end of the tenth century, yet somehow they soon became French in speech and law. After this, the unity of the West Franks fell even more rapidly apart. From confusion over the succession there emerged a son of a count of Paris who steadily built up his family's power around a domain in the Ile de France. This was to be the core of France. When the last Carolingian ruler of the West Franks died in 987, this man's son, Hugh Capet, was elected king. His family was to rule France for nearly four hundred years. For the rest, the West Franks were divided into a dozen or so territorial units ruled by magnates of varying standing and independence.

CONRAD OF FRANCONIA

Among the supporters of Hugh's election was the ruler of the East Franks. Across the Rhine, the repeated division of their heritage had quickly proved fatal to the Carolingians. When the last Carolingian king died in 911 there emerged a political fragmentation which was to characterize Germany down to the nineteenth century. The assertiveness of local magnates combined with stronger tribal loyalties than in the west to produce a half-dozen powerful dukedoms. The ruler of one of these, Conrad of Franconia, was chosen as king by the other dukes, somewhat surprisingly. They wanted a strong leader against the Magyars. The change of dynasty made it advisable to confer some special standing on the new ruler; the bishops therefore anointed Conrad at his coronation. He was the first ruler of the East Franks so to be treated. But Conrad was not successful against the Magyars; he lost and could not win back Lotharingia and he strove, with the support of the Church, to exalt his own house and office. Almost automatically, the dukes gathered their peoples about them to safeguard their own independence. The four whose distinction mattered most were the Saxons, the Bavarians, the Swabians and the Franconians (as the East Franks became known). Regional differences, blood and the natural pretensions of great nobles stamped on Germany in Conrad's reign the pattern of

its history for a thousand years: a tug-of-war between central authority and local power not to be resolved in the long run in favour of the centre as elsewhere, though in the tenth century it looked otherwise for a while. Conrad faced ducal rebellion but nominated one of the rebels his successor and the dukes agreed. In 919, Henry "the Fowler" (as he was called), Duke of Saxony, became king. He and his descendants, the "Saxon emperors", or Ottonians, ruled the East Franks until 1024.

THE OTTONIANS

Henry the Fowler avoided the ecclesiastical coronation. He had great family properties and the tribal loyalties of the Saxons on his side and brought the magnates into line by proving himself a good soldier. He won back Lotharingia from the West Franks, created new Marches on the Elbe

This 11th-century illustration, depicting St Peter receiving the keys of the Church, is from one of the many religious manuscripts commissioned by the Ottonian king Henry II.

instrument out of the German church; it was an advantage of the Saxon emperors that in Germany, unlike West Francia, churchmen tended to look with favour to the monarchy for protection against predatory laymen. A new archiepiscopal province, Magdeburg, was organized to direct the bishoprics established among the Slavs. With Otto ends, it has been said, the period of mere anarchy in central Europe; under him, certainly, we have the first sense of something we might call Germany. But Otto's ambition did not stop there.

In 936 Otto had been crowned at Aachen, Charlemagne's old capital. Not only did he accept the ecclesiastical service and anointing which his father had avoided, but he afterwards held a coronation banquet at which the German dukes served him as his vassals. This was in the old Carolingian style. Fifteen years later he invaded Italy, married the widow of a claimant to the crown of Italy, and assumed it himself. Yet the pope refused him an imperial coronation. Ten years later, in 962, Otto was back in Italy again in response to an appeal by the pope for help, and this time the pope crowned him.

EMPIRE REVIVED

Through Otto's coronation, the Roman and the Carolingian ideal of empire was revived. The German and Italian crowns were united again in what would one day be known as the Holy Roman Empire and would last nearly a thousand years. Yet it was not so wide an empire as Charlemagne's, nor did Otto dominate the Church as Charlemagne had done. For all his strength (and he deposed two popes and nominated two others) Otto was the Church's protector who thought he knew what was best for it, but he was not its governor. Nor was the structure of the

The emperor Otto II (973–1002) is depicted on this marble plaque with his wife Theophano, who is holding their son (the future Otto III) in her arms. The couple are shown kneeling at the feet of the enthroned figure of Christ.

after victorious campaigns against the Wends, made Denmark a tributary kingdom and began its conversion, and, finally, he defeated the Magyars. His son, Otto I, thus had a goodly inheritance and made good use of it. In disciplining the dukes, he continued his father's work. In 955 he inflicted on the Magyars a defeat which ended for ever the danger they had presented. Austria, Charlemagne's east March, was recolonized. Though he faced some opposition, Otto made a loyal empire very solid; it rested on the political manipulation of local magnates rather than on administration.

Nevertheless, the Ottonian Empire was a remarkable achievement. Otto's son, the future Otto II, married a Byzantine princess. Both he and Otto III had reigns troubled by revolt, but successfully maintained the tradition established by Otto the Great of exercising power south of the Alps. Otto III made a cousin pope (the first German to sit in the chair of St Peter) and followed him by appointing the first French pope. Rome seemed to captivate him and he settled down there. Like both his immediate predecessors, he called himself *augustus* but in addition his seals revived the legend "Renewal of the Roman Empire" which he equated with the Christian empire. Half Byzantine by birth, he saw himself as a new Constantine. A diptych of a gospel-book painted nearly at the end of the tenth century shows him in state, crowned and orb in hand, receiving the homage of four crowned women: they are Sclavonia (Slavic Europe), Germany, Gaul and Rome. His notion of a Europe organized as a hierarchy of kings serving under the emperor was Eastern. In this there was megalomania as well as genuine religious conviction; the real basis of Otto's power was his German kingship, not the Italy which obsessed and detained him. Nevertheless, after his death in 1002, he was taken to Aachen, as he had ordered, to be buried beside Charlemagne.

THE DECLINE OF THE OTTONIANS

Otto III left no heir, but the direct Saxon line was not exhausted; Henry II, who was elected after a struggle, was a great-grandson of Henry the Fowler. But his coronation at Rome masked the reality; he was a German ruler, not emperor of the West, at heart.

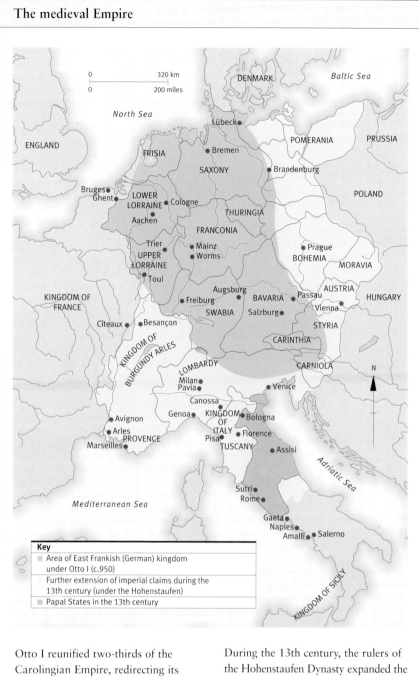

The medieval Empire

Otto I reunified two-thirds of the Carolingian Empire, redirecting its focus from France to the German regions. Only the western part of France remained outside his control.

During the 13th century, the rulers of the Hohenstaufen Dynasty expanded the territories of the empire, but 200 years of conflict with the papal monarchy had fatally weakened it.

His seal's inscription read "Renewal of the kingdom of the Franks" and his attention was focused on pacification and conversion in east Germany. Though he made three expeditions to Italy, Henry relied there not on government but on politics, the playing off of factions against one another. With him the Byzantine style of the Ottonian Empire began to wane.

Thus the eleventh century opened with the idea of Western empire still capable of beguiling monarchs, but with the Carolingian inheritance long since crumbled into fragments. They set out the lines of European history for ages to come. The idea of Germany barely existed but the country was a political reality, even if still inchoate. The curious federal structure which was to emerge from the German middle ages was to be the last refuge of the imperial idea in the West, the Holy Roman Empire. Meanwhile, in France, too, the main line of the future was settled, though it could not have been discerned at the time. West Francia had dissolved into a dozen or so major units over which the suzerainty of the Capetians was for

a long time feeble. But they had on their side a centrally placed royal domain, including Paris and the important diocese of Orleans, and the friendship of the Church. These were advantages in the hands of able kings, and able kings would be forthcoming in the next three centuries.

ITALY AND SOUTHERN EUROPE

The other major component of the Carolingian heritage had been Italy. It had gradually become more and more distinct from the territories north of the Alps; since the seventh century it had been evolving away from the possibility of integration with northern Europe and back towards re-emergence as a part of Mediterranean Europe. By the middle of the eighth century, much of Italy had been subjugated by the Lombards. This barbarian people had settled down in the peninsula and had adopted an Italianate speech, but they remained an aggressive minority, whose social tensions demanded release in frequent wars of conquest, and they had shaped the Catholicism they had adopted to their own needs and institutions. In spite of the theoretical survival of the legal claims of the Eastern emperors, the only possible balancing power to them in Italy until the eighth century was the pope. When the Lombard principalities began to consolidate under a vigorous monarchy, this was no longer enough; hence the evolution of papal diplomacy towards alliance with the Carolingians. Once the Lombard kingdom had been destroyed by Charlemagne, there was no rival in the peninsula to the Papal States, though after the waning of the Carolingians' power the popes had to face both the rising power of the Italian magnates and their own Roman aristocracy. The Western Church was at its lowest ebb of cohesion and unity

This is the title page of a copy of "The Edict of Rothari", a codification of Lombard customs that was still observed as law in Italy as late as the 11th century.

and the Ottonians' treatment of the papacy showed how little power it had. An anarchic Italian map was another result of this situation. The north was a scatter of feudal statelets. Only Venice was very successful; for two hundred years she had been pushing forward in the Adriatic and her ruler had just assumed the title of duke. She is perhaps better regarded as a Levantine and Adriatic rather than a Mediterranean power. City-states which were republics existed in the south, at Gaeta, Amalfi, Naples. Across the middle of the peninsula ran the Papal States. Over the whole fell the shadow of Islamic raids as far north as Pisa, while emirates appeared at Taranto and Bari in the ninth century. These were not to last, but the

Arabs completed the conquest of Sicily in 902 and were to rule it for a century and a half with profound effects.

The Arabs shaped the destiny of the other west Mediterranean coasts of Europe, too. Not only were they established in Spain, but even in Provence they had more or less permanent bases (one of them being St Tropez). The inhabitants of the European coasts of the Mediterranean had, perforce, a complex relationship with the Arabs, who appeared to

The Lombards' early relationship with the Church was not always a friendly one. This painting from the Theodolinda Chapel in Monza, near Milan, shows a Christian hermit (the blond figure to the left of the centre rider), about to go into battle against the Lombard troops.

We know that the Lombard architects tended to concentrate on restoration. Although few examples of original Lombard building and sculpture survive today, these stucco sculptures have been preserved in a small oratory in the church of St Mary of the Valley in Cividale, near Rome.

The discovery of
this gilt bronze
helmet of Swedish type
in a Saxon royal burial
ground at Sutton Hoo,
England, demonstrates
the strong Nordic
influence that pervaded
7th-century Saxon
England. The helmet
was part of a mainly
pagan treasure, which
was buried with a ship.
No trace of a body was
found, which suggests
that the ship burial was
intended as a memorial
rather than a tomb,
possibly in honour of
the East Anglian king
Redwald (599–625).

them both as free-booters and as traders; the mixture was not unlike that observable in the Viking descents except that the Arabs showed little tendency to settle. Southern France and Catalonia were areas in which Frankish had followed Gothic conquest, but many factors differentiated them from the Frankish north. The physical reminiscences of the Roman past were plentiful in these areas and so was a Mediterranean agriculture. Another distinctive characteristic was the appearance of a family of Romance languages in the south, of which Catalan and Provençal were the most enduring.

SCANDINAVIA

In 1000 CE, the peripheral Europe of the north barely included Scandinavia, if Christianity is the test of inclusion. Missionaries had been at work for a long time but the first Christian monarchs only appear there in the tenth century and not until the next were all Scandinavian kings Christian. Long before that, pagan Norsemen had changed the history of the British Isles and the northern fringe of Christendom.

For reasons which, as in the case of many other folk-movements, are by no means clear, but are possibly rooted in over-population, the Scandinavians began to move outwards from the eighth century onwards. Equipped with two fine technical instruments, a longboat which oars and sails could take across seas and up shallow rivers and a tubby cargo-carrier which could shelter large families, their goods and animals for six or seven days at sea, they thrust out across the water for

Until the 9th century, the Viking raids on England and Ireland were relentless and the violence and pillaging with which they were carried out were sometimes devastating. This staff originally belonged to an English bishop and was probably stolen during a raid: it was found in Helgö in Sweden.

four centuries, and left behind a civilization which in the end stretched from Greenland to Kiev. Not all sought the same things. The Norwegians who struck out to Iceland, the Faroes, Orkney and the far west wanted to colonize. The Swedes who penetrated Russia and survive in the records as Varangians were much busier in trade. The Danes did most of the plundering and piracy the Vikings are remembered for. But all these themes of the Scandinavian migrations wove in and out of one another. No branch of these peoples had a monopoly of any one of them.

The Viking colonization of remote islands was their most spectacular achievement. They wholly replaced the Picts in the Orkneys and the Shetlands and from them extended their rule to the Faroes (previously uninhabited except for a few Irish monks and their sheep) and the Isle of Man. Offshore, the Viking lodgement was more lasting and profound than on the mainland of Scotland and Ireland, where settlement began in the ninth century. Yet the Irish language records their importance by its adoption of Norse words in commerce, and the Irish map marks it by the situation of Dublin, founded by the Vikings and soon turned into an important trading-post. The most successful colony of all was Iceland. Irish hermits had anticipated Vikings there, too, and it was not until the end of the ninth century that they came in large numbers. By 930 there may have been 10,000 Norse Icelanders, living by farming and fishing, in part for their own subsistence, in part to produce commodities such as salt fish which they might trade. In that year the Icelandic state was founded and the *Thing* (which romantic antiquarians later saw as the first European "parliament") met for the first time. It was more like a council of the big men of the community than a modern representative body and it followed earlier Norwegian practice, but Iceland's continuous historical record is in this respect a remarkable one.

Colonies in Greenland followed in the tenth century; there were to be Norsemen there for five hundred years. Then they disappeared, probably because the settlers were wiped out by Eskimos pushed south by an advance of the ice. Of discovery and settlement further west we can say much less. The Sagas, the heroic poems of medieval Iceland, tell us of the exploration of "Vinland", the land where Norsemen found the wild vine growing, and of the birth of a child there (whose mother subsequently returned to Iceland and went abroad again as far as Rome as a pilgrim before settling into a highly sanctified retirement in her native land). There are reasonably good grounds to believe that a settlement discovered in Newfoundland is Norse. But we cannot at present go much further than this in uncovering the traces of the predecessors of Columbus.

This chalice, which dates from the beginning of the 8th century, was found in Ardagh in 1868 and constitutes one of the masterpieces of Irish gold and silver work. Treasures such as this were often seized by Viking raiders as booty.

VIKING RAIDS

In western European tradition, the colonial and mercantile activities of the Vikings were from the start obscured by their horrific impact as marauders. Certainly, they had some very nasty habits, spread-eagling among them, but so did most barbarians. Some exaggeration must therefore be allowed for, especially because our main evidence comes from the pens of churchmen doubly appalled, both as Christians and as victims, by attacks on churches and monasteries; as pagans, of course, Vikings saw no special sanctity in the concentrations of precious metals and food so conveniently provided by such places, and found them especially attractive targets. Nor were the Vikings the first people to burn monasteries in Ireland.

None the less, however such considerations are weighed, it is indisputable that the Viking impact on northern and western Christendom was very great and very terrifying. They first attacked England in 793, the monastery of Lindisfarne being their victim; the attack shook the ecclesiastical world (yet the monastery lived on another eighty years). Ireland they raided two years later. In the first half of the ninth century the Danes began a harrying of Frisia which went on regularly year after year, the same towns being repeatedly plundered. The French coast was then attacked; in 842 Nantes was sacked with a great massacre. Within a few years a Frankish chronicler bewailed that "the endless flood of Vikings never ceases to grow". Towns as far inland as Paris, Limoges, Orleans, Tours and Angoulême were attacked. The Vikings had become professional pirates. Soon Spain suffered and the Arabs, too, were harassed; in 844 the Vikings stormed Seville. In 859 they even raided Nîmes and plundered Pisa, though they suffered heavily at the hands of an Arab fleet on their way home.

One of the first victims of the Vikings in England was the 7th-century monastery of Lindisfarne. The Lindisfarne monks produced intricate miniatures, of which this Hiberno-Saxon-style page from the so-called Lindisfarne Gospels (c.696–698) is an example.

THE CONSEQUENCES OF THE VIKING CAMPAIGNS

At its worst, think some scholars, the Viking onslaught came near to destroying civilization in West Francia; certainly the West Franks had to endure more than their cousins in the east and the Vikings helped to shape the differences between a future France and a future Germany. In the west their ravages threw new responsibilities on local magnates, while central and royal control crumbled away and men looked more and more towards their local lord for protection. When Hugh Capet came to the throne, it was very much as *primus inter pares* in a recognizably feudal society.

Not all the efforts of rulers to meet the Viking threat were failures. Charlemagne and Louis the Pious did not, admittedly, have to face attacks as heavy and persistent as their successors, but they managed to defend the vulnerable ports and river-mouths with some effectiveness. The Vikings could be (and were) defeated if drawn into full-scale field engagements and, though there were dramatic exceptions, the main centres of the Christian West were on the whole successfully defended. What could not be prevented were repeated small-scale raids on the coasts. When the Vikings learnt to avoid pitched battles, the only way to deal with them was to buy them off and Charles the Bald began paying them tribute so that his subjects should be left in peace.

This was the beginning of what the English called Danegeld. Their island had soon become a major target, to which Vikings began to come to settle as well as to raid. A small group of kingdoms had emerged there from the Germanic invasions; by the seventh century many of Romano-British descent were living alongside the communities of the new settlers, while others had been driven back to the hills of Wales and Scotland. Christianity continued to be diffused by Irish missionaries from the Roman mission which had established Canterbury. It competed with the older Celtic Church until 664, a crucial date. In that year a Northumbrian king at a synod of churchmen held at Whitby pronounced in favour of adopting the date of Easter set by the Roman church. It was a symbolic choice, determining that the future England would adhere to the Roman traditions, not the Celtic.

ALFRED THE GREAT

From time to time, one or other of the English kingdoms was strong enough to have some sway over the others. Yet only one of them could successfully stand up to the wave of

Alfred the Great, King of Wessex (871–899), is depicted on this 9th-century Anglo-Saxon penny.

Danish attacks from 851 onwards which led to the occupation of two-thirds of the country. This was Wessex and it gave England its first national hero who is also an historical figure, Alfred the Great.

As a child of four, Alfred had been taken to Rome by his father and was given consular honours by the pope. The monarchy of Wessex was indissolubly linked with Christianity and Carolingian Europe. It defended the faith against paganism as much as England against an alien people. In 871 Alfred inflicted the first decisive defeat on a Danish army in England. Significantly, a few years later the Danish king agreed not only to withdraw from Wessex but to accept conversion as a Christian. This registered that the Danes were in England to stay (they had settled in the north) but also that they might be divided from one another. Soon Alfred was leader of all the surviving English kings;

eventually, none was left but he. He recovered London and when he died in 899 the worst period of Danish raids was over and his descendants were to rule a united country. Even the settlers of the Danelaw, the area marked to this day by Scandinavian place-names and fashions of speech as that of Danish colonization defined by Alfred, accepted their rule. Nor was this all. Alfred had also founded a series of strongholds ("burghs") as a part of a new system of national defence by local levies. They not only gave his successors bases for the further reduction of the Danelaw but set much of the pattern of early medieval urbanization in England; on them were built towns whose sites are still inhabited today. Finally, with tiny resources, Alfred deliberately undertook the cultural and intellectual regeneration of his people. The scholars of his court, like those of Charlemagne, proceeded by way of copying and translation:

The Nordic Sagas

The Sagas are legendary tales – transcriptions of traditional oral stories from ancient Nordic literature in narrative or verse form. The Sagas, many of which are about about heroic deeds and great Nordic warriors, fall into two groups: the family Sagas and the historical Sagas. The latter cover the period of Scandinavian expansion in the 9th to 11th centuries. Later historical Sagas recounted the lives of kings and queens and, following the arrival of Christianity in the 11th century, of bishops.

The tradition of writing and story-telling was extremely widespread in Scandinavia (and in the lands conquered by the Vikings) until the 13th century, when its popularity appears to have waned.

The Viking gods Thor, Odin and Freyr are represented in this 12th-century tapestry from the church of Skog in Halringland, Sweden.

This Thor's hammer amulet dates from the 10th century. Although Christianity became important in Sweden from this time, objects such as this are evidence of the co-existence, at least until the 10th century, of ancient Nordic religion and Christianity.

Canute I, King of England, Denmark and Norway, and his wife, Queen Emma of Normandy, are depicted on this 11th-century manuscript. The couple are installing an altar cross in the Abbey of Newminster (which originally belonged to Canute's enemy Ethelred II).

the Anglo-Saxon nobleman and cleric were intended to learn of Bede and Boethius in their own tongue.

THE SCANDINAVIAN LEGACY

Alfred's innovations were a creative effort of government unique in Europe, and marked the beginning of a great age for England. The shire structure took shape and boundaries were established which lasted until 1974. The English Church was soon to experience a remarkable surge of monasticism, the Danes were held in a united kingdom through a half-century's turbulence. It was only when ability failed in Alfred's line that the Anglo-Saxon monarchy came to grief and a new Viking offensive took place. Colossal sums of Danegeld were paid until a Danish king (this time a Christian) overthrew the English king and then died, leaving a young son to rule his conquest. This was the celebrated Canute, under whom England was briefly part of a great Danish empire (1016–35). There was a last great Norwegian invasion of England

The destruction of Barcelona in 985 by Al-Mansur's troops made it possible for the Counts of Barcelona to gain independence from the Carolingian monarch. Here, one of the counts, Ramón Berenguer I (1024–1076), is portrayed with his third wife, Almodis de la Marca, who was said to wield great influence over him.

in 1066, but it was shattered at the battle of Stamford Bridge. By that time, all the Scandinavian monarchies were Christian and Viking culture was being absorbed into Christian forms. It left many evidences of its individuality and strength in both Celtic and continental art. Its institutions survive in Iceland and other islands. The Scandinavian legacy is strongly marked for centuries in English language and social patterns, in the emergence of the duchy of Normandy, and, above all, in the literature of the Sagas. Yet where they entered settled lands, the Norsemen gradually merged with the rest of the population. When the descendants of Rollo and his followers turned to the conquest of England in the eleventh century they were really Frenchmen and the war-song they sang at Hastings was about Charlemagne the Frankish paladin. They conquered an England where the people of the Danelaw were by then English. Similarly, the Vikings lost their distinctiveness as an ethnic group in Kiev Rus and Muscovy.

The Iberian city of León in the Asturias was re-established in the reign of Ordoño II (914–924), the monarch who restored Christian unity in the region. He is depicted in this manuscript illustration.

CHRISTIAN SPAIN

The only other Western peoples of the early eleventh century who call for remark because of the future that lay before them were those of the Christian states of northern Spain. Geography, climate and Muslim division had all helped Christianity's survival in the peninsula and in part defined its extent. In the Asturias and Navarre Christian princes or chieftains still hung on early in the eighth century. Aided by the establishment of the Spanish March by Charlemagne and its subsequent growth under the new Counts of Barcelona, they nibbled away successfully at Islamic Spain while it was distracted by civil war and religious schism. A kingdom of León emerged in the Asturias to take its place beside a kingdom of Navarre. In the tenth century, however, it was the Christians who fell out with one another and the Arabs who again

Pagan and Christian imagery are combined in the decoration on this whalebone chest. The pagan scene on the left depicts Wayland the Smith awaiting his daughter Beadohild, after having murdered Nidhad's children. On the right, a Christian scene portrays the Adoration of the Three Kings.

made headway against them. The blackest moment came at the very end of the century when a great Arab conqueror, Al-Mansur, took Barcelona, León, and in 998 the shrine of Santiago de Compostela itself at which St James the Apostle was supposed to be buried. The triumph was not long-lived, for here, too, what had been done to found Christian Europe proved ineradicable. Within a few decades Christian Spain had rallied as Islamic Spain fell into disunion. In the Iberian peninsula as elsewhere, the age of expansion which this inaugurated belongs to another historical era, but was based on long centuries of confrontation with another civilization. For Spain, above all, Christianity was the crucible of nationhood.

THE CHURCH IN THE WEST

The Iberian example suggests just how much of the making of the map of Europe is the making of the map of the Church, but an emphasis only on successful missions and ties with powerful monarchs is misleading. There was much more to early Christian Europe and the Christian life than this. The Western Church provides one of the great success stories of history, yet its leaders between the end of the ancient world and the eleventh or twelfth century long felt isolated and embattled in a pagan or semi-pagan world. Increasingly at odds with, and finally almost cut off from, Eastern Orthodoxy, it is hardly surprising that Western Christianity developed an aggressive intransigence almost as a defensive reflex. It was another sign of its insecurity. Nor was it threatened merely by enemies without. Inside Western Christendom, too, the Church felt at bay and beleaguered. It strove in the middle of still semi-pagan populations to keep its teaching and practice intact while christening what it could of a culture with which it had to live, judging nicely the concession which could be made to local practice or tradition and distinguishing it from a fatal compromise of principle. All this it had to do with a body of clergy of whom many, perhaps most, were men of no learning, not much discipline and dubious spirituality. Perhaps it is not surprising that the leaders of the Church sometimes overlooked the enormous asset they enjoyed in being faced by no spiritual rival in western Europe after Islam was turned back by Charles Martel; they had to contend only with vestigial paganism and superstition, and

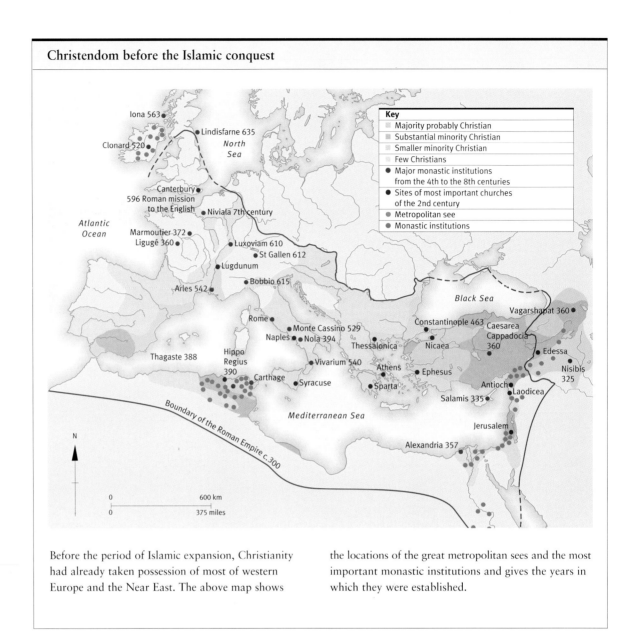

Christendom before the Islamic conquest

Before the period of Islamic expansion, Christianity had already taken possession of most of western Europe and the Near East. The above map shows the locations of the great metropolitan sees and the most important monastic institutions and gives the years in which they were established.

these the Church knew how to use. Meanwhile, the great men of this world surrounded it, sometimes helpfully, sometimes hopefully, always a potential and often a real threat to the Church's independence of the society it had to strive to save.

THE PAPACY

INEVITABLY, MUCH OF THE HISTORY which resulted is the history of the papacy. It is the central and best-documented institution of Christianity. Its documentation is part of the reason why so much attention has been given to it, a fact that should provoke reflexion about what can be known about religion in these centuries. Though papal power had alarming ups and downs, the division of the old empire meant that if there was anywhere in the West a defender of the interests of religion, it was Rome, for it had no ecclesiastical rival. After Gregory the Great it was obviously implausible to maintain the theory of one Christian Church in one empire, even if the imperial exarch did stay at Ravenna. The last emperor who came to Rome did so in 663 and the last pope to go to Constantinople went there in 710. Then came Iconoclasm, which inflicted grievous ideological damage. When Ravenna fell to the renewed advance of the Lombards, Pope Stephen set out for Pepin's court, not that of Byzantium. There was no desire to break with the Eastern Empire, but Frankish armies could offer protection no longer available from the East. Protection was needed, too, for the Arabs menaced Italy from the beginning of the eighth century, and, increasingly, the native Italian magnates became obstreperous in the ebbing of Lombard hegemony.

THE VULNERABILITY OF THE PAPACY

There were some very bad moments in the two and a half centuries after Pepin's coronation. Rome seemed to have very few cards in its hands and at times only to have exchanged one master for another. Its claim to primacy was a matter of the respect due to the guardianship of St Peter's bones and the fact that the see was indisputably the only apostolic one in the West: a matter of history rather than of practical power. For a long time the popes could hardly govern effectively even within the temporal domains, for they had neither adequate armed forces nor a civil administration. As great Italian property-owners, they were exposed to predators and blackmail. Charlemagne was only the first, and perhaps he was the most high-minded, of several emperors who made clear to the papacy their views of the respective standing of pope and emperor as guardians of the Church. The Ottonians were great makers and unmakers of popes. The successors of St Peter could not welcome confrontations, for they had too much to lose.

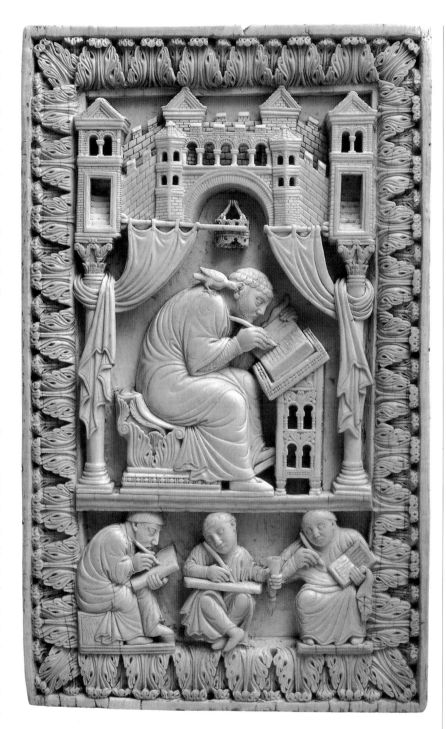

PAPAL PRETENSIONS

There was another side to the balance sheet, even if it was slow to reveal its full implications. Pepin's grant of territory to the papacy would in time form the nucleus of a powerful Italian territorial state. In the pope's coronation of emperors there rested veiled claims, perhaps

St Gregory the Great (540–604) is portrayed here working on one of his manuscripts. According to legend, the divine word was dictated to St Gregory by a dove (which is shown perched on his shoulder).

to the identification of rightful emperors; significantly, as time passed, popes withdrew from the imperial coronation ceremony (as from that of English and French kings) the use of the chrism, the specially sacred mixture of oil and balsam for the ordination of priests and the coronation of bishops, substituting simple oil. Thus was expressed a reality long concealed but easily comprehensible to an age used to symbols: the pope conferred the crown and the stamp of God's recognition on the emperor. Perhaps, therefore, he could do so conditionally. Leo's coronation of Charlemagne, like Stephen's of Pepin, may have been expedient, but it contained a potent seed. When, as often happened, personal weaknesses and succession disputes disrupted the Frankish kingdoms, Rome might gain ground.

More immediately and practically, the support of powerful kings was needed for the reform of local Churches and the support of missionary enterprise in the East. For all the jealousy of local clergy, the Frankish Church changed greatly; in the tenth century what the pope said mattered a great deal north of the Alps. From the *entente* of the eighth century there emerged gradually the idea that it was for the pope to say what the Church's policy should be and that the individual bishops of the local Churches should not pervert it. A great instrument of standardization was being forged. It was there in principle when Pepin used his power as a Frankish king to reform his countrymen's Church and did so on lines which brought it into step with Rome on questions of ritual and discipline, and further away from Celtic influences.

NICHOLAS I

The balance of advantage and disadvantage long tipped to and fro, the boundaries of the effective powers of the popes ebbing and flowing. Significantly, it was after a further subdivision of the Carolingian heritage so that the crown of Italy was separated from Lotharingia that Nicholas I pressed most successfully the papal claims. A century before, a famous forgery, the "Donation of Constantine", purported to show that Constantine had given to the Bishop of Rome the former dominion exercised by the empire in Italy; Nicholas addressed kings and emperors as if this theory ran everywhere in the West. He wrote to them, it was said, "as though he were lord of

the world", reminding them that he could appoint and depose. He used the doctrine of papal primacy against the emperor of the East, too, in support of the Patriarch of Constantinople. This was a peak of pretension which the papacy could not long sustain in practice, for it was soon clear that force at Rome would decide who should enjoy the imperial power the pope claimed to confer. Nicholas' successor, revealingly, was the first pope to be murdered. None the less, the ninth century laid down precedents, even if they could not yet be consistently followed.

Especially in the collapse of papal authority in the tenth century, when the throne became the prey of Italian factions whose struggles were occasionally cut across by the interventions of the Ottonians, the day-to-day work of safeguarding Christian interests could only be in the hands of the bishops of the local Churches. They had to respect the powers that were. Seeking the cooperation and help of the secular rulers, they often moved into positions in which they were all but indistinguishable from royal servants. They were under the thumbs of their secular rulers just

For the Roman Catholic Church, the papacy is a divine institution. In this fresco by Perugino (c.1450–1523) in the Vatican's Sistine Chapel, Christ is shown giving the keys of the Church to Peter, Bishop of Rome. The Catholic tradition recognizes the bishops of Rome as successors to St Peter and as the guardians of all authority over the universal Church.

Pope Nicholas I (c.858–867), who was determined to maintain papal authority, opposed the divorce of Lothair II, king of Lorraine, and his wife Theutberga. The famous crystal of Lothair (above), one of the best-known examples of engraving on rock crystal, tells the story of Theutberga.

as, often, the parish priest was under the thumb of the local lord and had to share his ecclesiastical proceeds in consequence. This humiliating dependency was later to lead to some of the sharpest papal interventions in the local Churches.

BISHOPS AND MONASTERIES

The bishops did much good, too; in particular, they encouraged missionaries. This had a political side to it. In the eighth century the Rule of St Benedict was well-established in England. A great Anglo-Saxon missionary movement, whose outstanding figures were St Willibrord in Frisia and St Boniface in Germany, followed. Largely independent of the East Frankish bishops, the Anglo-Saxons asserted the supremacy of Rome; their converts tended therefore to look directly to the throne

of St Peter for religious authority. Many made pilgrimages to Rome. This papal emphasis died away in the later phases of evangelizing the East, or, rather, became less conspicuous because of the direct work of the German emperors and their bishops. Missions were combined with conquest and new bishoprics were organized as governmental devices.

Another great creative movement, that of reform in the tenth century, owed something to the episcopate but nothing to the papacy. It was a monastic movement which enjoyed the support of some rulers. Its essence was the renewal of monastic ideals; a few noblemen founded new houses which were intended to recall a degenerate monasticism to its origins. Most of them were in the old central Carolingian lands, running down from Belgium to Switzerland, west into Burgundy and east into Franconia, the area from which the reform impulse radiated outwards. At the end of the tenth century it began to enlist the support of princes and emperors. Their patronage in the end led to fear of lay dabbling in the affairs of the Church but it made possible the recovery of the papacy from a narrowly Italian and dynastic nullity.

CLUNIAC MONASTICISM

The most celebrated of the new foundations was the Burgundian Abbey of Cluny, founded in 910. For nearly two and a half centuries it was the heart of reform in the Church. Its monks followed a revision of the Benedictine rule and evolved something quite new, a religious order resting not simply on a uniform way of life, but on a centrally disciplined organization. The Benedictine monasteries had all been independent communities, but the new Cluniac houses were all subordinate to the abbot of Cluny itself; he was the

Romanesque architecture

During the 19th century the term "Romanesque", previously used only by philologists to denote languages derived from Latin, began to be used by art historians and archaeologists to define an 11th-, 12th- and 13th-century architectural style which had clear links with Roman art. Early specialists studied Romanesque architecture as something homogeneous, although today it is recognized that there are variations in the Romanesque style found in different regions and historical periods.

Romanesque architecture – broadly recognizable by its round arches, thick walls with small windows, and massive vaulting – dates back to the first part of the 11th century in areas of southern Europe, first appearing in the Lombardy region and later spreading towards central Europe (the Ottonian Empire), the kingdom of France (Burgundy) and Catalonia. This early style, which is known as "First Romanesque", is characterized by vaulted spaces, devoid of sculpture or any other kind of decoration. Floor plans vary in Romanesque churches of this period: some constructions have only one aisle while larger basilicas may have three or five aisles. Some small buildings are circular in shape, although these are less common. A large bell-tower, adjacent to the main part of the church, is also typical of this style.

From the last quarter of the 11th century until the middle of the 12th, there emerged a style often called "Full Romanesque", which was influenced by the great monastic institutions, mainly the Abbey of Cluny, and by Pope Gregory VII's reforms. Full Romanesque churches are often vaulted buildings in which the use of a large amount of monumental sculpture is important. Although the sculpture has various motifs, the great theophanies were common in churches of this period.

The last stage, called "Late Romanesque", corresponds to the end of Romanesque art and many of its characteristics, such as the flying buttress, also form part of the early Gothic style. Pointed arches, substituting half-pointed arches, appeared during this phase.

The Church of St Martin Fromista, one of the most beautiful Romanesque buildings in northern Spain, is an example of the Full Romanesque architectural style.

This miniature from a Bible belonging to Charles the Bald (840–877) depicts scenes from the story of St Paul: his conversion to Christianity, his baptism and his subsequent role as a preacher. Most medieval art and literature was produced under the patronage of the Church, creating a rich legacy of religious material.

general of an army of (eventually) thousands of monks who only entered their own monasteries after a period of training at the mother house. At the height of its power, in the middle of the twelfth century, more than three hundred monasteries throughout the West and even some in Palestine looked for direction to Cluny, whose abbey contained the greatest church in Western Christendom after St Peter's at Rome.

CHRISTIAN CULTURE

Even in its early days, though, Cluniac monasticism was disseminating new practices and ideas throughout the Church. This takes us beyond questions of ecclesiastical structure and law, though it is not easy to speak with certainty of all aspects of Christian life in the early Middle Ages. Religious history is especially liable to be falsified by records which sometimes make it very difficult to see spiritual dimensions beyond the bureaucracy. They make it clear, though, that the Church was unchallenged, unique, and that it pervaded the whole fabric of society. It had something like a monopoly of culture. The classical heritage had been terribly damaged and narrowed by the barbarian invasions and the intransigent other-worldliness of early Christianity: "What has Athens to do with Jerusalem?" Tertullian had asked, but this intransigence had subsided. By the tenth century what had been preserved of the classical past had been preserved by churchmen, above all by the Benedictines and the copiers of the palace schools who transmitted not only the Bible but Latin compilations of Greek learning. Through their version of Pliny and Boethius a slender line connected early medieval Europe to Aristotle and Euclid.

Literacy was virtually coterminous with the clergy. The Romans had been able to post their laws on boards in public places, confident that enough literate people existed to read them; far into the Middle Ages, even kings were normally illiterate. The clergy controlled virtually all access to such writing as there was. In a world without universities, only a court or church school offered the chance of letters beyond what might be offered, exceptionally, by an individual cleric-tutor. The effect of this on all the arts and intellectual activity was profound; culture was not just related to religion but took its rise only in the setting of overriding religious assumptions. The slogan "art for art's sake" could never have made less sense than in the early Middle Ages. History, philosophy, theology, illumination, all played their part in sustaining a sacramental culture, but, however narrowed it might be, the legacy they transmitted, in so far as it was not Jewish, was classical.

CHURCH AND COMMUNITY

In danger of dizziness on such peaks of cultural generalization, it is salutary to remember that we can know very little directly about what must be regarded both theologically and statistically as much more important than this and, indeed, as the most important of all the activities of the Church. This is the day-to-day business of exhorting, teaching, marrying, baptizing, shriving and praying, the whole religious life of the secular clergy and laity which centred about the provision of the major sacraments. The Church was in these centuries deploying powers which often cannot have been distinguished clearly by the faithful from those of magic. It used them to drill a barbaric world into civilization. It was enormously successful and yet we have

The rise of Cluny, under the patronage of Rome, led to diverse local liturgies being substituted by Roman ones. In Spain's Christian kingdoms, this led to the emergence of new artistic trends and the abandonment of the Hispanic artistic tradition. One example of this can be found in the Bible of 960, now in the collegiate church of St Isadore of León. Self-portraits of the calligraphers who contributed to the work appear on the last page, which is shown here.

almost no direct information about the process except at its most dramatic moments, when a spectacular conversion or baptism reveals by the very fact of being recorded that we are in the presence of the untypical.

Of the social and economic reality of the Church we know much more. The clergy and their dependants were numerous and the Church controlled much of society's wealth. The Church was a great landowner. The

The monastic orders often received large donations of land or property, and many monasteries came to wield considerable economic power. The monastery of Santo Domingo de Silos in Spain, the 12th-century cloisters of which are pictured here, was an example of this trend.

revenues which supported its work came from its land and a monastery or chapter of canons might have very large estates. The roots of the Church were firmly sunk in the economy of the day and to begin with that implied something very primitive indeed.

ECONOMIC RECESSION IN THE WEST

Difficult though it is to measure exactly, there are many symptoms of economic regression in the West at the end of antiquity. Not everyone felt the setback equally. The most developed economic sectors went under most completely. Barter replaced money and a money economy emerged again only slowly. The Merovingians began to coin silver, but for a long time there was not much coin, particularly coin of small denominations, in circulation. Spices disappeared from ordinary diet; wine became a costly luxury; most people ate and drank bread and porridge, beer and

water. Scribes turned to parchment, which could be obtained locally, rather than papyrus, now hard to get; this turned out to be an advantage, for minuscule was possible on parchment, and had not been on papyrus, which required large, uneconomical strokes, but none the less it reflects difficulties within the old Mediterranean economy. Though recession often confirmed the self-sufficiency of the individual estate, it ruined the towns. The universe of trade also disintegrated from time to time because of war. Contact was maintained with Byzantium and further Asia, but the western Mediterranean's commercial activity dwindled during the seventh and eighth centuries as the Arabs seized the North African coast. Later, thanks again to the Arabs, it was partly revived (one sign was a brisk trade in slaves, many of whom came from eastern Europe, from the Slav peoples who thus gave their name to a whole category of forced labour). In the north, too, there was a certain amount of exchange with the Scandinavians, who were great traders. But this did not matter to most Europeans, for whom life rested on agriculture.

FARMING

Subsistence was for a long time to be almost all that most Europeans could hope for. That it was the main concern of the early medieval economy is one of the few safe generalizations about it. Animal manure or the breaking of new and more fertile ground were the only ways of improving a return on seed and labour which was by modern standards derisory. Only centuries of laborious husbandry could change this. The animals who lived with the stunted and scurvy-ridden human tenants of a poverty-stricken landscape were themselves undernourished and undersized, yet for fat, the luckier peasant depended upon the pig, or, in the south, on oil. Only with the introduction in the tenth century of plants yielding food of higher protein content did the energy return from the soil begin to improve. There were some technological innovations, notably the diffusion of mills and the adoption of a better plough, but when production rose it did so for the most part because new land was brought into cultivation. And there was much to exploit. Most of France and Germany and England was still covered with forest and waste.

URBAN LIFE

The economic relapse at the end of antiquity left behind few areas where towns thrived. The main exception was Italy, where some commercial relations with the outside world always persisted. Elsewhere, towns did not begin much to expand again until after 1100; even then, it would be a long time before western Europe contained a city comparable with the great centres of the classical Islamic and Asian civilizations. Almost universally in the West the self-sufficient agricultural estate was for centuries the rule. It fed and maintained a population probably smaller than that of the ancient world in the same area, though even approximate figures are almost impossible to establish. At any rate, there is no evidence of more than a very slow growth of population until the eleventh century. The population of western Europe may then have stood at about forty million – fewer than live in the United Kingdom today.

FEUDALISM

IN THIS WORLD, POSSESSION OF LAND or access to it was the supreme determinant of the social order. Somehow, slowly, but logically, the great men of Western society, while continuing to be the warriors they had always been in barbarian societies, became landowners too. With the dignitaries of the Church and their kings, they were the ruling class. From the possession of land came not only revenue by rent and taxation, but jurisdiction and labour service, too. Landowners were the lords, and gradually their hereditary status was to loom larger and their practical prowess and skill as warriors was to be less emphasized (though in theory it long persisted) as the thing that made them noble.

The lands of some of these men were granted to them by a king or great prince. In return they were expected to repay the favour by turning out when required to do him military service. Moreover, administration had to be decentralized after imperial times; barbarian kings did not have the bureaucratic and literate resources to rule directly over great areas. Thus the grant of exploitable economic goods in return for specific obligations of service was very common, and this idea was

These pictures illustrate an 11th-century copy of a text written by Beatus of Liebana, a monk who lived in late 8th-century Spain. Warriors are depicted in combat while their feudal overlord sits in state.

Feudalism

The word "feudal", from the Latin word *feudum*, meaning "fief", did not appear until the early 17th century. At the height of feudalism, the fief was a possession (usually a piece of land) granted by a lord (a noble of high standing) to a vassal (a noble generally of lesser standing than the lord) in exchange for a number of services – this was usually marked by an investiture ceremony.

The origins of the feudal system lie in 8th-century Frankish society, following the decline of the Carolingian Dynasty. The emergence of feudalism has been linked with the new military importance of heavy cavalry. The expense and level of expertise required by cavalry resulted in the emergence of a military élite, which gradually developed into a social élite and then a feudal nobility. From the Frankish lands, the feudal system was dispersed through Frankish conquests into northern Italy, Spain and Germany. In 1066 the Norman Conquest introduced it to England, and from there it spread to Ireland and Scotland. From the 12th century, however, the feudal system was threatened by the growth of the centralized state and the increasing power of towns. Feudalism's importance declined in the 14th century.

Various definitions of the term feudalism have been proposed. Some historians claim that it involved no more than the relationship between two free men – the lord and his vassal. This definition, however, is unsatisfactory, as it wrongly implies that the majority of the population were excluded from feudalism. Some medievalists see the feudal system as the precursor of

Agriculture was the basis for economic and social development under the feudal system. This manuscript illustration depicts a peasant harvesting grapes.

later socio-economic systems that favoured slavery and preceded capitalism.

Most experts agree, none the less, that the feudal system helped prevent absolutism and encouraged the development of increasingly powerful councils – one of the vassal's obligations was to provide counsel to the lord. Feudalism, therefore, formed the basis for the growth of the modern parliamentary system.

what lay at the heart of what later historians, looking back at the European Middle Ages, called feudalism.

Many tributaries flowed into this stream. Both Roman and Germanic custom favoured the elaboration of such an idea. It helped, too, that in the later days of the empire, or in the troubled times of Merovingian Gaul, it had become common for men to "commend" themselves to a great lord for protection; in return for his protection they offered him a special loyalty and service. This was a usage easily assimilated to the practices of Germanic society. Under the Carolingians, the practice began of "vassals" of the king doing him homage; that is to say, they acknowledged with distinctive ceremonies, often public, their special responsibilities of service to him. He was their lord; they were his men. The old loyalties of the blood-brotherhood of the warrior-companions of the barbarian chief began to blend with notions of commendation in a new moral ideal of loyalty, faithfulness and reciprocal obligation. Vassals then bred vassals and one lord's man was another man's lord. A chain of obligation and personal service might stretch in theory from the king down through his great men and their retainers to the lowest of the free. And, of course, it might produce complicating and conflicting demands. A king could be another king's vassal in respect of some of his lands. Below the free were the slaves, more numerous perhaps in southern Europe than in the north and everywhere showing a tendency to evolve marginally upwards in status to that of the serf – the unfree man, born tied to the soil of his manor, but nevertheless, not quite without rights of any kind.

SOCIAL ORGANIZATION

Some students of medieval history later spoke as if the relationship of lord and man could explain the whole of medieval society. This was never so. Though much of the land of Europe was divided into fiefs – the *feuda* from which "feudalism" takes its name – which were holdings bearing obligation to a lord, there were always important areas, especially in southern Europe, where the "mix" of Germanic overlay and Roman background did not work out in the same way. Much of

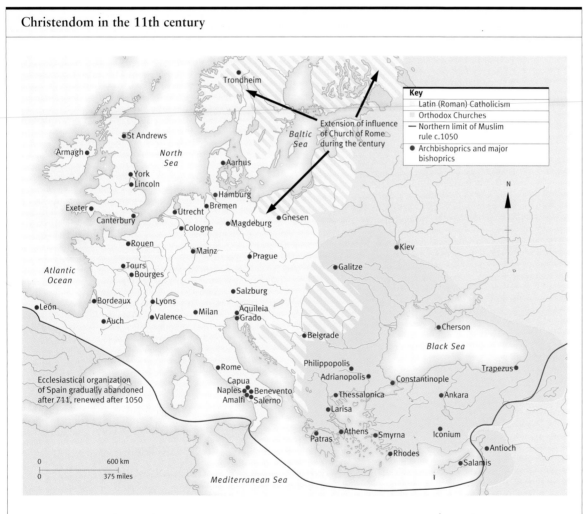

Christendom in the 11th century

Key
- Latin (Roman) Catholicism
- Orthodox Churches
- Northern limit of Muslim rule c.1050
- Archbishoprics and major bishoprics

At the beginning of the 11th century important events took place which were to have considerable repercussions for the future of medieval Europe: Islam was dispersed (the Fatimids in Egypt, the Abbasids in Baghdad and the Umayyads in Córdoba); the Byzantine Empire, Bulgaria and, finally, the legacy of the empire created by Charlemagne, all began to disintegrate and evolve into separate principalities.

A nobleman's commitment to vassalage was signified by two symbolic acts, usually performed in public. First the vassal, kneeling, would place his hands, clasped together, between those of his lord. This signified the establishment of a bond of peace between the vassal and the lord, as well as a mutual tie of friendship and fidelity. The vassal would then stand holding his hands above a sacred object and make an oath of loyalty to the lord. In this illustration from a 12th-century Spanish manuscript, Ramón Caldes and other noblemen pay homage to Alfonso II (791–842).

Italy, Spain and southern France was not "feudal" in this sense. There were also always some freeholders even in more "feudal" lands, an important class of men, more numerous in some countries than others, who owed no service for their lands but owned them outright.

For the most part, nevertheless, contractual obligations based on land set the tone of medieval civilization. Corporations, like men, might be lords or vassals; a tenant might do homage to the abbot of a monastery (or the abbess of a nunnery) for the manor he held of its estates, and a king might have a cathedral chapter or a community of monks as one of his vassals. There was much room for complexity and ambiguity in the feudal order. But the central fact of an exchange of obligations between superior and inferior ran through the whole structure and does more than anything else to make it intelligible to modern eyes. Lord and man were bound to one another reciprocally: "Serfs, obey your temporal lords with fear and trembling; lords, treat your serfs according to justice and equity" was a French cleric's injunction which concisely summarized a principle in a specific case. On this rationalization rested a society of growing complexity which it long proved able to interpret and sustain.

MILITARY ARISTOCRACIES

Mutual obligation also justified the extraction from the peasant of the wherewithal to maintain the warrior and build his castle. From this grew the aristocracies of Europe. The military function of the system which supported them long remained paramount. Even when personal service in the field was not required, that of the vassal's fighting-men (and later of his money to pay fighting-men) would be. Of the military skills, that which was most esteemed (because it was the most effective) was that of fighting in armour on horseback. At some point in the seventh or eighth century the stirrup was adopted; from that time the armoured horseman had it for the most part his own way on the battlefield until the

The investiture of two feudal knights is depicted in this 14th-century Castilian manuscript illustration. The English legal writer Henry de Bracton recorded one of the vows used in investiture ceremonies in his book *De Legibus Angliae*: "Hear this, lord, I promise my fidelity to your life and your limbs and your body and your possessions and your worldly honour, if God and these holy relics help me."

A "Tournament of English Knights before Richard II" is represented in this 15th-century illustration from the St Alban's Chronicle. In the tournament, military skills were perfected in what was intended to be a friendly and honourable encounter, although fatalities were not unusual.

coming of weapons which could master him. From this technical superiority emerged the knightly class of professional cavalrymen, maintained by the lord either directly or by a grant of a manor to feed them and their horses. They were the source of the warrior aristocracy of the Middle Ages and of European values for centuries to come. Yet for a long time, the boundaries of this class were ill-defined and movement into (and out of) it was common.

KINGS

Political realities often militated against theory. In the intricate web of vassalage, a king might have less control over his own vassals than they over theirs. The great lord, whether lay magnate or local bishop, must always have loomed larger and more important in the life of the ordinary person than the remote and probably never-seen king or prince. In the tenth and eleventh centuries there are everywhere examples of kings obviously under pressure from great men. The country where this seemed to present the least trouble was Anglo-Saxon England, whose monarchical tradition was the strongest of any. But pressure was not always effective against even a weak king if he were shrewd. He had, after all, other vassals, and if wise he would not antagonize all of them at once. Furthermore, his office was unique. The anointing of the Church confirmed its sacred, charismatic authority. Kings were set apart in the eyes

The Bayeux Tapestry (in fact an embroidery), dating from c.1077, tells the story of the events leading up to the Battle of Hastings of 1066 and the Norman conquest of England. In this detail, the Englishman Harold is depicted swearing an oath of loyalty to William, Duke of Normandy. In Norman eyes, Harold later broke his oath by usurping the English throne after the death of Edward the Confessor.

of most by the special pomp and ceremony which surrounded them and which played as important a part in medieval government as does bureaucratic paper in ours. If in addition a king had the advantage of large domains of his own, then he stood an excellent chance of having his way.

RESTRICTED LIVES

Not always in the technical and legal sense, but in the common sense, kings and great magnates were the only people who enjoyed much freedom in early medieval society. Yet even they led lives cramped and confined by

This scene from the Bayeux Tapestry represents the Battle of Hastings.

the absence of much that we take for granted. There was nothing much to do, after all, except pray, fight, hunt and run your estate; there were no professions for men to enter, except that of the Church, and small possibility of innovation in the style or content of daily life. Women's choices were even more restricted, and so they were for men as one went further down the social scale. Only with the gradual revival of trade and urban life as the economy expanded was this to change. Obviously, dividing lines are of almost no value in such matters, but it is not really until after 1100 that important economic expansion begins, and only then that we have the sense of moving out of a society still semi-barbarous, whose pretensions to civilization are sometimes negligible.

fuper miferuu̓ ↄ ↄmuniōat ↄ̄ ualde ↄ
larate ſuntos aic q̄ ↄinant i ſ̄ndo ↄ
dlamalāt uoce magna dic̄tes uñ
dicimus te ur̄ fili dei iuin q̄ dignat

es nob uchngenui dare lȳ dici ↄ bȳ nor
tis quam totuin teup̄ q̄ uniuius
tr̄ euā. bi ergo quu tuicho duit dic̄ uoin
quu ipi lic̄buit p̄tr̄ ai ſcis i ſc̄la ſc̄lor

Edward II, whose coronation ceremony is depicted here, was the first English heir-apparent to bear the title of Prince of Wales. His reign (1307–1327) was plagued with ill-advised favouritism, intrigue and constitutional conflicts, which ultimately resulted in his forced abdication and, a year later, his murder.

241
Shapur I takes
possession of
Antioch

320–c.550
The Indian
Gupta Empire

200

300

224
Ardashir I
founds the
Sassanid Empire

309–379
Reign of the
Sassanid king
Shapur II

330
Roman emperor
Constantine founds
Constantinople

A cameo representing the
defeat at Edessa in 260 of
the Roman emperor Valerian
(left) by the Sassanid ruler
Shapur I, who reigned from
241 to 272.

Defeat of Valerian I

This coin was minted during
the era of the Abbasid Islamic
caliphs, which began in 750. The
last Abbasid ruler was killed by
the Mongols in 1258.

Abbasid coin

c.570
Muhammad is
born in Mecca

615
Sassanid army
sacks Jerusalem

632
Death of
Muhammad

661–750
Umayyad
caliphate

726–843
Byzantine Iconoclast era

600

700

711
The Muslims take the
Iberian peninsula
from the Visigoths

732
Franks defeat
Muslims at Poitiers

The hunting scene on this
Sassanid plate depicts
Khusrau II, who became
emperor in 588. Khusrau
was defeated and killed
by the Roman emperor
Heraclius in 627.

Sassanid plate

The Dome of the Rock in Jerusalem was
built during the caliphate of Abd-al-Malik
(685–705). This great Islamic shrine, in
a city then firmly in the control of the
Damascus-based caliphate, provided
a secure focus for Muslim pilgrims.

The Dome of the Rock

962
Otto I crowned
Holy Roman Emperor

1071
The Seljuks defeat the
Byzantines in Asia Minor

1096–99
The First
Crusade

1000

1100

987–1328
Capetian Dynasty in France

The Bayeux Tapestry recounts events
surrounding the Battle of Hastings
of 1066 and the Norman Conquest of
England. Here, a scene from the
conflict is depicted.

The Bayeux Tapestry

Several artistic schools for the production
of icons were founded in Russia from the
beginning of the 12th century. The most
revered icon of all, however, the "Virgin of
Vladimir", was made in the Byzantine
capital, Constantinople.

The "Virgin of Vladimir"

1501–1736
Persia governed by
the Safavid Dynasty

1526–1530
Reign of Moghul
emperor Babur

1405
Death of Timur Lang

1400

1500

1379
Timur Lang
conquers Persia

1453
Constantinople is conquered
by the Ottoman Turks

1530–1556
Reign of Humayun

363
Shapur II's victory over
the emperor Julian

527–565
Justinian is
Byzantine emperor

400

500

531–579
Reign of Sassanid
emperor Khusrau I

In 793 the Vikings began to raid the
English coasts and went on to attack
other European countries, including
Ireland, France and Spain. This detail,
from an 8th-century Norse picture
stone, shows a Viking longboat.

Viking picture stone

871–899
Alfred the Great
is king of Wessex

910
Founding of the
abbey at Cluny

800

900

771–814
Charlemagne is
the sole ruler
of France

843
The Carolingian
Empire is divided

867–1025
Expansion of the
Byzantine Empire

909
Establishment of
the Fatimid Dynasty

Chinghis Khan founded the Mongol
Empire in 1206. Under his rule,
Mongol armies conquered southern
Russia, Burma, Central Asia, Iran
and the Near East.

Chinghis Khan

1171
Saladin destroys
Fatimid caliphate

1189–1192
The Third
Crusade

1258
The Mongols destroy
the Abbasid caliphate

1200

1300

C.1200
The Venetians monopolize
Byzantine trade with Europe

The Venetian Marco Polo, who travelled
around the Far East from 1271 to 1295, is
depicted kneeling before a servant of the
Mongol ruler Kubilai Khan, in whose
service he spent many years. Polo's
memoirs gained international renown.

Marco Polo at the court of Kubilai Khan

This brazier dates from the Persian
Safavid era. Shah Abbas the Great
(1588–1629) lowered taxes,
improved the road network and
encouraged the growth of trade.

Safavid brazier

1661
The British East India Trading
Company buys Bombay

1658–1707
Reign of Aurungzebe

1707
Death of Aurungzebe and
fall of the Moghul Empire

1600

1700

1556–1605
Reign of Akbar

1669
The emperor Aurungzebe
prohibits Hinduism

VOLUME 4 *Chapters and contents*

Chapter 1

Islam and the Re-making of the Near East

The Sassanids 8
Sassanid government 9
Zoroastrianism 10
The emergence of Manichaeism 11
Orthodox Christians in Persia 11
The Persian-Roman wars 12
Heraclius 12
The Asian nomads 13
Nomadic culture 14
The Scythians 14
The Hsiung-Nu 15
The Turks 16
Islam 18
The Prophet Muhammad 18
Mecca 19
The Koran and Muhammad's
  teaching 20
The *Hegira* 23
The Islamic brotherhood 23
Muhammad's legacy 24
The caliphs 24
Islamic conquests 24
Favourable conditions for Islam 26

Chapter 2

The Arab Empires

The Umayyad caliphate 28
Umayyad government 30
Taxation and commerce 31
Arab integration 31
The Shi'a 32
The Umayyad caliphate loses
  power 32
The Abbasid caliphate 32
Abbasid rule 33
Islamic civilization 34
Literary culture 35
Science and mathematics 37
Architecture 39
The arts 39
Umayyad Spain 41
The decline of the caliphs' power 43
The Islamic revolution 44
The dispersion of Islam
  worldwide 45

Chapter 3

Byzantium and its Sphere

The imperial office 48
Religion and emperors 50
Orthodox tradition 51
East and West grow apart 52
Theological disputes 53
The issue of Monophysitism 54
Byzantium and Asia 56
Medieval Byzantium 56
The problems of empire 58
A shrinking empire 60
The Isaurian recovery 61
Bulgaroctonos and the Late
  Isaurian Dynasty 62
Iconoclasm 63
The persecution of the
  Iconophiles 64
The sources of Iconoclasm 65
The increasing divisions between
  East and West 66
The splendour of Byzantium 70
The Byzantine economy 70
Internal power struggles 72

New enemies 72
The growth of Venetian power 73
The crusaders' threat to the
  Byzantine Empire 75
The "Franks" sack
  Constantinople 75
The Slavs 76
Slav origins 78
The Bulgars 79
The Bulgars convert to
  Christianity 79
The Cyrillic alphabet 79
Kiev and Byzantium 80
Viking Russia 81
Conflict and diplomacy 83
Early Russian Christianity 84
Vladimir 85
Society in Kiev Rus 87
The apogee of Kiev Rus 88
The northern princedoms 88
The emergence of Poland 91
Religious differences between Slav
  peoples 93
Slav Europe under strain 93

Chapter 4

The Disputed Legacies of the Near East

The caliphate dynasties 96
The Turkish peoples 97
The Muslim Turks 98
The Seljuk Empire 100
The structure of the Seljuk
   Empire 101
The threat of the crusades 102
Saladin 103
The Mongols and Tatars 103
Chinghis Khan 104
The Mongols in Europe 106
The Mongol onslaught on
   Islam 106
The khanates 107
Mongol rule 109
Mongol arrogance 110

Mongol culture 112
Persia under the Il-Khans 112
Persia turns to Islam 113
Timur Lang 114
The last phase of Byzantium 114
The shrinking empire 116
Christianity divided 118
The Ottomans 119
The Ottoman sultans 120
The fall of Constantinople 120
Ottoman expansion into
   Europe 120
The consequences of Ottoman
   victory 122
Religious tolerance under
   Mehmet 123
Safavid Persia 125
Shah Abbas the Great 125
Safavid decline 127

Chapter 5

The Making of Europe

The consolidation of Europe 130
Geographical limits 131
Western Christendom 134
The Frankish heritage 135
Papal recognition 135
Charlemagne 136
Charlemagne and the imperial
   title 138
Charlemagne's rule 140
The Carolingian Renaissance 140
Charlemagne's personal
   authority 143
The successors 145
The West and East Franks 146
Carolingian decline 146
Conrad of Franconia 147
The Ottonians 147
Empire revived 148
The decline of the Ottonians 149
Italy and southern Europe 150
Scandinavia 153

Viking raids 154
The consequences of the Viking
   campaigns 155
Alfred the Great 155
The Scandinavian legacy 157
Christian Spain 158
The Church in the West 159
The papacy 160
The vulnerability of the papacy 161
Papal pretensions 161
Nicholas I 162
Bishops and monasteries 164
Cluniac monasticism 164
Christian culture 167
Church and community 167
Economic recession in the West 169
Farming 170
Urban life 170
Feudalism 170
Social organization 173
Military aristocracies 175
Kings 176
Restricted lives 177

SERIES CONTENTS

Volume 1

**PREHISTORY
AND THE FIRST
CIVILIZATIONS**

Before History
The Foundations
Homo sapiens
The Possibility of
    Civilization

The First Civilizations
Early Civilized Life
Ancient Mesopotamia
Ancient Egypt
Intruders and Invaders:
    the Dark Ages of the
    Ancient Near East

Volume 2

**EASTERN ASIA AND
CLASSICAL GREECE**

**The Beginnings of
Civilization in Eastern Asia**
Ancient India
Ancient China
The Other Worlds of
    the Ancient Past
The End of the Old World

**The Classical
Mediterranean: Greece**
The Roots of One World
The Greeks
Greek Civilization
The Hellenistic World

Volume 3

**ROME AND THE
CLASSICAL WEST**

Rome
The Roman Achievement
Jewry and the Coming
    of Christianity
The Waning of the
    Classical West
The Elements of a Future

Volume 4

**THE AGE OF
DIVERGING
TRADITIONS**

Islam and the Re-making
    of the Near East
The Arab Empires
Byzantium and its Sphere
The Disputed Legacies of
    the Near East
The Making of Europe

Volume 5

**THE FAR EAST AND
A NEW EUROPE**

India
Imperial China
Japan
Worlds Apart
Europe: the First
    Revolution
Europe Looks Outward

Volume 6

**THE MAKING OF
THE EUROPEAN
AGE**

A New Kind of Society:
  Early Modern Europe
Authority and its
  Challengers
The New World of Great
  Powers
Europe's Assault on the
  World
World History's New
  Shape

Volume 7

**THE AGE OF
REVOLUTION**

Ideas Old and New
Long-term Change
Political Change in an Age
  of Revolution
A New Europe
The Anglo-Saxon World

Volume 8

**THE EUROPEAN
EMPIRES**

The European World
  Hegemony
European Imperialism and
  Imperial Rule
Asia's Response to a
  Europeanizing World
Strains in the System
The Era of the First
  World War

Volume 9

**EMERGING
POWERS**

A New Asia in the Making
The Ottoman Heritage and
  the Western Islamic
  Lands
The Second World War
The Shaping of a New
  World
Population, Economy and
  the Management of
  Nature
Ideas, Attitudes and
  Authority

Volume 10

**THE NEW
GLOBAL ERA**

The Politics of the New
  World
Inheritors of Empire
Crumbling Certainties
New Challenges to the
  Cold War World Order
The End of an Era
Epilogue: in the Light of
  History

INDEX

Page references to main text in roman, to box
text in **bold** and to captions in *italic*.

A

Aachen, Charlemagne's court 140, *140*, 141, 145
  Carolingian Renaissance at 137, 139, 140–43,
    141, *142*
  intellectual life at 136, 137, 139, 142–3
  Otto I at 148
  Otto III at 149
  thermal springs at 143
Abbas the Great (c.1557–1629), Safavid shah
    of Persia (1587–1629) 126–7, *126*, *127*
  Isfahan building programme and *126*, 127
  religious intolerance and 127
Abbasid caliphate 24, 32–41, *34*
  architecture of 38, 39, *39*, *40*, *47*
  army of 43–4
  arts of 39–41
  Buwayhid Dynasty 44
  Charlemagne, relations with 41, 140, *140*
  decline of 43–4, 96
  hereditary governorships of 34
  literature of 35–7
  mathematics in 37–8
  Mongols and 44, 107
  Persian influence upon 33, 34
  science in 37–8
  Sunnite orthodoxy of 33
  vizier, office of 34
  see also Islam; Islamic civilization;
    Islamic science; Umayyad caliphate
Abd-al-Malik, Umayyad caliph (685–705) *40*
Abd-ar-Rahman I, emir of Córdoba (756–788)
    39, **42**
Abd-ar-Rahman III, first caliph of Córdoba
    (912–961) **42**
Abraham, Hebrew patriarch 39
Abu-al-Abbas, first Abbasid caliph (749–754)
    32, *33*
Abu-Bakr (573–634), first caliph (632–634)
    24, *24*
Achaemenid Dynasty of Persia 8
  attacks on by Scythians 15
Aden 122
Aegean islands 75, 116
Afghans
  revolt of against Persia 128
Africa
  Islam and **42**, **43**, *43*, 44–5
  agriculture 170, *172*
Ahmed III, sultan of Turkey (1703–1730) *124*
Ahura Mazda, creator god 8, 10, *11*
Albania
  conquest of by Ottoman Turks 122
Alcuin (735–804), English scholar at Carolingian
    court 143
Aleppo
  conquest of by Mongols 113
Alexius I Comnenus (1048–1118), Byzantine
    emperor (1081–1118) **74**
Alfonso II, king of Asturias (791–842) *174*
Alfred the Great (849–899), king of Wessex
    (871–899) and England (886–899) 155–7, *155*
  defeat of Norsemen (Danes) by 156

Ali, cousin of Muhammad, fourth caliph
    (656–661) *24*
  assassination of 28
Alighieri, Dante (1265–1321), Italian poet 38
Almohads, Berber Dynasty 42
Almoravids, Berber Dynasty **42**, **43**
alms-giving (*sadaqa*) **22**
Amalfi (city-state) 151
Anatolia 44, 97, 100, 114
  absorption of by Ottoman Empire 120
  Arabs removed from 62
  Muslim settlement in 102
Antioch, principality of 62, 102
Aquitaine 146
  conquest of by Franks 136
Arabia 18–19, **20**
Arabic 20, 38
  as language of administration 31
  as lingua franca of Middle East 34
Arabs
  in China **25**, 26
  conquest of Sicily by 151
  conquests of under Islam 24–6, *24*, **25**, 61
  defeat of by Franks at Tours (Poitiers) 25, *25*,
    135
  in Sicily 102
  in Europe 151–3
  first Turkish empire and 98
  as nomadic pastoralists 19–20
  onslaught on Turks by 98
  as polytheists 19
  as seafarers 19
  see also Islam; Islamic civilization;
    Islamic science
Aragon, kingdom of **43**
architecture
  Byzantine **69**, 130
  Carolingian *142*
  Islamic 39, *39*, *99*
  Lombard 151
  Romanesque **165**
Ardashir I (Artaxerxes), Sassanid king of Persia
    (224–240) 8–9
Ardashir II, Sassanid king of Persia (379–383) *8*
Arghun, Il-khan of Persia (1284–1291) *113*
Arianism, Christian heresy 55, *135*
Aristotle (384–322 BCE), Greek philosopher
    34, 167
Armenia 62
  conquest of by Arabs 61
  conquest of by Sassanids 9
  recovery of by Byzantium 63
Armenian Church (Monophysite) 54
Armenians 12, 114
Arsacid Dynasty of Parthia 10
art
  Bulgarian icons *81*, *90*
  Byzantine **69**, *69*, 70, 72, 116
  in Iconoclastic period 67, **69**
  icons 63, **68**, *91*
  influence of on Carolingian court 142
  influence of on Christian Russian art *84*
  paintings *71*

Hispanic *168*
  Irish *154*
  Islamic 35, *131*
    calligraphy *38*
  Lombard 151
  Muslim 39–40
    pottery 39, *131*
    prohibition on figurative representation
      23, 31, 38, 39
  Russian icons *95*
  Sassanid *10*
Artaxerxes *see* Ardashir I
Asia, Central
  nomadic homelands in 13–14
  nomads from 13–18
Asia Minor 58, 62, 73
  conquest of by Seljuk Turks 72, 100
  conversion of from Christianity to Islam 100
  manpower reserves in 57
  Osmanlis in 116
Assassins, Islamic sect
  destruction of by Mongols 107
Assyria 13, 14
astrolabes *34*
astronomy 36
Asturias 158, *158*
Athens, Catalan duchy of 118
Attila (c.406–453), Hun chieftain 16
Augustine, St (354–430), bishop of Hippo
    (396–430) 143
  Manichaeism and 11, *11*
Austria 148
Avars 58, 79
  in Balkans 12, 93
  conflict between Charlemagne and 138
  displacement of from Mongolia 16
  as Sassanid allies 13, 17
  in south Russia 78
  stirrup introduction of by 16
Averroës 38
Avicenna (Ibn-Sina) 38
Ayyubid Dynasty in Egypt and Levant 103
al-Aziz, Fatimid caliph of Egypt (975–996) 97

B

Bactria
  overrunning of by Scythians 15
Baghdad, centre of Abbasid caliphate 24, 32, *33*,
    34, 43
  sacking of by Mongols 107
  conquest of by Turks 127
  Varangians 81–2
Baldwin I (1171–1205), Count of Flanders and
    Latin Emperor of the East 118
Balkans, Slavs and Avars in 12
barbarians
  Euro-Asiatic nomads **17**
  incorporation of within caliphates 44
Barcelona
  destruction of by Al-Mansur *158*, 159
Barcelona, county of **43**

Bari, emirate 151
Basil I the Macedonian (c.812–886), Byzantine
    emperor (867–886) 71
Basil II (*Bulgaroctonos*) (c.958–1025), Byzantine
    emperor (976–1025) 62–3, *62*
  as patron of the arts **69**
Basil, St (c.330–379) *91*
Basra 31
battles
  Adrianopolis (1205) *118*
  Edessa (260) *12*
  Goliath Spring (1260) 107
  Hastings (1066) *177*
  Horns of Hattin (1187) *102*
  Manzikert (1071) 72, 100
  Mohács (1526) 122
  Nehavand (642) *9*
  Stamford Bridge (1066) 158
  Tours (Poitiers) (732) 25, *25*, 135
Bavarians 147
Bayeux Tapestry *177*
Beatus of Liebana, 8th-century Spanish
    monk *171*
Bedouin 18–19, 31
beer 169
Benedict, St
  Rule of 140, 142, 164
Benedictine monasteries 164
Berber peoples
  as allies of Arabs 25
Bible 142
Black Sheep Turks 114
Boethius, Anicius Manlius Severinus (c.480–524),
    Roman philosopher 143, 157, 167
Bogomil heresy 72
Bohemia 92, 138
Bokhara 13, 14
  sacking of by Mongols 105, **105**, 108
Boleslav I, ruler of Poland (992–1025) 92
Boniface, St (680–754), evangelist in Germany
    135, 164
Book of Marco, The (Marco Polo) **110**
Book of the Thousand and One Nights, The
    (Haroun-al-Raschid) 35, *35*
Book of the Wonders of the World, The
    (Marco Polo) *108*, **110**, *112*
Bosnia and Herzegovina
  conquest of by Ottoman Turks 122
Brittany 146
Buddhists 105
Bulgaria
  conquest of by Ottoman Turks 120
  as first Slav state 79, 84
  relations between Byzantium and 79, 114
Bulgars 58, 61, 62, 78, *78*, 79–80, *79*, 87
  conversion of to Christianity 62, 79
  defeat of by Basil II 62–3
  priests of in Kiev Rus 88
  revolts of 72, 75
  siege of Thessaloniki and *78*
burial rites *14*
Buwayhid Dynasty, Abbasid caliphate 44, 97
  overcoming of by Seljuk Turks 100

Byzantine army
  Greek fire 56, 57, 61, 84
  Iconoclasm and 65, 66, **67**
  underfunding of 72
Byzantine Empire (Byzantium) **17**, 48–95
  alliance between Umayyad caliphate and 43
  Arab conquests within 25–6, 60–61
  Western assistance sought by 116–19
  Christian heritage of 51
  clerical intransigence in 118–19
  confinement of to Anatolia 44
  Constantinople regained by 116
    decline and extinction of 114–20
  defeat of by Turks at Manzikert 72
  divergence of from West 51–2
  dynasties of
    Comneni 72–3, *73*
    Isaurian 62–3
    Macedonian 63, **69**
    Palaeologus 116
    Phrygian 63
  declining economy of 70–71
  expansion of under Isaurian Dynasty 62–3
  Hellenistic influences on 56
  imperial court in 70
  Islam seen as heresy in 51
  medieval characteristics of 56–7, 58–60
  Orthodox Church in 51–2
  Osmanli Turks and 116, 120
  papal primacy accepted in 118–19
  plague in 118
  internal power struggles of 72
  resources of 57, 58
  Roman Catholic Church, union with 118–19
  Sassanid conflict in 8, *9*
  Serbian attacks on 116
  splendour of 70
  territorial extent of in 600 CE 58
  territorial losses of 60–61, 116–18
  Trebizond and 116
  see also Constantinople

C

Cairo, seat of Fatimid caliphate 43, *43*
calendar, Muslim 23, *23*
caliphs 24, *24,*
Canute I (c.995–1035), king of England
  (1016–1035) 157, *157*
Capet, Hugh (c.938–996), king of France
  (987–996) 147, 155
Capetian Dynasty 147, 150
caravanserais *13*
Carinthia 138
Carolingian Dynasty 136–47, 147
Carolingian Empire **149**
  decline of 146–7
  legacy of 150
  partitioning of 145–6
  territorial expansion of 137–8
Carolingian Renaissance 140–43, *141, 142*
  copying of Bible during 142
Carthage
  conquest of by Arabs 25
Castile and León, kingdom of **43**
Celtic Church 155
Chaldea
  conquest of by Islam *24*
Charlemagne (742–814), king of Franks and
  emperor (800–814) 136–45, *136, 137,* **137**
  Alcuin, tutor of 143
  Church and State under 138–140, *142,* 161

code of law and **137**
coronation of by Leo III 136, 138–9, 162
cultural renaissance under **137**, 140–43, *141,*
  142–3, *142*
death of 145
defence of against Norse raiders 155
Denmark and 138
as Frankish warrior-king 136, 139, 142
Haroun–al-Raschid and 41, 140, *140*
personality of 143–5
imperial title and 138–9
reformation of the Frankish Church by 135,
  140, 143
Byzantium and 139, 140
Saxon March and 137–8
Spanish March and 138, 158
successors to 145–6
sword of *138*
Charles I the Bald, king of the Franks and
  emperor (840–877) 144, 146, *166*
  payment of tribute to Norsemen by 155
Charles III the Simple (879–929), king of
  Western Franks (893–922) 146
Cheibanid khanate 107
China
  Chinghis Khan and 104
  defence of against Huns 15
  Great Wall of 15
  paper money in 109
  Sung Dynasty of 112
  T'ang Dynasty of 98
Chinghis (Genghis) Khan (c.1162/1167–1227),
  Mongol conqueror and emperor (1206–1227)
  campaigns of *104,* 105, 105–106, *106*
  death of **105**
  defeat of Chin State by 104
  divine mission of 104–5
  Mongol language and 109
  religious tolerance under 105
  successors to 106
Chioggia, War of 74
Chionites *see* Hsiung-Nu
Christendom, Western
  geographical extent of 131, 134–5
  insecurity of 159–60
  Norse influences on 153–5
Christian missionary activity 52, 162
  Slavs and 79–80, *80,* 93
  Anglo-Saxon 164
  in Bulgaria 79
  encouragement of by bishops 164
  in Germany 135
  in Scandinavia 153
Christianity
  Byzantine emperors 50–51
  Islam and 103
  Manichaeism 11
  Muhammad and 23
  in northern Spain 158–9
  in Scandinavia 153
  in Persia 11–12
  Easter festival and 155
  Slavs and 76–7
  Irish missionaries and 155
  symbolism of *131*
Church and State
  in Byzantine Empire 50–53
  under Lombards *151*
  under Charlemagne 138–40
  under Otto I 148–9
churches
  enriching of by Charlemagne **136**
  St Apollinare the New (Ravenna) 58

St Clement (Rome) *80*
St Dmitri (Vladimir–Suzdal) *88*
St Eugene (Trebizond) *69*
St Irene (Constantinople) *75*
St Isadore (León) *168*
St John (Ephesus) *75*
St Mark (Venice) *75*
St Martin Fromista (Spain) *165*
St Mary, (Llugo de Llanera) *131*
St Mary of the Valley (Cividale) *151*
St Saviour, Chora Monastery (Istanbul) *91, 116*
St Sophia (Constantinople) *see* St Sophia
St Sophia (Kiev) *85,* 93
St Sophia (Novgorod) *87,* 93
St Vitale (Ravenna) *49, 51,* 67
St Vitus (Prague cathedral) *92*
St Vicente basilica (Córdoba) *39*
Theodolinda chapel (Monza) *151*
Clovis (465–511), Merovingian king of the
  Franks (481–511) 135
  conversion of to Catholicism *135*
Cluniac monasticism 164–5, 168
  influence of on Romanesque architecture **165**
Cluny, Abbey of **165**, 167
coinage
  Anglo-Saxon *155*
  Arabic 31, *31, 34*
  Byzantine *54, 63,* 70, *70*
  Merovingian *169*
  of Ottoman Turks 120
  reformation of under Charlemagne **137**
  short supply of *169*
  Venetian *74*
Conrad I, king of Franconia (911–918) 147
Constantine I the Great (Flavius Valerius
  Constantinus) (c.274–337), Roman emperor
  (306–37) 49, *50,* **51,** *70*
Constantine V (718–775), Byzantine emperor
  (741 and 743–775) 63, 65, *67*
Constantine XI, Byzantine emperor (1448–1453)
  fall of Constantinople and 48, 120
Constantinople 12, 13, 17, *17,* *87*
  besieged *17,* 26, 41, 57, 61, 62
    by Ottoman Turks 120
  defences of 57
  emperors restored in 75
  Norsemen penetrate defences of 79, 81
  Ottoman building programme in 129
  Ottoman Turks' conquest of 48, *48,* **51,**
    53, 120
  raiding of by the Rus 80–81
  Fourth Crusade and **51,** **74,** 75–6, 76, 94
  see also Byzantine Empire
Coptic Church, in Egypt and Ethiopia 54, *55*
Córdoba
  caliphate of in decline 43
  caliphate established in 41, **42**
  Great Mosque of *38,* 39, 43, 47
  Madinat al-Zahara, caliphate palace of *42*
  Umayyad emirate in 41, **42**
Crete
  conquest of by Ottoman Turks 122
  recovery of by Byzantium 62
crusades 44, *103*
  First (1096–1099) 102
  Third (1189–1192) 103
  Fourth (1202–1204) **74,** 75–6, 76, 94
  Seljuk Turks and 100, 102
Ctesiphon, Sassanid capital 31
Cuman peoples 16, 94
Cyclades 75
Cyprus
  conquest of by Arabs 61

conquest of by Ottoman Turks 122
raiding of by Arabs 25
recovery of by Byzantium 62
Cyril, St (9th century)
  Cyrillic alphabet 79–80, *91*
  Slavs and 79–80, *80,* 93

D

Dalmatia 140
Damascus, centre of Umayyad caliphate 24,
  28–9, *29,* 31, **42**
  Great Mosque of *29, 30,* 39, 113
  surrender of to Mongols 107
Danegeld 155, 157
Danelaw 156, 158
Danes *see* Norsemen (Vikings)
Dante Alighieri (1265–1321), Italian poet 38
De legibus Anglae (Bracton) *175*
Delhi
  sacking of by Timur Lang 114
Denmark (Dane Mark) 138, 148
Derbent 128
Discovery of the World, The (Marco Polo) *110*
Dome of the Rock, Jerusalem 39, *40*
Donation of Constantine 162

E

East India Company
  in Ormuz 127
Eastern Roman Empire *see* Byzantine Empire
economic developments
  medieval recession 168–70
Edessa, county of 102
education
  clerical monopoly of 167
Edward II (1284–1327), king of England
  (1307–1327) *179*
Edward the Confessor, St (c.1003–1066),
  king of England (1042–1066) *177*
Egypt
  Alexandria 61
  conquest of by Muslims 24, 25, *25*
  conquest of by Ottoman Turks 122
  Coptic Church in 54, *55*
  Fatimid caliphate of 43, *43,* 96, 97, 102
  invasion of by Persians 12
  religious disaffection in 26
  Saladin's seizure of power in 102
Einhard (c.770–840), Carolingian intellectual
  136, 143
El-Andalus (Islamic Spain) 41–3, **42**
Emma, queen of Normandy *157*
England
  under Alfred 156–7
  Norse raids of 154, 156
  as part of Danish empire 157
  shire structure of 157
  system of defensive burghs in 156
English
  Shah Abbas and 127
Eskimos 154
Ethelred II, king of England (978–1016)
  157
Ethiopia
  Muslims emigrate to 23
Euclid (323–283 BCE), Greek geometrician
  34, 167
Europe
  Arab incursions into 25, **25,** 26

geographical limits of 131, 134–5, **139**
map of **139**
medieval shaping of 132–6
military aristocracies in 175
population levels of 170
post-Roman backwater of 130–31
Turks at Gallipoli 11

F

farming
  subsistence 170
Faroes
  colonization of by Norsemen 153
fasting (*sawm*) 22
Fatima, daughter of prophet
  Muhammad *43*
Fatimid caliphate in Egypt 43, *43*, 96, 97
  Saladin and 102
  see also Egypt
feudalism 170–77, *171*, **172**
  chain of obligation in 173–6
  knights and 175
  landowners and 170–72
  military aristocracies and 175–6
  origins of **172**
  slavery and 173
  tournaments and 176
  vassalage and 172–3, **172**, *174*, 175–6
Flanders 146
Florence, Council of 118–19
food and diet 169
France
  Capetian Dynasty of 146–7
  Norse raids on 154
  Paris 146–7, 150
  roots of in West Francia 146, 150
Franconia (East Francia) 147
Frankish Church
  reformation of 135, 140, 143, 162
Franks *134*
  defeat of Arabs by at Tours (Poitiers) 25, **25**, 26, 135
  colonization of Germany by 135
  Constantinople and 75–6, 76, 116
  East Francia 146, *146*
  king crowned emperor 68–9
  Merovingian Dynasty of 135
  northeast Spain recaptured by 41–3
  origins of feudal system in **172**
  support of papacy by 135
  West Francia and 146–7, 150
    effect of Norse raids on 155
  see also Carolingian Dynasty;
    Carolingian Empire; Charlemagne
Freyr, Norse god *83*, *156*
Frisia
  missionary work in 164
  Norse raids on 154

G

Gaeta (city-state) 151
Gascony 146
Genghis Khan *see* Chinghis Khan
Genoa 74, 77, 116, 119
Germanic peoples 93, 135, *135*
  Saxons 135, 137–8, 147
Germany
  colonization of by Franks 135
  political fragmentation of 147

roots of in East Francia 146
Ottonian Empire and 148
Ghazan (1271–1304), Mongol Il-khan
  (1295–1304), 113, *113*
ghazis (petty princes) 119, 125
Ghaznavid Dynasty in Iran 99
  eviction of 100
Gibraltar 25
Golden Horde khanate 107, 112
  defeat of by Timur Lang 114
government and administration
  of Abbasid caliphate 33–4
  of Byzantine autocracy 49–51, 56
  in city-states 77, 151
  divine kingship and 8
  in feudal system 170–76
  Mongols and 107, 109
  Sassanid system in 9–10
  Seljuk Turks and 99, 101
  of Umayyad caliphate 30–31
Granada, kingdom of 42
Greece
  conquest of by Ottoman Turks 120
Greek fire 56, 57, 61, 84
Greenland
  colonization of by Norsemen 154
Gregory I the Great, St (540–604), pope
  (590–604) 71, *91*, 160, *161*
Gregory VII (Hildebrand) (c.1023–1085),
  pope (1073–1085) 165
Guide for the Perplexed (Maimonides) 37
Guy de Lusignan, king of Jerusalem (1186–1192)
  102
Güyük Khan, successor of Chinghis Khan
  (1246–1248) **105**

H

Hadrian I, Pope 136
hajj, pilgrimage to Mecca 22
Hamdanid Dynasty 96–7
Hanse, German trade league 88
al-Hariri, Maqamat, Islamic warrior *27*
Harold II (c.1020–1066), king of England (1066)
  177
Haroun-al-Raschid (c.766–809), Abbasid caliph
  (786–809) 34, *35*, 41, 43
  as gift to Charlemagne 140, *140*
Hegira (Muhammad's flight to Yathrib) 23
Hellenistic civilization
  Byzantium influenced by 56
  Persian damage of 60
  Turkish annihilation of 121
Henry I the Fowler (c.876–936), king of
  Saxony (912–936) 147, 149
Henry II (973–1024), king of the Saxons
  (1002–1024), Holy Roman Emperor
  (1014–1024) *147*, 149–50
Heraclius (c.576–641), Roman emperor in East
  (610–641) 12–13, *13*, 17, 60–61, *70*, 79
  Monophysitism debate and 54–5
History of the Conquest of the World, The
  (Ala-al-Din) *111*
Hohenstaufen Dynasty **149**
Holy Roman Empire 150
  degradation of 77
  roots of in Ottonian Empire 148
  see also Charlemagne; Ottonian Dynasty;
    Ottonian empire
Honorius, Pope (625–638) 54–5
Hsiung-Nu *see* Huns
Hulugu, Mongol khan 112

Hungary
  defeat of by Mongols 106
  defeat of by Ottoman Turks 122
Huns, Asian nomads (Hsiung-Nu)
  15–16, *15*, **17**, 78, 79
  invasion of Sassanid Empire by 16
  threat to China of 15
  westward movements of **9**, 15, 16

I

Ibn-Sina (Avicenna) 38
Iceland
  colonization of by Norsemen 153–4
  Norse legacy of 158
  Sagas (epic poems) of 154, **156**, 158
Iconoclasm movement in Orthodox Church
  56, 63–6, *65*, 67, **67**, 161
  causes of 66
  papacy and 135
  persecution of Iconophiles during 65
icons
  Annunciation of Ustjug 95
  consecration ceremonies **63**
  creation of 66, *86*
  destruction of by Iconoclasts 63–4, *65*, 67
  "Virgin of Vladimir" *86*
  see also art
India
  ravaged by Timur Lang 114
Ionian islands
  occupation of by Ottoman Turks 122
Iraq 31, 32, 41
  Arab conquest of 24, *24*, 25, **25**
  Buwayhid Dynasty of 97
Ireland
  art of *154*
  Norse raids on 154
  Norse settlement in 153
Irene (c.752–803), Byzantine empress (797–802)
  65, 69
Isaurian Dynasty, Byzantium 62–3
Isfahan 99, *126*, 127–8
  massacre of Safavid sympathizers in 128
Islam
  all-embracing nature of 45
  brotherhood of believers (*umma*) in 23
  cultural stability of 96, 101
  divorce in *44*
  Christianity and 103
  non-Arab converts to 31, 32
  origins of 18
  Orthodox view of 51
  pillars of the faith **22**
  rejection of by Jews at Medina 23
  local government and 101
  religious hierarchies in 31
  schism in 28
  spread of 24–6, *24*, **25**, 32, 44–6, *45*
  status of women in 44, 45
Islamic civilization 34–41
  architecture of 39
  astronomy in *36*, 37
  commerce and 38
  literature of 31, 35–7
  music of 41
  Arabic and 34, 38
Islamic Empire
  decline of 96
  defeat of by Franks at Tours (Poitiers)
  25, *25*, 26
  Italy and 151

lack of records in 30–31
Mongol offensive against 106–7
slavery in 45
territorial conquests of 24–6, *24*, **25**, 131, 151
Islamic science 37–8, *37*, 130
  astronomy 36, *37*, 38
  mathematics 37–8
  medicine 38
  navigation *34*
Isle of Man
  colonization of by Norsemen 153
Ismail I (1486–1524), Safavid ruler of Persia
  (1501–1524) 125, 127, **127**
Istria 140
Italy
  Attila's threatened invasion of *16*
  city-states in 151
  invasion of by Otto I 148
  Arabs and 161
  Norse raids on 154
  subjugation of by Lombards 150
  Ottonian Empire and 148–9

J

Jacobite Church (Syria) 54, 114
James, St (d.44 CE), apostle of Jesus 159
Janissaries 120, *121*
Jaxartes River 14
Jerusalem
  capture of by Muslims 25
  as crusader kingdom 102
  Dome of the Rock 39, *40*
  recapture of by Saladin 103
  sacking of by Persians 12
jihad (defence of the faith) **22**
John II Comnenus (1088–1143), Byzantine
  emperor (1118–1143) *73*
John II Kalojan, king of Bulgaria (1197–1207)
  118
John VI Cantacuzenus (d.1383), Byzantine
  emperor (1347–1354) *115*
John VIII, Byzantine emperor (1425–1448)
  118
Justinian I (c.482–565), Roman emperor in East
  (527–565) 48, *50*, 51, *51*, *53*, 57

K

Kaaba *18*, 19, *19*, *21*
Kabul
  conquest of by Arabs 25
Khadijah, wife of prophet Muhammad *21*
Khazaria, khanate of *see* Khazars
Khazars, Central Asian tribe 16, *17*, *26*, 78, 81
  conversion to Judaism 60, *60*
  decline of 84
  Islam held back by 85, 98
  St Cyril and 80
Khiva oasis
  conquest of by Ardashir I 8
Khurasan
  conquest of by Arabs 25, 97
Khusrau I, Sassanid king of Persia (531–579)
  9, *10*, *12*, 140, *140*
Khusrau II, Sassanid king of Persia (590–628)
  10, *12*, 13, *13*
Al-Khwarizmi (d.835), Islamic astronomer 38
Kiev 81, 83
  Mongol capture of 94, **105**, 106, 108
Kiev Rus 83

absorption of Norsemen 158
adoption of Orthodox Christianity in 87–8
as capital of Russian Empire *85*
Byzantium and 83–4, 88
Cyrillic alphabet introduced into 88
decline of 89–91, 94
defeat of by Chinghis Khan 94, **105**, 106
links between the West and 88
map of **89**
rule of succession in 83, 88
society of 87–8, 91
territorial expansion of 93
Al-Kindi (d.870), Islamic philosopher 38
Koran 20–21, **21**, *22*, 44
Muhammad's recital of 20–21
see also Arabs; Islam; Shi'ites; Sunnites
Krum, Bulgarian king (803–814) 79, *79*
Kubilai Khan (1216–1294), Mongol emperor of China (1259–1294) 107, 110, **110**
death of 113
Peking palace of 108
Kufa 31, 32, *33*
Kurdistan
conquest of by Ottoman Turks 122

L

La Chanson de Roland, epic poem **138**
languages 31, 102
Arabic 31, 34, 38, **42**
influence of Koran on 20
Charlemagne's mastery of 143
Greek 31, *52*, 56
Hebrew **42**
Latin
decline of 52
official status of **137**
written 109
Norse influences on Irish 153
Persian 31
Romance (Catalan, Provençal) **42**, 153
translations
from Arabic and Persian to Turkish 100
from Arabic to Latin 38
into Arabic 34, 38
Leo I the Great (c.390–461), pope (440–461) 16
Leo III, Byzantine emperor (717–741) 62, 64
Leo III, pope (795–816) 136, 138–9, *142*, 162
Leo IV, Byzantine emperor (775–780) 65, 66
Leo V, Byzantine emperor (813–820) *65*
León (city) 158
conquest of by Al-Mansur 159
León, kingdom of 158
Levant 44, 75, 103, 112
Muslim reconquest of 103
Lindisfarne monastery
raids on by Norsemen 154, *155*
literacy
clerical monopoly of 167
Islamic 35
literature
Arabic 31, 35–7, 100
Carolingian 142
Norse Sagas 154, **156**, 158
Russian 88
Lombards 61, *150*
Catholicism adopted by 150
defeat of by Pepin the Short 135
Charlemagne and 150
conquest of Ravenna by 161
Lothair I (795–855), Holy Roman Emperor (817–877) 145, *145*

Lothair II (825–869), king of Lotharingia (855–869) *164*
Lotharingia 145, 146, 147, 162
Louis I the Pious (778–840), Holy Roman Emperor (814–831 and 835–840) **137**, 145, *145*
Norse raiders and 155
Louis II the German (805–876), king of East Francia (817–876) 145–6

M

Macedonian Dynasty, Byzantium 63, **69**
Magyar tribes 84, 93–4, 130, 132, 134, 147, 148
Mahmud, Afghan ruler of Persia (1722–1725) 128
Maimonides, Moses (1135–1204), philosopher 37
Mamelukes, Turkish mercenaries 98, *98*, 103, 107
defeat of by Timur Lang 114
Mongol advance and 103, 112, 113
Ayyubid Dynasty in Egypt and 103
Mani (Manichaeus) (c.216–c.276), founder of Manichaeism 11, *11*
Manichaeism, Christian heresy 11
Al-Mansur (939–1002), Arab conqueror in Spain *158*, 159
maps
Arabia in the 7th century **20**
Byzantine Empire, The **61**
Charlemagne's Europe **139**
Chinghis Khan, The Mongol Empire of **106**
Christendom in the 11th century **173**
Christendom before the Islamic Conquest **160**
growth of Venice as a Mediterranean power, The **74**
Islam beyond the Arabic world until 1800 **45**
Islamic Iberia **43**
Islam, The early spread of **25**
Kiev Rus **89**
medieval Empire, The **149**
Ottoman expansion in the 14th and 15th centuries **122**
political situation in western Europe during the 12th and 13th centuries, The **77**
Sassanid Empire at the time of Khusrau I, The **9**
Western world in the year 1000, The **133**
Marco Polo (1254–1324), Venetian merchant traveller *108*, 109, **110**, *111*, 112
Martel, Charles (c.689–741), Frankish warrior 135, 159
mathematics
Arabic 37–8
Maurice (582–602), Byzantine emperor 12
Mecca, holy city of Islam 18, 19–20, *19*, *40*
Kaaba 18, 19, *19*, 21
Muhammad and 23
as place of pilgrimage (*hajj*) 19, **22**, 23, 96, 126
trade in 20, *20*
Medina, City of the Prophet 23, *23*, *40*, 96, 126
mosque of *47*
Mehmet I, sultan of Turkey (1413–1421) *119*
religious tolerance of 123
Mehmet II the Conqueror (1429–1481), sultan of Turkey (1451–1481)
capture of Constantinople by *48*, 120–21
Merovingian Dynasty 135
silver coinage of *169*
Merv (city) 14
Merv oasis
conquest of by Ardashir I 8
Mesopotamia 8, 13, 62, 102
conquest of by Islam 24

conquest of by Timur Lang 114
Black Sheep Turks and 114
Arabs in 17
Methodius, St (9th century)
mission to the Slavs of 79–80, *80*, 93
Michael II, Byzantine emperor (820–829) 63
Mieszko I, king of Poland (960–992) 91–2
mihrab (niche in wall indicating direction of Mecca) 39, *47*, *124*
military techniques
archery 14–15
Avars introduce stirrups 16
Greek fire 56, *57*, 61, 84
heavy cavalry **172**, 175–6
of Mongol army **105**, 108
see also weapons
millennial beliefs 132, *132*
Mithras, god 8
monasteries
Chora *91*, *116*
Cluny 164–7, **165**
Grand Lavra **69**
Lindisfarne 154, *155*
Mount Athos **69**
Patleina *81*
Santo Domingo de Silos *169*
monasticism
Cluniac order 164–7
early medieval reform of 164
in England 157
Orthodox tradition of 53
money, paper
in China 109
in Persia 109
Möngke Khan, successor of Chinghis Khan (1251–1259) *105*, 106
Mongol Empire 104, **105**, 106
decline of 113–14
disintegration into khanates of **105**, **106**, 107
Persian Il-khans in 112
success of 107–8
territorial extent of under Chinghis Khan **105**
Mongolia 15, 16, 104
Mongols 6, 104–14, *107*
Abbasid caliphate and 44
army discipline of **105**
assumption of supremacy of 110–11
Chin state defeated by 104, **105**
conquest of Kiev by 94, **105**
Europe and 106
Islam and 45, 106–7, 112, 113, *113*
Mamelukes and 107
paper money and 109
religion of 110
religious tolerance of 105, 108, 112
Timur Lang and 114
warfare and 111, *111*
see also Chinghis (Genghis) Khan
Monophysitism, Christian heresy 54–5, *55*
Monothelitism 54–5
Morocco, emirate of 41
Moscow 89
mosques
al-Azhar (Cairo) 97
Ala-al-Din (Konya) *101*
at Kufa (Iraq) 32, *33*
Dome of the Rock (Jerusalem) 39, *40*
Friday Mosque (Isfahan) *99*
Great Mosque (Córdoba) *38*, 39, *43*, *47*
Great Mosque (Damascus) *29*, *30*, 39
Great Mosque (Mecca) *19*
Lutfullah (Isfahan) *126*

Sulaimaniye (Istanbul) *123*
Mosul 102
Mu-Awiyah, first Umayyad caliph (661–680) 28, *29*
Muhammad, prophet (c.570–632) 18–24, *23*
ascent to Heaven of 39
birth of 18, *18*
death of 24, **25**
flight of to Yathrib 23
marriage of 20, *21*
in Mecca 19
succession of 24, *24*
al-Muizz, Fatimid caliph of Egypt (953–975) 97
Muscovy 94, 158
Muslims, population pressures on 26
Mustafa I, sultan of Turkey (1617–1618) *124*
Al-Mutanabbi, poet 28

N

Nadir Kali (1688–1747), shah of Persia (1736–1747) 128
Naples 118
Naples (city-state) 151
Navarre, kingdom of *43*, 158
Nestorians, Christian heretics 12, *55*, 114
Mongols and 105, 106, 112
Nicaea, Council of 54
Nicephorus I, Byzantine emperor (802–811) 79, *79*
Nicholas I, Pope (858–867) 162–4, *164*
Njörd, Norse god 83
nomadic peoples
culture of 14, *14*, 15
Euro-Asiatic 13, **17**
Huns (Hsiung-Nu) 9, 15–16, *15*, *16*, **17**, 78, 79
Mongols 94, 103–14
Oghuz Turks 99–100
Pechenegs 16, 72–3, 84, 85, 89–91
Scythians 14–15, *14*
Tatars 104
Normandy
duchy of 158
grant of future duchy to Rollo 146
Normans
Bayeux Tapestry *177*
conquest of England by **172**, *177*
in Mediterranean 72, 74, 75
pressure of on Byzantine Empire 72, *72*
Norsemen (Varangians) 81–4, *89*, 153
Norsemen (Vikings) 81–4, *82*, 130, 134
absorption of into local cultures 158
colonization by 153–4, 156
conflict between Byzantium and 80–81, *82*
at Kiev 81
longboats of *82*, 153
mythology of **83**
Newfoundland settlement of 154
at Novgorod 81
piracy and plunder by 153, *153*, 154–5, *154*, 156
settlement in England of 156
Slavs subjugated by 81
trade of 153–4
West Francia and 146
Novgorod 81, 83, 88, 89, *89*

O

Odin, Norse god 82, **83**, *156*
Oghuz Turks
migration of 99, 100
see also Seljuk Turks; Turkish peoples

Ogoday Khan, son of Chinghis Khan
    (1229–1241) **105**, 106
Ormazd, creator god *11*
Oleg (10th century), prince of Russia 83–4
Olga (d.968), ruler of Kiev (945–962)
    conversion to Christianity of 84
Oljeyetu, Mongol Il-khan (1302–1317) *113*
Ordoño II, king of León (914–924) *158*
Orkhan (1288–1359), first sultan of Turkey
    (1326–1359) 119, 120, *121*
Orkneys and Shetlands
    colonization of by Norsemen 153
Ormuz, port of 127
Orthodox Church
    Bogomil heresy in 72
    characteristics of 51–2
    divergence of from Roman Catholic Church
        52–4, 66–70
    Iconoclast movement of 56, 63–6, **67**, 135, 161
    icons of 63–6, **63**, 65, **67**, 86, 90
    conversion of Slav peoples to 76–7, 87–8
    theological disputations in 53–4, 56, 63–6, 118
    Vladimir's conversion to 87
Osman I (1259–1326), Ottoman sultan
    (1299–1326) 119
Osmanli Turks 116
Otto I the Great (912–973), Holy Roman
    Emperor (936–973) *143*, 148–9, **149**
Otto II (955–983), Holy Roman Emperor
    (973–983) 148, *149*
Otto III (980–1002), Holy Roman Emperor
    (983–1002) 148, *149*
Ottokar I, king of Bohemia
    (1192–1193; 1197–1230) 92
Ottoman Dynasty (of Osmanli Turks)
    119–20, *119*
Ottoman Empire 44, 122–3
    Bursa, capital of *119*
    military organization of 119
    multiracial policy of 123
    Safavid Dynasty and 125
    territorial expansion of 120, 122, **122**
Ottoman Turks
    defeat of by Timur Lang 114, 120
    fighting spirit of 119
    Janissaries 120
    siege of Constantinople and 120
Ottonian Dynasty 147–50
    decline of 149–50
Ottonian Empire 149–50, **149**
    intervention in papacy by 148, 149, 151, 161, 163
    territorial expansion of 147–8
Oxus River 14, 17, 26, 100, 107

P

Palaeologus Dynasty, Byzantium 116–19, *116*
    John VI Cantacuzenus *115*
Palestine
    conquest of by Muslims *24*, 25
    occupation of by Seljuk Turks 100
papacy 160–64, *163*
    authority of 163
    Byzantine emperor and 135–6
    Church policy and 162
    Lombards and 150
    Ottonian interventions in 148, 149, 151,
        161, 163
    Temporal Power of 135
    see also popes
Papal States 135, 150, 151
papyrus 169

parchment 169
Parthia 10
    Ardashir I and 8
    Scythians in 15
Pechenegs, Russian nomads 16, 72–3, 84, 85,
    89–91
Peking conquered by Chinghis Khan **105**
Peloponnese
    occupation of by Ottoman Turks 122
Pepin the Short (714–768), king of the Franks
    (751–768) 135, **137**, 161
    coronation of by Stephen II 135, 162
    Ravenna and 135, 161
Persia
    conflict with Rome 11–13
    conquest of by Islam 24
    conquest of by Timur Lang 114
    defeat of by Arabs 25, 26
    destruction of cities in Levant and Asia
        Minor by 60
    dismemberment of by Russia and Turkey 128
    gods of *8*
    Il-khans in 112–14
    paper money in 109
    persecution of Christians in 11–12
    Safavid Dynasty of 97, 125–8
    Sassanid Dynasty *see* Sassanid Dynasty
Persian khanate 107
Phrygian Dynasty, Byzantium 63
Picts
    replacement of by Norsemen 153
pilgrimage
    to Jerusalem (Catholic) 70
    to Jerusalem (Islamic) *40*
    to Mecca (*hajj*) **22**
Pisa 77, 151, 154
Plato (c.428–c.348 BCE), Greek philosopher 34
Pliny the Younger (62–113 CE), Roman
    administrator 167
Poland
    conversion of to Roman Catholicism 85, 91–2
    defeat of by Mongols 106
    Slav origins of 85
    territorial expansion of 92
political systems
    autocracy (Byzantium) 49–51, 56
    autocracy (Mongol) 110–11
    city-states 77, 151
    feudalism 170–77
popes
    Pope Gregory the Great 160, *161*
    Pope Gregory VII **165**
    Pope Hadrian I 136
    Pope Honorius 54–5
    Pope Leo III 136, 138–9, *142*, 162
    Pope Nicholas I 162–4, *164*
    Pope Stephen II 135, 161
Portugal
    traders from 127
    trading ships from 123
Premysl, founder of first Bohemian dynasty 92
Prester John (c.12th–13th century), legendary
    Christian king 102, **105**
Primary Chronicle, The, Russian historical
    text 88
Provence 151

Q

Quraysh, Bedouin tribe 18, 20, 24
    opposition to Muhammad by 23, 28
    patriarchal caliphs drawn from 24, 28

R

Ramón Berenguer I, Count of Barcelona
    (1024–1276) *158*
Ravenna 62, 142
    churches of *49, 51, 58,* 67
    conquest of by Lombards 161
    as gift to St Peter 135
    imperial exarch of 160
Redwald, king of East Anglia (599–625) 152
religion
    Arab polytheism 19
    Bogomil heresy 72
    Byzantine theological disputations 53–4,
        56, 63–6
    Christianity *see* Christianity
    Iconoclasm 63–6, *67*, 135, 161
    Islam *see* Islam
    Manichaeism 11
    missionary activity *see* Christian missionary
        activity
    Mongol 110
    monotheistic 18, 21, 23, 31
    Orthodox Christianity *see* Orthodox Church
    Zoroastrianism 10
    see also Shi'ites; Sunnites
Rhodes
    capture of by Sassanids 12
Richard I the Lionheart (1157–1199), king of
    England (1189–1199) *103*
Rollo, first duke of Normandy (c.911–c.925)
    84, 146, 158
Roman Catholic Church
    cultural monopoly of 167
    daily impact of 167–8
    divergence from Orthodoxy of 52–4, 66–70, 85
    economics of 168–9
    insecurity of 159–60
Romanesque architecture **165**
Rum, Turkish sultanate of 72, 100, *101*, 119
    defeat of by Mongols 106
Rurik (d.879), prince of Russia 83, **89**
Russia 119
    conversion of to Christianity 84–7, *85, 87*
    Isfahan and 127
    origins of 81, 83
    trading privileges of 83, 84

S

sadaqa (alms-giving) **22**
Safavid Dynasty in Persia 125–8
    anti-Ottoman position of 125
    art and literature of *126*, 127, **127**, *127*
    decline of 127–8
    origins of 125, *125*
al-Sahli, Ibrahim ibn Saud, instrument maker 34
St Sophia, Constantinople 48, *51*, 70, 80, 84,
    120, *123*
    construction of ordered by Justinian I **51**, *53*
    desecration of by crusaders 75
    Islamic alterations to *124*
    mosaics in *50*, 73
Saladin (Salah al-Din al-Ayyub) (1137–1193),
    Sultan of Egypt and Syria (1174–1193) 38,
    75, 103, *103*
    battle of the Horns of Hattin and *102*
    in Egypt 102
    recapture of Jerusalem by 103
salat (prayers) **22**
Samanid Dynasty, Abbasid caliphate 97
    conversion of Seljuk Turks to Islam 99, 100

Samarkand 14, 25
    sacking of by Mongols 105, **105**
Santiago de Compostela, shrine
    taken by Al-Mansur 159
Sassanid Dynasty in Persia 8–13, *8, 12, 13*
    Ardashir I, founder of 8
    invasion of Syria and Egypt by 12
    Khusrau I *9*, *10, 12*, 140, *140*
    Khusrau II 10, 12, 13, *13*
    sacking of Jerusalem by 12
    Shapur I *12*
Sassanid Empire
    collapse of 13, 17–18
    conflict between Byzantines and 8, **9**
    conquest of by Arabs 9, 18, 25, **44**
    map of **9**
    Mesopotamia and 25
sawm (fasting) **22**
Saxons 135, 147
    conversion of by Charlemagne 137–8
    in England *152*
Scandinavians *see* Norsemen
Scotland
    Norse settlements in 153
scripts
    Carolingian minuscule 142, 169
    Cyrillic 79–80, 88
    Turkish 109
Scythians 14–15, *14*, 78
    displacement of by Huns 15
Seljuk Turks *34*, 73, 99, 100–102,
    armies of 101
    crusades and 100, 102
    defeat of Byzantines by 100
    government of 101
    ulema (religious leaders) 101
    see also Oghuz Turks; Ottoman Turks;
        Turkish peoples
Septimania 146
    conquest of by Franks 136
Serbia 78
    attack on Byzantine Empire by 116
    conquest of by Ottoman Turks 120, *121*
shahada **22**
Shapur I, Sassanid king of Persia (241–272)
    defeat of Valerian by 12
Shi'a, party of the Shi'ites 32
Shi'ites, Islamic sect 28, 32, 33
    Abbasid caliphate and 43
    Abu-al-Abbas and 32
    Buwayhid Dynasty of 100
    Fatimid caliphate and 43, *43*
    Safavid Dynasty of Persia and 125, 127, 128
    Umayyad caliphate and 30
shipping
    Norse 153
Sicily
    conquest of by Arabs 151
Sinan (Ottoman architect) 123
Slav peoples 58, 61, 76–81
    in Balkans 12
    in Bohemia and Moravia 93
    Bulgars *see* Bulgars
    civilization of 77–8, 79–80
    conflict between Charlemagne and 138
    conversion of to Orthodox Christianity
        76–7, 80, 85
    in Croatia and Serbia 93
    Greek influence on 52
    movements of into Balkans 78
    origins of 78
    in Poland 85
    powers of survival of 78

raids on Byzantium by 79
in Russia 81
"slavery" and 169
topography and culture of 76–8
slavery
in early Russia 91
in feudal society 173
in Seljuk armies 101
as sign of reviving economy 169
under Islam 45
Spain
conquest of by Arabs **25**
El-Andalus and 41–3, **42**
Norse raids in 154
political entities of **43**
reconquest of 102
Spanish March 138, 158
Umayyad rule of 41–3, **42**
Stephen II, pope (752–757) 135
stirrups 16, 175
Sulaiman I the Magnificent, sultan of Turkey
   (1520–1566) *123*
Sunnites, Islamic sect 28
   Afghans 128
   Ottoman Turks 125
   Seljuk Turks 100
Sutton Hoo burial ground *152*
Sviatoslav, prince of Russia (962–972) 84–5
Swabians 147
Syria 62
   conquest of by Arabs 24, 25, **25**
   conquest of by Islam *24*
   conquest of by Ottoman Turks 122
   invasion of by Sassanids **9**, 12
   Mamelukes in 103, 112, 113
   occupation of by Seljuk Turks 100, 102
   Umayyad caliphate and 24, 28–30

T

Tabriz 125
Tamberlane *see* Timur Lang
Tamir River 17
T'ang Dynasty in China
   collapse of 98
Taranto, emirate of 151
Tariq (d.c.720), Berber commander 25
Tatars (Mongolian tribe) 104, 119
taxation 31
   on Arab land 34
   Byzantine 57
   Mongols and 109
   Muslim 28
   Persian 10
   Shah Abbas and *127*
   tax-farming 43
technological innovations 170
Tengri, Mongol sky god 110
Tertullian (c.152–222), Christian churchman 167
Theodora, Byzantine empress (c.500–548) *49*
Thessaloniki
   besieged by Bulgars 78
Thor, Norse god *82, 83*, **83**, *156, 157*
Thrace 62, 116
Tiflis 128
Timur Lang (c.1336–1405), Mongol emperor
   (1369–1405) **106**, 114
trade 34, 43, 70, *127*
   Anglo-Persian 127
   decline 169
   in Kiev Rus 87
   Mongol protection of 109

trade routes 9, 14, 19, **20**
   to East 123
   of Kiev Rus **89**
   Mongol 109–10
   Silk Road 39, 56
Trans-Jordan
   conquest of by Islam *24*
Transoxiana 97, 98, 114
   Chinghis Khan and 105, 106
   Seljuks and 99, 102
transport and travel
   in Mongol Empire 109
Trebizond 58, *72,* 109
   as ally of Byzantium **51**, 116
   conquest of by Ottoman Turks 121
Tripoli, county of 102
Tunisia, emirate of 41
   caliphate *43*
Turkestan khanate 107
Turkish peoples 97–101
   art of writing and 98
   of first Turkish Empire 17, 98
   Ghaznavid Dynasty in Iran 99–100
   iron-workers 16, **17**
   lack of records of 98
   of second Turkish Empire 100
   siege of Constantinople and 17
   see also Oghuz Turks; Ottoman Turks;
      Seljuk Turks

U

Umar, second caliph (634–644) *24*
Umayyad caliphate 24, 26, 28–32, *29, 30*
   Africa and **42, 43, 43**
   army of 28
   Charlemagne and 140
   end of 32, *33*
   sea power of 43
   siege of Constantinople by *57*
   Spain and 41–3
   see also Abbasid caliphate; Islam; Islamic
      civilization; Islamic science
urbanization 170
Uthman, son-in-law of Muhammad, third caliph
   (644–656) *24*

V

Valerian (Publius Licinius Valerianus), Roman
   emperor (253–60)
   defeat of by Sassanids *12*
Varangians (Norsemen) 81–4, **89**, 153
Venice, republic of 73–6, **74, 77**, 116–17,
   119, 151
   Aegean islands and 115–16
   Byzantium and 140
   commercial empire of 75
   naval power of 74
   sack of Constantinople by **74,** 75
Verdun, Treaty of 145, 146
Vienna
   Ottoman sieges of 122, **122**
Vikings *see* Norsemen
Vinland 154
Vladimir 89
Vladimir (c.956–1015), Christian prince of
   Russia (980–1015) 85–7
   conversion of to Christianity *85,* 87
   marriage of to Byzantine princess Anna
      85, 87

W

weapons
   cannon 120
   Greek fire *56, 57, 61, 84*
   see also military techniques
Wends 138, 148
Wessex, Anglo-Saxon kingdom of 155–6
Whitby, Synod of 155
White Horde khanate 107, 112
White Sheep Turks 125
William II, duke of Normandy (1035–1087) *177*
William of Roebruck (13th century), Franciscan
   friar 112
Willibrord, St (658–739), Anglo-Saxon
   missionary 164
women
   divorce and *44*
   under Islam **44,** 45
writing, Turkish 98, 109

Y

Yaroslav I the Wise, prince of Kiev Rus
   (1019–1054) *87,* 88, 89, *93*
Yathrib (Medina)
   Muhammad's flight to 23, *23*
Yueh-chih people 15

Z

zakat (alms-giving) **22**
Zoroastrianism 10, 12, 18, 38

ACKNOWLEDGMENTS

The publishers wish to thank the following for their kind permission to reproduce the illustrations in this book:

KEY

b bottom; **c** centre; **t** top; **l** left; **r** right
AAA Ancient Art & Architecture Collection, London
ADO Agence Dagli Orti, Paris
AGE A.G.E. Fotostock, London
AISA Archivo Iconografico S.A., Barcelona
AKG AKG, London
BAL Bridgeman Art Library, London
BL British Library, London
BM British Museum, London
BN Bibliothèque Nationale, Paris
BNM Biblioteca Nacional, Madrid
ET e.t. Archive, London
KM Kunsthistorisches Museum, Vienna
MAN Museo Arqueologico Nacional, Madrid
ON Osterreichische Nationalbibliothek, Vienna
RHPL Robert Harding Picture Library, London
RMN Réunion des Musées Nationaux, Paris
SHM Statens Historiska Museum, Stockholm
WFA Werner Forman Archive, London

Front cover: Oronoz
3 BN (Pers.113, f.107)
7 AKG / Real Monasterio, El Escorial
8 AISA
10t RMN / Chuzeville / Louvre, Paris
10b AISA
11b Giraudon / Bibliothèque Sainte-Geneviève, Paris
12 BN
13t MAN
13b RHPL
14 AAA
15 Römisch-Germanisches Museum, Cologne
16 Alinari-Giraudon / Pina Coteca Vaticana, Vatican
17 ET / Sucevita Monastery, Moldovita, Romania
18 Topkapi Palace Museum, Istanbul (Ms.H.1221)
19 BAL / Fitzwilliam Museum, Cambridge
21 Topkapi Palace Museum, Istanbul (Ms.1222)
22 Giraudon-Index / Museé Condé, Chantilly
23 Spencer Collection / The New York Public Library (Astor, Lenox and Tilden Foundations)
24 Reproduced by kind permission of the Trustees of the Chester Beatty Library, Dublin
27 BN (Ar.5847, f.94v)
28 Oronoz / BN
29 Oronoz
30 ADO
31 MAN
33 Corbis / Nik Wheeler
34t MAN

34b MAN
35 AISA / BN
36 Giraudon-Dost Yayinlari / University Central Library, Istanbul
37 AISA / BN
38 WFA
39 AISA
40 AISA
42 Corbis / Sheldan Collins
43 MAN
44 BN (Ar.5847, f.125)
47 AISA / BN
48 Oronoz / Topkapi Palace Museum, Istanbul
49 AISA / Ravenna
50 AISA / Ravenna
51 Oronoz
52 AISA
54 MAN
55 1997 Dumbarton Oaks, Trustees of Harvard University, Washington DC
56 BNM (Vit.26.2, f.34v)
57 Index / Biblioteca Apostolica, Vaticana
58 Scala / S Apollinare Nuovo, Ravenna
60 Oronoz / Colección Duques de Alba, Madrid
62 WFA / Biblioteca Nazionale Marcuana, Venice (Gr.Z17)
63 MAN
64 Lauros-Giraudon / Basilica San Marco, Venice
65b Biblioteca Vaticana (Gr.372-43v)
65t MAN
66 Scala / S Francesca Romana, Rome
67 S Vitale, Ravenna / Scala / Art Resource, New York
68 BAL / Richardson & Kailas Icons, London
69 Scala / Galleria Fresaka, Belgrade
70t MAN
70b MAN
71 BN (Gr.510, f.438v)
72t MAN
72b BNM (Vit.26.2, f.97v)
73 Oronoz
75 AISA
76 BAL / Giraudon / Louvre, Paris
78 WFA / BNM (f.217r)
79 Biblioteca Apostolica Vaticana (Vat. Slavo 2, f.145v)
80 Scala / San Clemente, Rome
81 National Archaeological Museum, Sofia
82 Michael Holford / SHM
83 Nationalmuseum, Stockholm
84 BAL / Kremlin Museum, Moscow
85t AKG / Erich Lessing / Academy of Science, St Petersburg
85b Marco Polo / J de Vergara
86 Scala / State Tretyakov Gallery, Moscow
87 AGE
88 AISA
90 Lauros-Giraudon / National Art Gallery, Sofia
91 CM Dixon
92 AKG / Erich Lessing
93 Corbis / Dean Conger / Santa Sofia, Kiev
95 RHPL / State Tretyakov Gallery, Moscow

96 MAN
97 AAA / B Norman
98 BL (Add.18866, f.140r)
99 Fiorepress-Firo Foto
100 Metropolitan Museum of Art, New York (Francis M Weld Fund, 1950)
101 AGE
102 Corpus Christi College, Cambridge (Ms.26, f.279)
103 BL (Cot. Faust B, f.72v)
104 BN (Per.1113, f.44v)
105 AAA / Ronald Sheridan
107 BN
108 BN
109 BN (Pers.1113, f.107v)
110 Oronoz
111 AISA / BN
113 Corbis / Roger Wood
115 BN (Grec.2144, f.11)
116 AISA / Kariye Camii, Istanbul
118 The John Work Garrett Library, Johns Hopkins University, Baltimore
119 Sonia Halliday Photographs, Weston Turville
121 ON (Cod.8.626, f.63)
123 AISA
124 BAL / Hagia Sophia, Istanbul
125 MAN
126t AISA
126b Spencer Collection / The New York Public Library (Astor, Lenox and Tilden Foundations)
127 MAN
129 Giraudon-Dost Yanyinlari / Topkapi, Palace Museum, Istanbul
130 MAN
131t MAN
131b Imagen Mas / Museo Arqueológico, Oviedo
132 BN (Lat.8878, f.145v)
134 BN (Lat.8878, f.193)
135 Bibliothèque Municipale, Castres, France
136 Giraudon / Musée Condé, Chantilly
137 Bibliothèque Municipale, Castres, France
138 RMN / Willi / Louvre, Paris
140t BAL / Giraudon / BN
140b BAL / Giraudon / BN
141 AKG /Schatzkammer, Aachen
142b Index / Biblioteca Nazionale, Turin
142t Oronoz
143 BAL / KM
144 BN (Lat.1, f.423)
145 BON (Cod.908, f.3v)
146 Bibliothèque Municipale d'Arras (Ms.1045, f.8)
147 Bayerische Staatsbibliothek, Munich (Nr.335, Css.4452, f.152v)
148 Scala / Castello Sforzesco, Milan
150 BNM (Ms.413, f.16r)
151t AISA
151b Scala
152 BM
153 BAL / SHM
154 National Museum of Ireland, Dublin
155l BL Cott Nero

155r BM
156 SHM
157l SHM
157r BAL / BL
158t AISA / Archivo de la Corona de Aragón, Barcelona
158b Oronoz
159 BM
161 KM
162 Scala / Pinoteca Vaticana
164 BM
165 Imagen Mas
166 BAL / BN (Lat., f.386v)
168 Oronoz / San Isidoro, León
169 AISA
171 BNM
172 Oronoz / San Isidoro, León
174 Oronoz / Archivo de la Corona de Aragón, Barcelona
176 BN (Esp.36, f.72v)
176 BAL / Lambeth Palace Library, London
177d Giraudon / Musée Bayeux
177t Michael Holford / Musée Bayeux
179 Corpus Christi College, Cambridge (Ms.20, f.68r)

MAPS
Maps copyright © 1998 Debate pages 9, 77 and 133
Maps copyright © 1998 Helicon/Debate pages 20, 25, 43, 45, 61, 74, 89, 106, 122, 139, 149, 160, 173

TEXT CREDITS
The publishers wish to thank the following for their kind permission to reproduce the translations and copyright material in this book. Every effort has been made to trace copyright owners, but if anyone has been omitted we apologize and will, if informed, make corrections in any future edition.

pp.21 and 44 extracts from the Koran translated by Arthur J. Arberry (Oxford University Press 1964) copyright © 1955. Reproduced by permission of HarperCollins Publishers Ltd.; p.35 extract from *The Book of the Thousand Nights and One Night* by Haroun-al-Raschid, rendered into English from the literal and complete French translation of Dr J. C. Mardrus by Powys Mathers (Routledge & Kegan Paul 1986) copyright © 1964. Reproduced by permission of Routledge.